South Harting
Hill Climb

1905-1924

South Harting Hill Climb
1905-1924

"The Premier Hill Climb of the Year"
THE LIGHT CAR AND CYCLECAR

Graham J. Orme-Bannister

Newlands Press
ALRESFORD • HAMPSHIRE

**South Harting Hill Climb
1905-1924**

First Published in the United Kingdom in 2006 by

NEWLANDS PRESS
Hillcroft, Bighton Lane, Bishop's Sutton
Alresford, Hampshire SO24 0AU UK

Tel: 01962 734988
E-mail: GJOrmeB@aol.com

Copyright © Graham J. Orme-Bannister 2006

The right of Graham J. Orme-Bannister to be identified as the author of
this work has been asserted by him in accordance with the Copyright,
Designs and Patents Act 1988.

All rights reserved. No part of this publication may be reproduced,
stored in a retrieval system or transmitted, in any form or by any
means, electronic, mechanical or otherwise without prior permission in
writing from the copyright holder.

ISBN-10: 0-9552485-0-7
ISBN-13: 978-0-9552485-0-4

Produced and printed by members of
THE GUILD OF MASTER CRAFTSMEN

Cover Design by RPM Print & Design
Book Design and Typesetting by Cecil Smith
Typeset in Century Old Style

Printed and bound in Great Britain by
RPM PRINT & DESIGN
2-3 Spur Road, Quarry Lane, Chichester
West Sussex PO19 8PR

Title page:
DOROTHY LEVITT, DRIVING A MINERVA,
WHO FINISHED 14th IN THE YELLOW TROPHY EVENT. (1907)
LAT PHOTOGRAPHIC

This book is dedicated to:

**The National Motor Museum Trust
Reference and Motoring Picture Libraries**

Without whose facilities and assistance it would not have happened.

This work is published with the assistance of

The Michael Sedgwick Memorial Trust

The Michael Sedgwick Memorial Trust
was founded in memory of the famous
motoring researcher and author

MICHAEL SEDGWICK, 1926–1983

The Trust is a registered charity to encourage new
research and the recording of motoring history.
Suggestions for future projects, and donations, should be sent to:

Honorary Secretary
The Michael Sedgwick Trust
c/o John Montagu Building
Beaulieu, Hampshire SO42 7ZN

SOUTH HARTING HILL CLIMB 1905-1924

CONTENTS

Preface	9
Introduction	11
1. The Early Years – 1904 to 1906	
1904 – The Portmouth Trials	14
1905 – The First ACGBI (The Automobile Club of Great Britain & Ireland) Event	17
1906 – The Second ACGBI Event	27
2. The Handicap Formula Debate	42
3. The ACGBI Handicapping System	55
4. The Yellow Trophy – 1907	61
5. "The R.A.C. Abolition of Hill-Climbs"	78
6. The Middle Years – 1913 and 1914	
1913 – The First Cyclecar Club Event	81
1914 – The Inter Club Meeting	89
1914 – The Second Cyclecar Club Event	95

A PANORAMIC VIEW NEAR THE SUMMIT OF THE HILL

(1907)

LAT PHOTOGRAPHIC

CONTENTS

7. The Post War Years – 1919 to 1924
    1919 – The First Junior Car Club Meeting — 102
    1920 – The Second Junior Car Club Meeting — 113
    1921 – The Third Junior Car Club Meeting — 124
    1922 – The Fourth Junior Car Club Meeting — 133
    1923 – The Fifth Junior Car Club Meeting — 145
    1924 – The Surbiton Motor Club Meeting — 153
    1924 – The Sixth Junior Car Club Meeting — 161

8. The End of the Road – 1925 and Kop Hill — 172

Appendices
I   Schedule of Events held – 1904 to 1924 — 177
II   Contemporary Reports Found — 178
III   Tables of Entries and Results — 179
IV   Earl Russell – The Father of The South Harting Hill Climb — 220
V   Earl Russell and the Motor Car — 236
VI   A Brief History of Speed Limits — 247
VII   The Organising Clubs — 250
    The Automobile Club of Great Britain & Ireland (ACGBI) — 250
    The Cyclecar Club — 252
    Junior Car Club — 254
VIII   Source Documents, Picture Credits & Acknowledgments and Further Reading — 257
IX   Index of Motoring Personalities — 259
X   Index of Motor Cars — 262

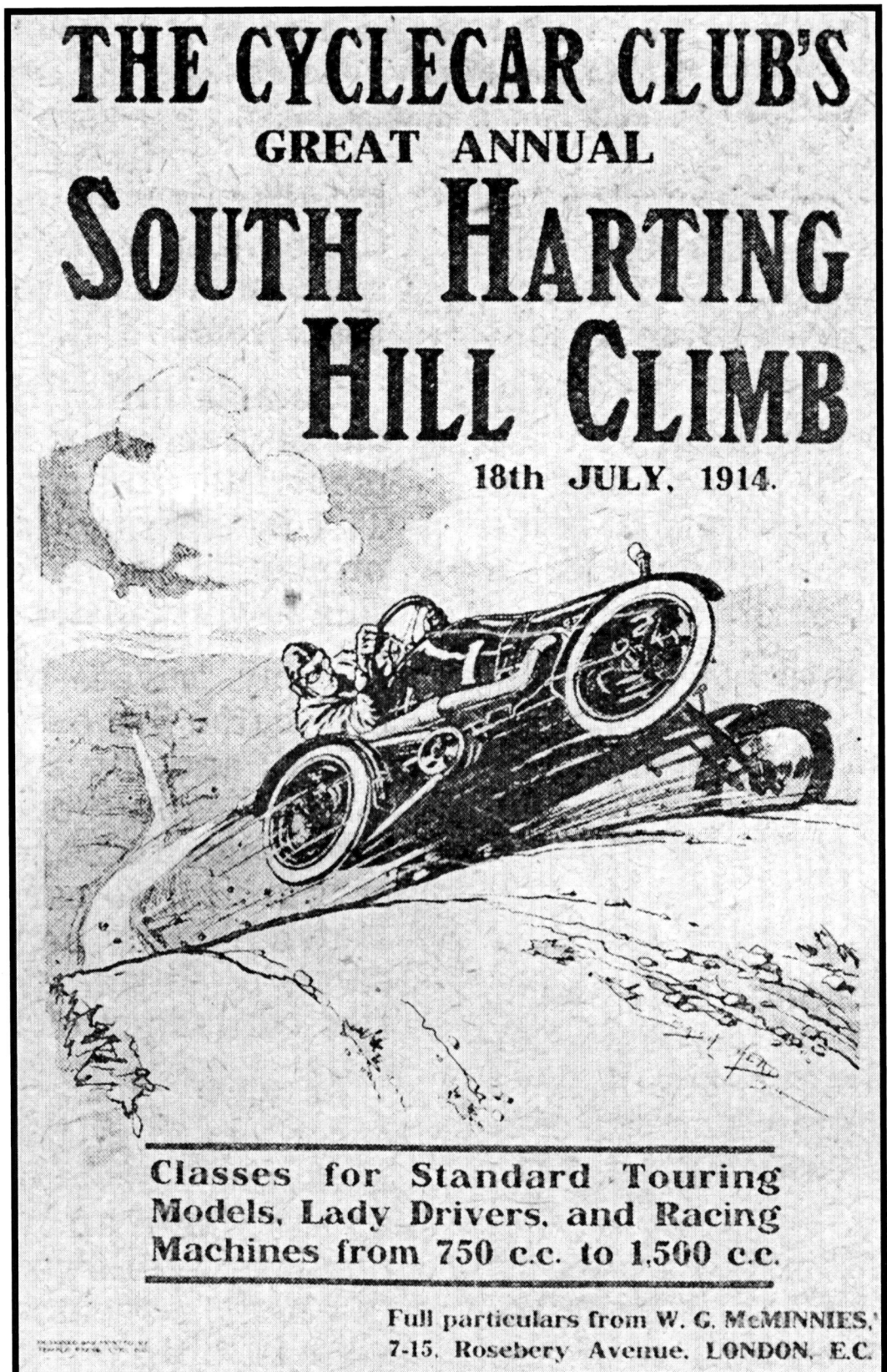

PREFACE

For the last twenty five years of their lives my parents lived in the seaside town of Rustington in West Sussex. For the latter part of this period I was living near Odiham in north Hampshire and my journeys down to Rustington took me through the village of South Harting and up over the South Downs to Goodwood.

My father was an engineer and instilled in me from a very early age a love of all things mechanical. As a teenager, my introduction to motor sport was at Brands Hatch in the days when it was still a motor cycle grass-track with the racing lap run anti-clockwise. When the tarmac surface was first laid in 1950, for 500cc Formula 3 racing, I recall a very young Stirling Moss in his Cooper winning all five races he entered at only the second ever car meeting held there. Having then spent most of my working life in the oil industry, on the technical sales aspects of fuels and lubricants, the epithet "petrol head" is perhaps doubly appropriate.

Against this background, every time I climbed that glorious hill out of South Harting and up over the South Downs I used to think what a superb location it would be for a hill climb event. Some years later, when working as a volunteer in the Reference Library at Beaulieu, to my astonishment and delight I stumbled across a reference to a "South Harting Hill Climb" having being held in 1905. Slowly, over a period of some three years, I then pieced together the story which is the subject of this book.

Graham Orme-Bannister
2006

C.H. COOPER ON HIS 16-20hp BEESTON HUMBER
CHANGING GEAR AT THE TOP OF THE STEEPEST GRADIENT.
(1905)

INTRODUCTION

The "quintessentially English"[1] village of South Harting in West Sussex lies on the northern edge of the South Downs, some four miles south of Petersfield on the B2146. Just beyond the village the B2141 forks off to the left and climbs over the downs heading towards Chichester. The first mile or so of this gloriously twisty and scenic road has a gradient of up to 1 in 7 and was, in the period from 1905 to 1924, the venue for the South Harting Hill Climb.

Within this period reports of thirteen separate events have been found, with at least twelve different organising clubs having been involved. Chronologically the events break down into three groups, with no events being held in the years from 1908 to 1912 and 1915 to 1918. As a prelude to these thirteen events, the Portsmouth Motor Car Trials were held in 1904, including a hill climb on a private road in adjoining Up Park.

The twenty year period from 1904 to 1924 saw huge changes in the role and nature of motoring in Great Britain, going from the motor car being essentially a rich mans toy, to being popular middle class, if not quite working class, transport. The number of cars on the roads of Britain increased from less than 8,500 in 1904 to over half a million in 1925. The typical car changed from a "veteran" eligible now for the Brighton run, to that archetypal "vintage" car, the Alvis 12/50. As in so many other fields of human activity, the First World War was a major catalyst for technical development and social change.

As with motoring in general, the nature of motor sport in Britain also changed during that twenty year period. Almost the only organised motoring events in Britain up until 1900 were general efficiency trials, sometimes with timed sections, of which the 1,000 Mile Trial in the year 1900 is undoubtedly the best known. Since the timed sections were frequently up hills, to increase the severity of the test, hill climbs became a common format for early motoring competitions, along with some short timed sprints on the level.

[1] The Central Office of Information issued a film in 1957 which featured South Harting as a "quintessentially" English village. Humphrey Sladden, parish councillor and local historian, through a relative working in India, reports that the film was being shown there as recently as 1995.

SOUTH HARTING HILL CLIMB 1905-1924

Petersham Hill near Richmond, Westerham Hill in Kent, Mucklow Hill at Halesowen and Tilburstowe Hill in Surrey were a few of the early venues even before South Harting Hill was first used in 1905. In those very early days the braking test staged coming down the hill was often more exciting than the climb up. Some twenty six separate hill climb events were reported in Britain in 1903.

In continental Europe, and France in particular, actual racing on public roads was allowed, whether on closed circuits or from town to town. This was, however, forbidden in Britain and proper motor racing did not arrive, Crystal Palace, Gilmorehill and Bexhill not withstanding, until the opening of the Brooklands track at Weybridge in 1907. This remained the only venue until Donnington Park opened in 1933.

Thus the only speed based competitive motoring events held on public roads in Britain in the period up to 1925 were hill climbs and sprints. It was, however, illegal to close any public road for any reason during that time, so that these competitive timed events were held on roads still technically open to normal traffic. In the very early days this problem was more apparent than real, since the venues were normally in quiet rural locations and normal traffic almost non existent. We must assume that the few local car owners would have been supportive, and that most other local residents initially welcomed the novelty and the visitors money. Nevertheless some farmers insisted on exercising their right to drive a horse-drawn cart very slowly up the tracks during the event.

However, as the years passed, the general level of traffic increased and the spectator crowds grew; so proportionately did the event management problems. Eventually in 1925 safety issues brought an end to all speed events on public roads. Like circuit racing, the future of hill climbing and sprinting lay in events held on private land where admission, parking, crowd control, and safety could all be effectively managed. In fact Shelsley Walsh had already been operating since 1905.

There is another extraordinary twist to this scenario. It is perhaps not generally realised today that the 20mph speed limit introduced in the 1903 Motor Car Bill remained in force until 1930. Before that, since 1896, the general speed limit had been only 12 mph. Thus all speed events held on public roads until 1925 were increasingly illegal and only proceeded in a bizarre legal limbo.

One practical consequence of this surreal state of affairs on the running of the South Harting Hill Climb, and other similar speed related events held on public roads, was in the reporting of the results. Only once in the twenty years that the events were run were speeds officially published.

Police attitudes to speed events on public roads were ambivalent, reflecting their lack of clear objectives. They had no power to close roads, or deny access to them by the general public. They were, however, directly responsible to local authorities who, on the one hand, sanctioned the events, but also encouraged them to enforce with speed traps a widely discredited speed limit, often as a fund raising exercise to pay for road maintenance.

This narrative started out with the simple objective of telling the largely forgotten story of the South Harting Hill Climb. It soon became apparent however that the twenty year period from 1904 to 1924 was a time capsule which defined a particular phase in the development of motor sport in Britain. The phase can perhaps be defined by three changes which took place progressively over the period.

INTRODUCTION

LAT PHOTOGRAPHIC

A 15hp DARRACQ DRIVEN BY A. RAWLINSON HALF WAY UP THE HILL WITH
A PANORAMIC VIEW BACK TO THE START LINE AT ENGINE FARM.

The fundamental evolution was from trials on public roads run for the express purpose of helping buyers decide which car to buy, to competitive events on private roads for mainly sporting reasons. Along the route of this change was a heated debate on developing technically sound formulae for comparing cars, in order to move away from the initial price-only comparison. This can be seen as the first step along the long path to modern Formula racing. The third change was from the early dominance by trade entries trying to sell cars, to predominantly private owners indulging their competitive instincts.

The period was also characterised by a rapid growth in the vehicle population in Britain and the social penetration of the motor car. The legislators however effectively stood still, in large part paralysed by the First World War. It has therefore been all but impossible to tell the story of the South Harting Hill Climb without invoking some of the legal, political and social environment in which the story developed.

The story of the individual events has been told mainly as reported with minimum comment; the temptation to add modern perspective has mostly been resisted. If there appear to be inconsistencies in the narrative in the spelling of peoples names, the naming and power rating of cars and reporting of results it is because that is the way they was reported at the time. Changes have only been made where the information as reported would be either incorrect or misleading.

CHAPTER 1

THE EARLY YEARS
1904 to 1906

1904 – The Portsmouth Trials

The first recorded hill climb near South Harting was part of an event held on October 16th 1904, and mostly reported in the motoring press under the heading "Motor Car Trials at Portsmouth". The event was split into two sections. The first was a 22½ mile run from the Granada Motor Garage at Southsea to South Harting via Petersfield; this was primarily a fuel consumption test but also incorporated a self timed climb of Portsdown Hill. The second section was an independently timed hill climb on a private road near South Harting.

The event was almost entirely a naval affair. Ten out of the fifteen competitors, and all of the nine officials, were naval officers. And senior officers at that: three Commanders, three Captains and twelve Lieutenants. The Senior Service seniors at play.

Among the list of competitors one car and driver pairing stands out, one without any known naval connection. The name was J. D. Siddeley and the car a 40 hp Mercedes; the latter among a run of Humbers, Renaults and Oldsmobiles of between 5 and 20 hp.

John Davenport Siddeley, later Sir John Siddeley and eventually Lord Kenilworth, was to become one of the giants of British industry, being associated with such names as Siddeley-Deasy, Wolseley-Siddeley, Armstrong Siddeley, Bristol Siddeley and lastly (although by this time no longer personally involved) with Hawker Siddeley. In the context of the Portsmouth Trials however, the question is:- why was he driving a Mercedes. The Siddeley Autocar Company Ltd. had been formed in 1902 and their first cars, made for them by Vickers, were introduced at the Crystal Palace Show in 1903. Why was Siddeley not promoting his own cars?

To add to the mystery, the report of the event in the *Automobile Club Journal*, under the heading "A NAVAL OFFICER'S MOTOR RUN", omits his name completely, listing only fourteen entrants. As the self appointed controllers of motor sport, perhaps the ACGBI

THE EARLY YEARS 1904 TO 1906

thought the Mercedes not to be eligible, or perhaps they objected to John Siddeley's professional status against the amateur naval Commanders and Captains. Although the ACGBI reported the Trials, they were not the organising club and the event was not run under their regulation.

For the first section of the Trials fuel tanks were brimmed at the start and then refilled at the finish, measuring the quantity of petrol used to the nearest half pint. In addition, an observer in each car timed the ascent of Portsdown Hill en route.

The second section of the Trials was an independently timed ascent of a private road near South Harting kindly lent by Col. Hon. Turnour Featherstonhaugh of Up Park. Up Park is the estate in which the famously restored National Trust house Uppark is situated. Much was made in the press reports of the fact that a telephone was installed half way up the hill to enable the competitors to follow each other more closely.

No map was published in any of the contemporary reports to identify the actual road used. However in the comments column of the results table reference is made to some cars also "climbing both steep hills south of Harting" which "both had portions of 1 in 6½". The inference clearly is that the Trial was not run on either of these roads, which are taken to be the present B2146 and B2141, but on a private road within Up Park. The secondary inference is that the track used was not as steep as either of the two public roads. The most likely track is the one which runs from the Bridgers Pond entrance off the B2146 up to the house. This track runs for about a mile and rises from 100 feet above sea level to some 180 feet.

The results make fascinating reading and again highlight the presence of John Siddeley. The 40hp Mercedes was dramatically both the fastest car in the timed sections and the thirstiest car in the fuel consumption test. The most frugal car was a 6½hp Humberette

AN UNNAMED GROUP OF THE NAVAL OFFICERS AND THEIR PASSENGERS
TAKING PART IN THE PORTSMOUTH TRIALS.

SOUTH HARTING HILL CLIMB 1905-1924

driven by one Professor Dykes. It is instructive to compare these two cars:

	Humberette	**Mercedes**
Unladen weight	10cwt.	25cwt.
Fuel tank capacity	3 gallons	24 gallons
Passengers carried	2	5
Miles per gallon	70	11.3
Portsdown Hill time	3mins. 42secs.	2mins. 19secs.
South Harting time	2mins. 37.6secs.	1min. 5.6secs.

The performance of the Mercedes is impressive but not altogether surprising, the line between Mercedes racing cars and production cars was a fairly thin one in those heady, Gordon Bennett winning, days. Mercedes cars of this period were, by any standard, technically very advanced vehicles. It is the 6½hp Humberette which surprises. The fuel consumption, on a run including Portsdown Hill, is frankly amazing. The next best car achieved only 45mpg, and a 5hp Humberette in the same event could do no better than 30mpg. This is even more astonishing when you take into account the fact that the 6½hp Humberette was also fourth fastest up the South Harting hill. Whoever Professor Dykes was he either knew something special about tuning and driving motor cars, or perhaps how to manipulate half pint measures.

Five separate reports of the Portsmouth Trials were found (see App.II) but they were all clearly transcribed almost verbatim from one original report. Since the results were the major part of the reports, and the remainder largely a detailed account of the naval involvement, we should perhaps assume that the Senior Service issued a press release and that no independent reporters were present.

The frustrating thing about the reports is that they are all, with one very minor exception, completely devoid of comment. The only minor exception was *The Autocar*, who thought that separate observers in each of the cars timing the ascent of Portsdown Hill was "an unsatisfactory method". When you look at the results you can understand their dissatisfaction. Six of the eleven cars which made the climb had times quoted which were an exact number of minutes to the second. One wonders whether those times were anything more than estimates based on pocket watches. The times up the South Harting hill were all to the nearest fifth of a second. However since the times up Portsdown Hill were not treated as a separate trial, they were perhaps not material, just indicative.

For some reason four of the cars which took part in the South Harting hill climb Trial had not taken part in the Fuel Consumption Trial. There is nothing in the reports to indicate why.

THE EARLY YEARS 1904 TO 1906

CARS IN CLASS A WAITING TO START AT
THE FOOT OF THE HILL.
(1905)

1905 – The First ACGBI Event

The first proper South Harting Hill Climb was held on Saturday 10th June 1905. It was organised by the Automobile Club of Great Britain and Ireland, (ACGBI), supported by the Sussex County Automobile Club.

A detailed map of the course was published in *The Autocar* a week before the event and showed the start to have been on the present B2146 about a quarter of a mile before the junction with the B2141. The building shown in contemporary photographs at the start line is the Engine House, which is still there today at the entrance to Engine Farm. The "engine" in question used to pump water from the adjacent ponds up the hill to Uppark. The course turned left up the B2141 and then ran for just under a mile further to give a total course length of 1833 yards with an average gradient of 1:9 and a maximum of 1:7.

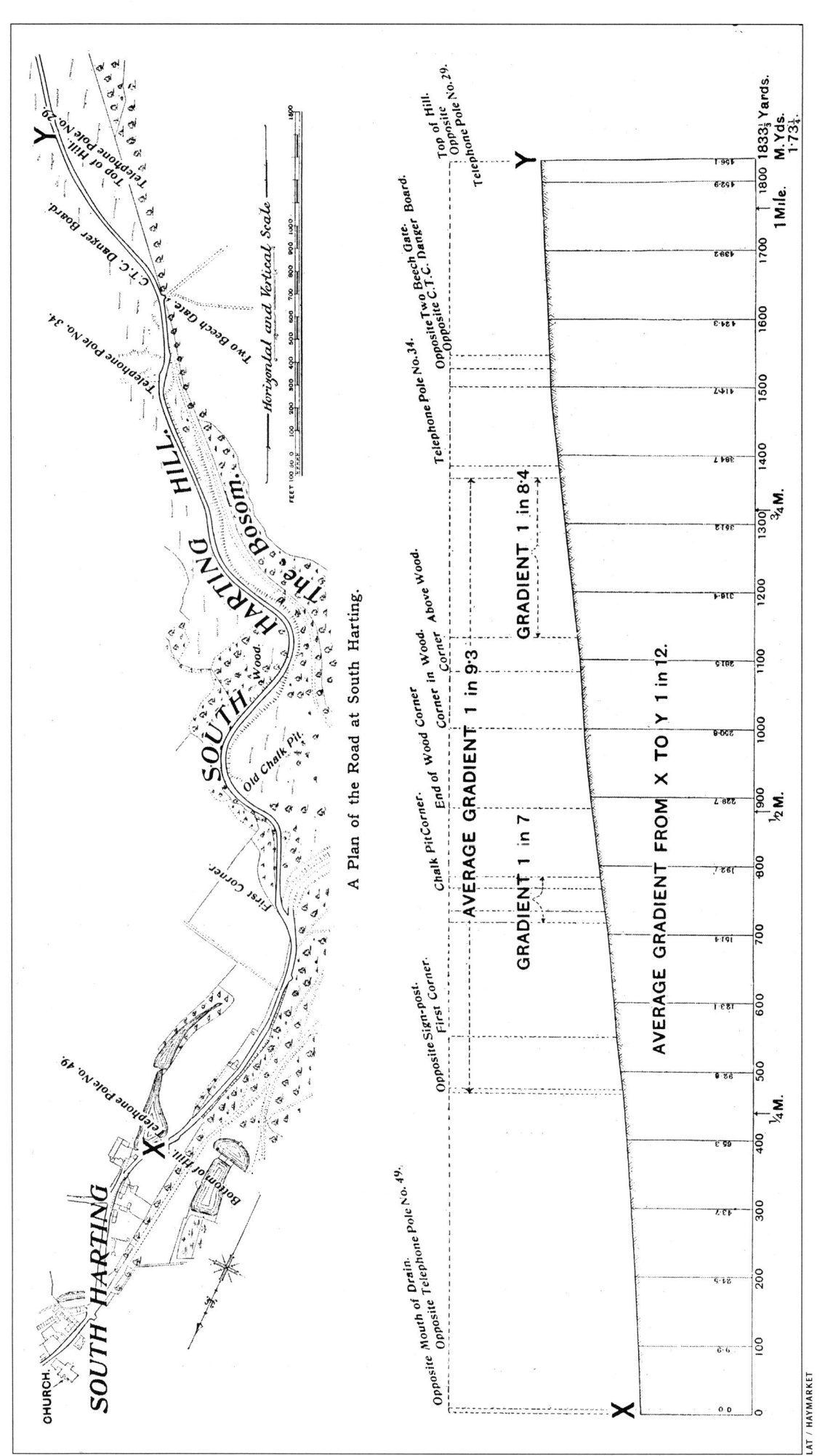

THE EARLY YEARS 1904 TO 1906

The surveying and layout of the course was credited to Earl Russell, who lived at Telegraph House, high on North Marden Down just south of the three Hartings. A prominent motoring pioneer, and an early member of the Automobile Club, Earl Russell was, by any standards, a colourful character. The elder brother of renowned academic Bertrand Russell, he removed himself from Oxford because of some scandalous, but unsubstantiated, allegations; later in 1901 he was jailed for bigamy. When car registration numbers were introduced in 1903 he reportedly queued all night to get the very first London number, A 1. (see Appendices IV and V)

In the context of the first South Harting Hill Climb, he was Clerk of the Course, a member of the Races Committee of the ACGBI, and Vice Chairman of the Sussex County Automobile Club. He also donated two of the three trophies to be competed for. Probably inspired by the Portsmouth Trials in 1904, he should surely be considered as the father of the South Harting Hill Climb.

Entry to the event was open to members of the Automobile Club, and all affiliated clubs. Entrants were divided into three classes based on vehicle price. Steam cars were eligible:

Quote:

CLASS A   For cars, the list price of which is £150.00 and not more than £350.00; and in this class, cars costing not more than £250.00 must carry two passengers, and cars costing over that and up to £350.00 must carry four passengers.

CLASS B   For cars the chassis price of which is £300.00 and not more than £500.00, to carry four passengers.

CLASS C   For cars the chassis price of which is over £500.00 and not more than £850.00, to carry four passengers.

Unquote:

We see clearly in these Class definitions the heritage from Motor Trials. The purpose of the event was primarily to test the relative performance of production cars. Cars which had "competed in open events for racing cars" were specifically excluded. Efficiency was not a factor in the Class awards since price was the only criteria, but it would have been in the Gold Medal Handicap, in which all cars were awarded marks against an unpublished handicap formula. However, referred to as "the Club formula", it would almost certainly have been based on the then widely accepted ratio of (weight) divided by (run time x horse power).

Forty nine entries were received, which disappointed the ACGBI but was considered quite sufficient by *The Autocar*. Entrant and driver were quoted separately and threw up some historically interesting names. Mr. Louis Coatalen, later to be a respected designer for

THE ONLY PUBLISHED MAP OF THE COURSE WAS THIS ONE IN
THE AUTOCAR BEFORE THE FIRST EVENT. EARL RUSSELL WAS CREDITED
PERSONALLY WITH SURVEYING AND DESIGNING IT. SUBSEQUENT
EVENTS SOMETIMES USED A SLIGHTLY SHORTER COURSE.
(1905)

SOUTH HARTING HILL CLIMB 1905-1924

COMPETITORS LINING UP AT
PETERSFIELD STATION FOR WEIGHING-IN.
(1905)

Sunbeam, was driving a Humber, for whom he was a designer in 1905. Miss Dorothy Levitt, pioneer lady racing driver, drove both a De Dion and a Mors. Capt. Sir R.K. Arbuthnot, R.N. was driving his own Sunbeam again, and Tom Thornycroft was driving a 24hp Thornycroft in Class C. The Hon. C.S. Rolls was an entrant, not a driver, and the car a 15hp Orleans. The driver was Claude Johnson, who had been the first Secretary of the Automobile Club, but now worked for Rolls selling imported French cars. Later in 1905 they would both be involved in marketing the new car being made by Henry Royce. The entry included three White steam cars. Most entrants were either manufacturers or British agents for imported cars.

Weighing-in was at Petersfield Station on the Saturday morning. The cars were weighed twice, once empty and then again with passengers; this data was needed for the Gold Medal Handicap calculations. The person entrusted with these calculations was W. Worby Beaumont. *The Automotor Journal* thought he was "deserving of sympathy for his invidious position. This extraordinary arrangement of introducing a qualifying factor based on personal observation in order to level up mechanical results, appears to us to be not only undesirable,

THE EARLY YEARS 1904 TO 1906

but even more open to question than the numerous formulae which have figured so conspicuously in confusing the issues of other similar events." This foreshadowed the huge row which was to break out a year or so later.

Earl Russell was in charge at the start line, although the actual starter was Julian Orde, who was also Secretary of the Meeting, as well as the current Secretary of the ACGBI itself. A new electric timing system was being tried, but back up manual timing was available since flag signals were visible between start and finish lines. There were virtually no trees anywhere up the hill at that time, compared to the continuous wooded cover that exists today. Earl Russell had also installed a telephone link up the hill.

There had been heavy rain the day before the event as well as on the day itself. The chalk road surface was very treacherous and the start line had frequently to be brushed clear of mud. Weighing-in had been delayed and there were further delays at the start, and throughout the event, caused by normal traffic. The Automobile Club thought this very inconsiderate of the non-competitors.

Before the event *The Autocar* was fairly upbeat about the whole affair: "The villagers are taking the liveliest interest in the competition, and consider themselves honoured that the hill overlooking their tiny burgh should have been selected for so important a competition."

After the event their tone changed somewhat: "As a spectacle, nothing slower has ever been operated by the Club. Smartly handled, the whole trial could have been run through in half the time. The waits between cars were at times dreary in the extreme; and this in addition to the fact that, barring the climbing of half a dozen of the vehicles in Class C, the cars taking this hill at long intervals produced a spectacle which could not be described as thrilling even by the most enthusiastic."

To avoid antagonising the police or the anti-motoring lobby, the ACGBI had decided to publish only the winner and runner up in each Class with no actual times or speeds quoted. *The Autocar* described this system as "foolish" on the basis that anti-motorists would remain anti-motorists whether the times were published or not. *Motoring Illustrated* equally expressed "much dissatisfaction" with the system and even did some private timings, recording average speeds from 7 to 27½mph. The latter illegal speed would have equated to a run time of 2mins. 16secs., whereas the slower speed would have taken 8mins. 55secs.

Apart from *The Autocar* and *Motoring Illustrated*, the other three reports found were largely uncritical if not wholly enthusiastic. *Automobile Club Journal*, not surprisingly, was the most enthusiastic: "Notwithstanding the weather, the Club held a most successful meeting at South Harting on Saturday last. From first to last everything went smoothly and well , thanks to the efforts of all concerned."

Could this be the same event *The Autocar* described?

Despite their overall misgivings, *The Autocar* was the only journal to give a detailed account of proceedings, positioning themselves at Chalk Pit Corner. This was, at 1:7, both the steepest and bumpiest part of the hill. The Peugeot entered and driven by Mr. Cutler in Class A managed to stall its engine and could not be restarted without setting down one passenger. The highlight for *The Autocar* seemed to have been Dorothy Levitt who climbed successfully and with style on both her 8hp De Dion in Class A and the 12hp Mors in Class B. Frank Churchill in his own 14hp Hallamshire stopped at Chalk Pit Corner with a slipping clutch. Apart from these minor happenings, reporting on the uneventful climbs of the other forty five cars must have taxed the ingenuity of even the most creative journalist.

SOUTH HARTING HILL CLIMB 1905-1924

TOM THORNYCROFT ON THE 24hp THORNYCROFT
NEAR THE START LINE.

Humber had a good day winning Classes A & B, and so did Daimler, gaining 1st and 2nd in Class C. The Humber that won Class A was driven by Louis Coatalen. A 13hp Dixi, entered by Mrs. E. Bennett-Stanford and driven by her husband, won the Gold Medal Handicap with an 18hp Peugeot second.

When the last car had ascended, Earl and Countess Russell invited all competitors and officials back to Telegraph House for tea. One of the duty policemen was quoted by the Automobile Club as saying "I have enjoyed the day very much".

THE EARLY YEARS 1904 TO 1906

DOROTHY LEVITT ON HER 8hp DE DION
WAITING TO START IN CLASS A.

E.M.C. INSTONE
ON HIS 30hp
DAIMLER
AT THE START
LINE IN CLASS C.
(1905)

xxiv. The Autocar. ADVERTISEMENTS.—Supplement. June 17th, 1905.

HILL-CLIMBING.

10 H.P.
SPEEDWELL

takes **2nd place** in the

South Harting Hill-climb,

BEATING CARS OF HIGHER PRICE AND HORSE-POWER.

FULL PARTICULARS AND LIST FREE:

The Speedwell Motor Co.,
LIMITED,
151, KNIGHTSBRIDGE, S.W.

THE EARLY YEARS 1904 TO 1906

OFFICIALS AND SPECTATORS AT THE
FINISH LINE. THE COURSE TELEPHONE IS
HOUSED IN THE CAR ON THE RIGHT.
(1905)

SOUTH HARTING HILL CLIMB 1905-1924

THE LONG QUEUE FOR THE START,
ALMOST BACK TO THE VILLAGE CENTRE.
(1906)

THE EARLY YEARS 1904 TO 1906

1906 – The Second ACGBI Event

The second South Harting Hill Climb was held on Saturday June 23rd 1906 and on paper was almost a rerun of the 1905 event. A closer analogy however would be to consider the 1905 event as a rehearsal for the 1906 event, which turned out to be bigger, better run, in much better weather and on dry roads. The ACGBI had clearly taken on board the criticisms of the first event and even *The Autocar* was moved to report: "The climb was well organised, and those officiating did an immense amount of good work".

Eighty four entries had been received, of which sixty four actually appeared on the start line. To cope with these larger numbers the weighing-in at Petersfield had to be started at 8.00am on the Saturday, under the close scrutiny of the "clerk of the scales" Mr. Lyons Sampson. This meant that some of the more distant competitors needed to be in the area the day before. To this end the West Sussex Motor Co. of Chichester offered free overnight garaging, and then set up shop in South Harting on the Saturday to supply petrol, oil, batteries and tyres.

The influx of competitors and spectators clearly put a considerable strain on local resources. Every hotel room in Petersfield had been booked a week in advance and there was a reported "black market" in Bed & Breakfast accommodation. *Automotor Journal* noted many people sleeping in their cars. Two hundred cars were counted in and around South Harting; a somewhat flowery paragraph from *Motoring Illustrated* captured the atmosphere:

> "South Harting, with its magnificent panoramas, its picturesque cottages, is a place where every prospect pleases, and on Saturday only the dust from the caravanserai of cars and the works of the road-hog were vile. And the only road-hogs we saw were coachmen with a fatal fascination for the wrong side of the road, and sleepy-eyed waggoners too weary or churlish to pull aside for swifter vehicles to pass. Narrow tortuous lanes brought us to South Harting, where the open spaces of the village were crammed with cars, the natives regarding the event as justification for a general holiday."

To overcome the delays experienced the year before several changes were made to the way the actual runs were organised. Firstly the hill was divided into four sectors which were all connected by telephone so that any problems were immediately common knowledge. Secondly, and slightly controversially, the fastest cars were sent up the hill first which tended to make the later afternoon runs a bit anticlimactic.

The method of recording the results was also different. Instead of just reporting the winner and runner up in each class, all competitors were awarded marks which, while not themselves actual times, the differences were actual time differences. Although not explained, the mechanism would appear to have been that the actual times in seconds were deducted from some arbitrary higher common number. Thus the quickest time would translate into the highest number of marks. Using the unofficial timings published by *Motoring Illustrated* the number used can be calculated as 400. In the event, however, the number should have been at least 550, since the slowest cars in CLASS A had to be credited with substantial negative marks. There was also a separate handicap event based on a still unpublished formula, but kept within individual Classes rather than between all entrants.

SOUTH HARTING HILL CLIMB 1905-1924

A.C. EARP ON HIS 35HP IRIS WAITS PATIENTLY IN LINE.
(1906)

THE EARLY YEARS 1904 TO 1906

The entries for 1906 were divided into four Classes, instead of three as in 1905, and the order of listing was reversed to reflect the running order:

Quote:

CLASS D   For cars the chassis price of which is over £850.00, to carry four passengers. The chassis price includes the tyres.

CLASS C   For cars the chassis price of which is over £500.00 and not more than £850.00, to carry four passengers. The chassis price includes the tyres.

CLASS B   For cars the chassis price of which is £300.00 and not more than £500.00, to carry four passengers. The chassis price includes the tyres.

CLASS A   For cars the list price of which is £150.00 and not more than £350.00; and in the Class cars costing not more than £250.00 to carry two passengers, and cars costing over that and up to £350.00 to carry four passengers. The price of any chassis in this Class to be less than £300.00

Unquote:

JEREMY BACON COLLECTION

ONE OF ONLY TWO PICTURES FOUND
ACTUALLY SHOWING A POLICE PRESENCE.
(1906)

SOUTH HARTING HILL CLIMB 1905-1924

CARS WAITING THEIR TURN NEAR THE START LINE.
(1906)

The extra Class was CLASS D at the top end of the price range, and appears to have been created to allow in Napiers and the bigger Daimlers, which an official said had deliberately been kept out the previous year. This attracted two notable new names, Cecil Edge (co-driver with his cousin, S.F. Edge, of the winning Napier in the 1902 Gordon Bennett race) driving his own 60hp Napier, and Charles Jarrott as entrant of a 60hp De Dietrich. Mr. Algernon Lee Guinness was driving his own Darracq in CLASS B, along with Mr. J.T.C. Moore-Brabazon in a Minerva. Many names from 1905 were also present, including Dorothy Levitt as the only female name in the list.

Among the familiar names in the list of officials were Mr. J.W. Orde as Secretary of the Meeting, Earl Russell as Judge, Mr. W. Worby Beaumont as Handicapper and Mr. A.V.

– 30 –

THE EARLY YEARS 1904 TO 1906

Ebblewhite (later to become well known as the handicapper at Brooklands) as Timekeeper.

Early on Saturday morning, long before the scheduled start time, several competitors drove to the hill to put in a few practice runs. Officials of the ACGBI and the Sussex County A.C. however soon put a stop to this on the grounds that they would damage the road surface before the event had even begun. Whilst this logic was probably sound it is not clear on what grounds they could prevent them using a public road, particularly as they were powerless to stop normal traffic using the road during the later timed runs by competitors.

The first car up the hill at 11.00am was Cecil Edge on his 60hp, six cylinder Napier. Instone, on his 35hp Daimler, hit a pair of posts on the first corner, put two wheels on the grass verge, swerved violently, and was lucky not to crash. However Class D was won by Manville on his 35hp Daimler. Second was Davenport Powell in another 35hp Daimler, with Edge third. The 45hp Daimlers, which had been entered, were scratched. Manville was unofficially timed at 1min. 57.4secs.

On the handicap formula Cecil Edge was the winner, with Mieville second in a 30-40hp Peugeot. Mieville had been eleventh against the clock. Manville dropped to fifth.

Class C was between Dorothy Levitt in a 50hp Napier and George Barwick in his 30hp Daimler. The latter won. On handicap formula a 28hp Pipe driven by G. Dumont won; he had been tenth fastest against the clock. The Class should have been enlivened by Coleman's 18hp White steam car but a repeated link motion breakage before the event prevented him getting to South Harting in time for his scheduled start. Two Rolls-Royce entries also failed to make the start line.

After the lunch break there was high drama in Class B. Darracq cars swept the board taking the first five places, but the first and second 20hp cars, both entered by Warwick J. Wright, were subject to several protests, although no reasons were reported. A later meeting of the Competitions Committee upheld the protests, which made Sydney Girling in a 20-32hp Darracq the winner, with a similar car second. On handicap formula a 12-16hp Clement-Talbot driven by T.H. Woollen won; he had been eighth fastest against the clock. Girling was reduced to twelfth on handicap. The Whitlock-Aster driven by W.H. Arnold had suffered clutch slip all the way up and the engine overheated to such an extent that the radiator exploded as the car crossed the finishing line.

Fastest time in Class A was posted by a 10hp Stanley steam car driven by A.H. Bruck, with Louis Coatalen second in a 10-12hp Coventry-Humber. The Stanley was also later placed first on handicap formula, although the ACGBI admitted that they had no rational formulaic basis on which to compare the performance of a steam car with a petrol engined car. The Stanley was the only car in any Class to win both on time and handicap.

When all the programmed events had been completed the crowd were treated to a £25.00 charity match race, organised in order to give the White steam car, which had not made the scheduled start, a chance to show its paces. To add spice to the occasion the match was against Dorothy Levitt in her 50hp Napier. Mr. F. Coleman not only beat Dorothy Levitt, but also beat Manville's fastest time of the day by 0.2sec. It was calculated that, at the finish line, Coleman was doing over 50mph.

Mr. Coleman, already carrying 29 stones of passengers, said he could have done even better with more ballast since he was losing traction on the corners. The same car had, the previous week, won its class at Shelsley Walsh.

When the competition was over, Countess Russell presented the prizes in the judges tent

J. M. GORHAM, 30hp DAIMLER, WAITING TO START.
(1906)

at the top of the hill. Competitors and officials were then invited back to Telegraph House for tea.

In complimenting the officials for a well run event *Motoring Illustrated* added:

> " Special thanks are due to the police, who assisted the officials in safeguarding the public, and wisely observed the spirit rather than the letter of the law."

THE EARLY YEARS 1904 TO 1906

J. M. GORHAM, 30hp DAIMLER, ABOUT TO START HIS ASCENT.
(1906)

THE EARLY YEARS 1904 TO 1906

THE AUTOMOTOR JOURNAL

MONTAGUE NAPIER, S. F. EDGE AND W. H. WHITE DISCUSS THE
ACTION FROM THEIR OWN VANTAGE POINT.
(1906)

left
W. H. ARNOLD
ON HIS 18-22hp
WHITLOCK-ASTER
ROUNDING THE
FIRST BEND.
(1906)

LAT PHOTOGRAPHIC

right
COMPETITORS
RELAXING DURING
THE LUNCH BREAK
IN THE VILLAGE.
(1906)

THE AUTOMOTOR JOURNAL

SOUTH HARTING HILL CLIMB 1905-1924

MOTORING ILLUSTRATED.　　　ADVERTISEMENTS.　　　JUNE 30, 1906.

BY APPOINTMENT TO
HIS MAJESTY THE KING.

BY APPOINTMENT TO
H.R.H. THE PRINCE OF WALES.

Daimler

Sussex Automobile Club Hill=Climb, South Harting, June 23rd.

Daimlers First and Second in Class D, First in Class C, Beating high-powered cars of nearly all leading makes.

Also Hill=Climb for Dupre Cup, June 23rd,

Competed for by Notts, Leicester and Derby Clubs.

Three fastest times made on Daimlers. The continued success of Daimler cars in all competitions is the most striking proof of their claim to be the MOST REPRESENTATIVE BRITISH CAR.

The Daimler Motor Co. (1904), Ltd.,

Coventry : Daimler Works.　　　Manchester : 60, Deansgate.
London : 219-229, Shaftesbury Avenue, W.C.
Bristol : 18, Victoria Street.　　　Nottingham : 96-98, Derby Road.

AGENTS :

MESSRS. CHAPMAN VON SOBBE & Co., LTD., Mulberry Street, LIVERPOOL.
ALBERT FARNELL, 50, Manningham Lane, BRADFORD.
MESSRS. SANDERSON & SANDERSON, 65, Percy Street, NEWCASTLE-ON-TYNE.
MESSRS. SCOTTISH AUTOMOBILE Co., LTD., The Velodrome, Leith Walk, EDINBORO.
MESSRS. ROSSLEIGH MOTOR Co., LTD., 44, Sauchiehall Street, GLASGOW.
SOUTH WALES MOTOR Co., 94, St. Mary Street, CARDIFF.
JOHN HUTTON, SONS & Co., 115, Summer Hill, DUBLIN.
ANGLIAN MOTOR Co., LTD., BECCLES, SUFFOLK.

WHEN COMMUNICATING WITH ADVERTISERS, PLEASE MENTION MOTORING ILLUSTRATED.

iii.

THE EARLY YEARS 1904 TO 1906

A GENERAL VIEW NEAR THE TOP OF THE HILL,
SHOWING THE RETURN ROAD TO THE VILLAGE.
(1906)

SOUTH HARTING HILL CLIMB 1905-1924

DOROTHY LEVITT, 50hp NAPIER, AND
FREDERICK COLEMAN, WHITE STEAM CAR,
LINE UP FOR THEIR MATCH RUN.
COLEMAN WON.
(1906)

ii. The Autocar. ADVERTISEMENTS.—Supplement. June 30th, 1906.

THEY WERE SEEN AT
FROME,
THEY WERE SEEN AT
SOUTH HARTING,
THEY WILL BE SEEN AT
ASTON.

SIMMS
PNEUMATIC BUFFERS
FITTED TO THE TWO
SIMMS-WELBECK CARS,
BUT THEY WILL FIT
ANY CAR.

Prices—Small car, £8:8:0. Large Car, £10:10:0.

Simms-Welbeck Four-cylinder Cars, Side-entrance,

12-15 H.P.	.. ..	£425.
20-24 ,,	.. ..	£500.
26-30 ,,	.. ..	£575.

IMMEDIATE DELIVERY
FROM
SIMMS MANUFACTURING CO., LTD.,
Welbeck Works, Kilburn, LONDON, N.W.

SOUTH HARTING

HILL CLIMB.

(Class B.)

DARRACQ 1st

Warwick J. Wright.

DARRACQ 2nd

A. Huntley Walker.

WARWICK J. WRIGHT and A. HUNTLEY WALKER

can give **IMMEDIATE** Delivery of

1906 DARRACQS.

Your visit to their handsome Showrooms,

483, OXFORD ST., W.,

will be esteemed.

THE AUTOMOTOR JOURNAL

OFFICIALS AT THE FINISHING LINE. EARL RUSSELL,
THE JUDGE, SEATED ON THE LEFT OF THE PICTURE.
(1906)

JEREMY BACON COLLECTION

JOHN COURAGE, 24hp ROCHET-SCHNEIDER, AND
ERNEST OWERS, 60hp NAPIER, WAIT AT THE TOP OF THE HILL
FOR CLEARANCE TO RETURN TO THE VILLAGE.
(1906)

CHAPTER 2

THE HANDICAP FORMULA DEBATE

On the 30th June 1906 *Automotor Journal* published a lavishly illustrated and uncritical report of the South Harting Hill Climb which had been held the previous week end. Shorter accounts of four other hill climb events appeared in the same issue. Two weeks later the same journal published a full page editorial piece under the banner headline "HILL CLIMBS – THEIR QUESTIONABLE VALUE". It contained the comment " we regard most contests of this kind as worse than useless in their present form". What on earth was going on.

Whilst the chattering classes may well have been muttering over their gin and tonics for some time, the first salvo in the published debate seems to have been a letter from S.F. Edge in *The Autocar* on the 23rd June 1906. This was the same day the South Harting Hill Climb was being held, where Edge was watching his cousin Cecil compete on his 60hp Napier.

The premiss behind Edge's letter was that the prime function of hill climb events was to "demonstrate the relative merits of the cars". Given this premiss he complained that the value of the events was being severely diminished because the organising clubs all used different classification systems and handicap formulae. Some of the handicap formulae were not even published. His main concern with known formulae was the diverse methods used to calculate horse power; he particularly decried those formulae based on piston area only and which ignored stroke. He was completely dismissive of South Harting where the classification system was based purely on chassis price. The Edge letter was a plea for debate rather than a specific proposal; it should be remembered however that his business was selling Napier cars, which were both expensive and had relatively short stroke engines.

The *Automotor Journal* editorial on the 14th July started from the same premiss and covered similar ground, but had a few additions and a different spin. They made the sweeping statement that both the motoring public and the event organisers had "failed to grasp the fundamental principles which are of vital importance to their (hill climbs) practical utility".

THE HANDICAP FORMULA DEBATE

Further "the results are arrived at by the use of some unknown or unsatisfactory formulae, and practically no steps are taken to see that the competing cars are replicas of any standard model".

Then they homed in on their prime target. They argued that to judge the measured performance of any given car, be it on speed or time, it was necessary somehow to compute the weight and power of that car. The unknown in the computation was power. The manufacturers advertised power figures lacked any common logic, and there was no industry agreed standard or method for engine rating. In fact the suspicion was that the advertised horse power figures had more to do with sales promotion than fact. There was no correlation between cylinder dimensions and quoted horse power.

Some proposed engine rating formulae were based on piston area alone, some then compensated for long stroke, others schemes were based on the cubic contents of the cylinders and yet another on the piston displacement per minute. Each of these systems was thought to favour a particular type of engine.

The ACGBI Tourist Trophy Race for production cars, run in the Isle of Man, had adopted a fuel consumption basis for calculation specifically to avoid the engine rating argument, and this was the way *Automotor Journal* wanted a standard hill climb formula to go. By defining "a suitable fuel allowance" and a minimum (loaded) vehicle weight, it was thought that a realistic basis for comparing cars could be devised. To add urgency to the debate, *Automotor Journal* suggested that the ACGBI should act on the advice given by its own Expert and Technical Committee eight months earlier and stop sanctioning any hill climb events until a sound technical basis for a formula could be found. The Committee in fact expressed doubt that any such basis existed.

In the same issue of *Automotor Journal* another letter from Edge was published, a copy of one that he had sent to the ACGBI on 4th July. This letter went well beyond the simple plea for debate in his previous one to *The Autocar*, and actually proposed a standard classification system and handicap formula for running hill climb events.

His starting point was the already familiar observation that the horse power claimed by manufacturers bore no consistent relationship to the cubic inch capacity of the engine. This resulted in "apparently small horse-powered cars beating others of much greater horse-power". He tabulated the catalogue horse power of some leading cars against their cylinder dimensions and produced some startling numbers.

The results were expressed as cubic inches of engine capacity per catalogue horse power. The benchmark was the 40hp Napier which produced 1hp for every 7.25 cu.ins. The worst was the 24hp Fiat at 1hp for every 18.5 cu.ins.. Daimler, Peugeot, Darracq and De Dietrich were grouped in the middle at around 10-12 cu.ins. per 1hp.

Edge's shrewd proposal based on these findings was that all manufacturers should be required to classify their engines on the basis of a minimum of 1hp for every seven cubic inches of capacity. Thus the 24hp Fiat would immediately become the 63hp Fiat, and the 60hp De Dietrich would become the 104hp De Dietrich. Edge believed from known laboratory data that this would still understate the actual horse power of some cars, but it would at least create an approximately level playing field. Given this definition of power, Edge was then quite prepared to accept a basic hill climb formula of:

$$\frac{\text{Time x Power}}{\text{Weight}} \quad \text{or:} \quad \frac{T \times P}{W}$$

– 43 –

Most versions of this formula used the inverse ratio. Cars would then run in classes determined simply by engine capacity in cubic inches, such as:

> Any number of cylinders up to 150 cubic inches
> 150 cubic inches to 350 cubic inches
> 350 cubic inches to 500 cubic inches
> Over 500 cubic inches

The weight figure would not be that of the car alone but would be a minimum, to include a payload, related to engine capacity. The figure suggested was 1cwt per 10 cubic inches of capacity. Thus a car weighing 30cwt with a 400 cubic inch engine would have to carry a payload of 10cwt, which equates roughly to five passengers plus luggage.

Automotor Journal then went into overdrive. On the 21st July 1906 they published their own detailed, three page, proposal for a classification system and handicap formula. They clearly sensed that the ACGBI would be forced to act soon and they intended to make sure that their own preferences would have to be taken into consideration.

Their starting point again was that calculating potential horse power was the nub of the problem. Actual engine rating was seen as a separate issue and made the subject of a second "Yellow Cover" proposal; "Yellow Cover" being a descriptive euphemism for *The Automotor Journal*. The first essential was to get rid of the "fictitious horse power evil", and the way to do that was seen as the application of the Tourist Trophy principles, which were based on fuel consumption, to hill climbs. To enable the general motoring public to better understand the issues, *Automotor Journal* published a separate series of technical articles under the title "What is Horse Power", which they tactfully suggested should be required reading before trying to understand their handicap formula.

They argued that, beyond the bore, stroke and the number of cylinders of a particular engine, it was necessary to look at engine speed (rpm) and carburettor tuning. The latter could be set up for normal road performance or short burst sprints or hill climbs.

High engine speed was seen as a basic design parameter which could only be achieved at high manufacturing cost. To make engines run at high speed needed lighter rotating components, precision machining and better materials. This added cost was seen as uneconomic for the "average" car with its (by inference) heavy and crudely made engine. It should be remembered however that "high speed" in 1906 meant around 1300rpm, a fast tickover for a modern engine.

Despite these caveats *Automotor Journal* insisted that no formula should be adopted which would stifle engine development. They had stated in their original "mend or end" editorial that all the proposed horse power formulae favoured different types of engine; they therefore concluded that no one horse power formula could be satisfactory. Echoes of the ACGBI Technical Committee conclusions.

The crux of the *Automotor Journal* argument was thus that it was necessary to avoid calculating potential horse power completely. Their way of doing this was to claim that the "rate of fuel consumption" was equivalent to power, and that "fuel used" could therefore be substituted for horse power in any handicap formula. Important to their mathematics was the concept of "rate" of fuel consumption rather the total "quantity" of fuel used.

This logic led to the bizarre conclusion that it was completely unnecessary to time the cars up the hill at all. The generally accepted basic handicap formula for hill climbs was

W/(P x T). If you substituted (fuel used divided by time) for P, then the two "time" factors cancelled each other and you were left with simply W/F, where F = fuel used. For a given rate of fuel consumption, a longer run time would mean a higher (Fuel used).

The main snag with the system was that all competing cars would have to be fitted with a standard fuel measuring device. The *Automotor Journal* proposal, supported by drawings, meant that the only permanent fitment required on the cars would a three way tap in the fuel line. For competition a small standard vertical container would be plumbed into the branch connection with an accurate burette type measuring tube incorporated. The tap positions were fuel tank to engine for normal running, fuel tank to engine and container, and container to engine. By selecting the second tap position the container would be filled at the start line and the reading noted. At the start, an official would set the tap to feed the engine from the container and at the finish line an official on the car would close the tap to isolate the container again. A second reading would then allow the actual amount of fuel used on the run to be calculated.

The second *Automotor Journal* proposal was that all new engine types should be bench tested in the presence of an independent inspector and issued with a Certificate of power produced. The ACGBI would maintain a Register of these Certificates, and every individual engine would be stamped with an identification mark recording bore, stroke, normal speed, normal bhp and Certificate number. Normal (engine) speed was defined as the speed at which fuel consumed per hp is lowest. Thus calibration curves correlating engine speed, fuel consumption and power produced would need to be plotted.

By "a remarkable coincidence", to quote *Automotor Journal* a week later, *The Autocar* published a "A Hill-Climbing Formula" on exactly the same day as *Automotor Journal*; to add to the coincidence the basic formula was remarkably similar. *The Autocar* formula was credited to J.W. Roebuck, whereas the *Automotor Journal* proposal had no named author and was therefore presumably a team effort.

Mr. Roebuck briefly covered the same ground to explain why a standard formula was needed, and why the definition of horse power was the core problem. He then claimed to have originated the idea of using fuel consumption rather than calculated horse power in the formula, but also added the idea that oil consumption should be taken into account as well. This was not pursued in the actual formula however. As with the *Automotor Journal* proposal, cars would have to be fitted with small auxiliary fuel tanks during competition to facilitate actual measurements. Mr. Roebuck envisaged "an ordinary glass tube…graduated in tenths of cubic centimetres so that even while climbing the driver could note exactly what petrol he was using". There was no facility for cutting the fuel supply from the auxiliary tank at the end of the run apart from stopping the engine.

The Autocar formula was W/(T x F). Thus they stayed with timed runs but substituted F for P in the basic formula. There were no limitations on vehicle weight, and the cars would run in classes based purely on the number of engine cylinders, whatever the capacity. Finally Mr. Roebuck claimed that by adding an experimentally derived constant on the top line of the formula it could apply to steam cars as well as petrol.

The Autocar proposal took up less than one page, lacked detail, had no originality and had not been thought through. Whatever may be thought of the principle of the *Automotor Journal* proposal, it was thought through, professionally presented, and supported with engineering drawings of the fuel measurement system required. It is difficult not to see *The Autocar* piece as a simple, hurriedly prepared, journalistic spoiler. Over the ensuing few weeks in that summer of 1906 a quite bad tempered spat was played out between the two rival journals.

The *Automotor Journal* response was a further weekly series of four, minimum one page, editorial articles as well as pages of informed correspondence. On 28th July they confronted by name both J.W. Roebuck and *The Autocar*, and Henry Royce.

Royce got into the debate through a letter in *Automotor Journal* published in the same 21st July issue as their proposal. The letter was written by Claude Johnson, who with the Hon. C.S. Rolls was marketing the cars that Royce made, but he quoted discussions with Royce and a formula that he had proposed.

The first proposal in the Johnson letter was that all cars wishing to enter hill climb events should have their "normal" fuel consumption measured under standard conditions and independently certified by the ACGBI. An observed route from the General Post Office in London to Oxford and back was suggested. This figure, combined with factors related to cylinder dimensions, would then be taken as a measure of engine efficiency to be used in the Royce handicap formula.

The Royce formula was a variant on the basic permutation of weight, horse power and run time. The weight was to be divided by the product of the efficiency factor and the run time. The efficiency factor was (square of the cylinder diameter) x (square root of the stroke) x (certified fuel consumption).

The *Automotor Journal* article on 28th July started off by talking of "remarkable coincidences" and "telepathy", but was generally welcoming of the support for their proposal from all quarters. Then they put the knife in; the composure evident in their original proposal seemed to evaporate.

The basis on which they tried to demolish both the Roebuck and Royce formulae was convoluted indeed. They created a scenario where five cars with different sized engines, running at different gross weights, and taking different times to complete the theoretical hill climb run, nevertheless scored identical marks according to their simple W/F formula. They then applied the Roebuck and Royce formulae to the same set of data to see how they would rank them. Not surprisingly they produced totally different results, on which basis they accused both Roebuck and Royce of being incompetent mathematicians. The sheer arrogance of *Automotor Journal* was breathtaking:

> "So conclusively does our table demonstrate the correctness of the *Automotor Journal* formula, and the incorrectness of the others that nothing more need be said concerning the bare facts of the case".

With the benefit of hindsight, and some of the ensuing correspondence, it can be seen that *Automotor Journal* made some fundamental mistakes in their argument. Firstly, in creating their five car scenario, they made certain technical assumptions which are not valid. They assumed, for instance, that if you doubled the weight of a given car it would take exactly twice as long to climb the hill, and that if you doubled the power you would exactly halve the time.

To compare the results of applying different mathematical formulae to a data set based on such false assumptions would seem unlikely to generate meaningful conclusions.

Despite this, in subsequent correspondence, Henry Royce ate humble pie and accepted the *Automotor Journal* criticism. He acknowledged that previously used hill climb formulae encouraged "absurdly high speed engines" which were "not usually very delightful to ride

THE HANDICAP FORMULA DEBATE

behind". He also acknowledged that, in discussion with Claude Johnson before he wrote to *Automotor Journal* quoting Royce, he "did not give the subject the attention it evidently deserved". He then stated that he "wished to admit the imperfection of my own proposal and the correctness of your criticism". Royce proposed two modified formulae, the first of which gave "marks of merit in proportion to the good use of the fuel" and the second "marks of merit for the good use made of a given engine".

These two formulae could be used separately or in conjunction. Royce then proceeded to endorse the idea of small temporary fuel tanks to measure the actual fuel used on a hill climb run, saying that Rolls-Royce had obtained much valuable data using exactly the same technique on test chassis. He was also sympathetic to the idea of fuel based formulae in general since a Rolls-Royce had been the fastest 4 cylinder car in the previous years Tourist Trophy race, which was run on a "fuel allowance " basis.

The Autocar of the 28th July amplified their skeletal proposal of the previous week, mainly by making the fuel measuring device needed on the cars slightly more credible, and remarkably similar to the *Automotor Journal* design. They also argued against the idea of eliminating the time factor, even though it might be done "theoretically". It would lead to the "production of freak engines (which) would certainly follow". Cars powered by such engines "would perhaps climb the hill in two hours time, whereas another might climb the hill in two minutes; yet the petrol consumption in the two cases could be arranged to be the same, or even slightly lower on the car which took the longer time. In the result the slower car would be returned the winner, which is quite absurd".

The Autocar ended this particular editorial with a plea for the establishment of standard fuel consumption data for each type of engine, much as Johnson had done. But they qualified this with the baffling observation that "it is the exception rather than the rule to find really first class technical and practical men engaged in scientific workshop tests. It is only such men who can intelligently avail themselves of the information resulting by the above suggested tests". Whether this was more than a statement that insufficient skilled people were available is not clear.

Before publication of the 4th August issue, the editors at *The Autocar* would have seen the hatchet job done on their formula by *Automotor Journal* the week before. Acknowledging the "peculiar coincidence" that *Automotor Journal* and *The Autocar* had published formulae "having many points in common" on the same day, they then dismissed the *Automotor Journal* "five car scenario" by saying that "if a formula were produced which would give every competing car an equal figure of merit, it would be futile to hold competitions at all". It was rapidly degenerating into a dialogue between the deaf and the blind.

On the 4th August *Automotor Journal* significantly upped the stakes. This they did by

"offering to place a Challenge Cup or Trophy at the disposal of the ACGBI for the purpose of instituting an annual international event of this character, provided that the general lines advocated by us meet with their approval".

They then published the text of a letter which they had sent to the Secretary of the ACGBI.

The letter proposed an event

"open to touring cars of any standard type, irrespective of their size, power, or system of propulsion, and that the Cup should be held each year by the car which proves itself to be the most efficient – regardless of its class or price".

The preferred formula was their own simple W/F but, perhaps in deference to some of the opposition, they considered (P x T) as a satisfactory alternative to F, where P was the certified horse power of the engine and T the run time. They added a new factor to the debate by suggesting that an allowance should be made for "windage", or wind resistance. Thus was body design entered into the equation.

The following week *Automotor Journal* devoted a whole page to countering *The Autocar's* response to their hatchet job on the Roebuck and Royce formulae. This was, however, almost entirely a linguistic exercise and added no new information or arguments.

The whole polemic revolved around subtle differences in meaning between efficiency and performance, and between theoretical and actual. This was simply verbal fisticuffs and moved the argument forward not one iota.

On the 18th August *Automotor Journal* returned to the subject of windage. Virtually all the previous debate had been about the value of the "P" term in the basic hill climb formula and how it was derived. However it was recognised that, since the drag caused by wind resistance increased with the square of the speed, there was a built in advantage to slow, small cars compared to fast, large ones. In that situation there might be a temptation for large, powerful cars to run below their true maximum speed in order to reduce windage and fuel consumption when using the W/F formula.

Automotor Journal then shot themselves in the foot. They argued that, since relative run times were normally published anyway, such skulduggery would be evident to the interested observer. Thus having argued that the timing of hill climb runs was unnecessary, since the holy grail was efficiency not performance, they now argued that timing data needed to be published before it would be possible to fully understand the results.

To factor windage into the basic hill climb formula it was proposed that an allowance should to be added to the "W" factor for each car. This allowance would take the form: $C(0.005V^2 \times \text{area})$, where C was a constant for each hill depending mainly on gradient, and V the speed of the car up the hill. This would have the effect of increasing the actual marks calculated by the formula. To measure speed, however, it would be necessary to time the cars up the hill.

In order to demonstrate the effect of windage on the results of hill climbs, *Automotor Journal* again set up a theoretical "five car scenario" as they had done to justify their basic W/F formula. The cars varied from one with a 6bhp engine, weighing 1500lbs, with a cross sectional area of 10 sq.ft., to one with a 72bhp engine, weighing 4500lbs, and a cross sectional area of 22 sq.ft. The cars, which were all deemed to be of equal efficiency, were then run at two laden weights up three theoretical hills with gradients of 1 in 5, 1 in 10 and 1 in 15.

The speeds which each would have theoretically achieved were then calculated, with no allowance made for wind resistance, i.e. "in vacuo". This was effectively what was happening in practice. The speeds were then recalculated with the windage allowance built into the formula.

At the extremes the calculations showed that the smallest and least powerful car would run up the steepest gradient at 3.5mph and be completely unaffected by wind resistance, whereas the largest and most powerful car running up the shallowest gradient would have

THE HANDICAP FORMULA DEBATE

achieved 46.15mph "in vacuo", but only 34.6mph in still air. This speed "penalty" would have reduced a 100 mark score to 75 marks. The effect of a 12mph headwind was not calculated.

Automotor Journal, however, recognised that the complications of measuring the cross sectional area of every car, measuring average speeds, and then doing all the calculations could, in that computerless age, only be justified for the most important national events.

For lesser events, a "rough and ready" chart based method of estimating the weight allowance was proposed. A set of charts would be needed for different gradients so that clubs could select the chart appropriate to their hill. Each chart would show a family of curves, one for each particular weight of car, plotting the "weight allowance" against (certified) engine bhp. For example, a car weighing 3000lb, with a 30bhp engine, running up a 1 in 10 gradient would qualify for a weight allowance of 220lbs. The assumptions made in the production of the charts would be refined as real data from real events was accumulated. The biggest assumption was that there was a linear relationship between engine power and the cross sectional area of the car.

In conclusion *Automotor Journal* admitted that this method of calculating results would not in itself remove the temptation for large fast cars to run below their maximum performance when the simple W/F formula was being used. They left it to the "average motorist" to make a judgement based on a combination of formula marks, actual speeds, and price.

In the penultimate article in the series, on the 25th August, *Automotor Journal* turned to the subject of steam cars. Central to their concept of hill climbs as demonstrations of vehicle efficiency for potential buyers was the notion that all types of touring car should be eligible to compete. In practice this meant steam cars, which were a sensitive issue because when they did compete against petrol engined cars they frequently won.

As with electric power, steam power produces maximum torque at low speed and is therefore ideal for hill climbing. In those very early days of the motor car it was by no means a foregone conclusion that the petrol engine would become the standard source of motive power.

Automotor Journal recognised that no formula based solely on cylinder dimensions could be meaningful for a steam engine. The temperature and pressure of the steam had additionally to be taken into account. For a simple flash boiler vague analogies could be made between steam temperature and pressure, and mixture strength and compression ratio in a petrol engine. For a compound steam engine, with a low pressure cylinder as well, the analogy was lost. It was concluded that no acceptable mathematical basis for comparison was available. For the time being therefore there was no alternative to actual measurement of engine power as a basis for comparison.

A fuel consumption based formula was theoretically possible but the practical implications of doing this were too complex. To make the basic W/F formula work for different types of engine it would be necessary to establish a constant, C, for each type of engine as a multiplier for W, and this could only be done when a sufficiently large body of experimental data was available. No such database existed for steam engines. The constant would be a function of the ratio of fuel consumed per bhp produced. Even if the value of C were known for steam engines it would be necessary to have a very strict regime of scrutineering to ensure that individual cars were run in the same configuration as used to derive the data.

There were further complications in that steam engines arrived at the start line with a reserve of stored energy in the boiler which would give an unfair advantage over a petrol engine which generated similar power at the back wheels. A loose analogy could be drawn with a heavy flywheel on a petrol engine, assuming no "free engine" device were fitted. However quantifying this, and putting the cars on an equal footing, would be yet another mathematical complication.

The last in the series of *Automotor Journal* editorial articles on hill climbs and formulae was on 1st September 1906 and headed " Summary and Some Further Side Issues".

Distancing themselves from some of the more domestic aspects of the debate, they decided that the overall main conclusion had to be that some form of official, independent, laboratory based engine rating system needed to be established, recorded and monitored. The "fictitious horse power evil" had to be eliminated. From this distance we need to remind ourselves that the "evil" was usually under reporting horse power rather than over reporting.

Automotor Journal also played up the aspect that they were educating motorists to understand the issues involved, and also preparing them for the vagaries of the increasingly important second hand market in cars. The documentation that went with early cars would become increasingly misleading as the claims made by manufacturers for new cars became more controlled.

It must be stressed however that the entire logic of the *Automotor Journal* campaign was based on the concept that the sole purpose of hill climbs was to evaluate production cars for prospective purchasers. They must serve a "useful purpose" and be tests of "efficiency". The word "sport" was never mentioned.

Trying to square the circle, they observed that such things as power, carrying capacity, speed and cost were all important but they said nothing about efficiency. Different people were influenced by different aspects of vehicle design and performance, and it was probably impossible to find one formula that would satisfy the needs of all spectators at all hill climbs. As a compromise they proposed that three categories of hill climb events be recognised and different degrees of stringency applied to the calculation of results in each case.

For the "most pretentious events" all competing cars should have a certified horse power rating, which should be the "normal" horse power at the engine speed at which the fuel consumed per bhp was lowest, the full formula should be applied, the run speed should be measured, and a windage factor calculated by actual vehicle measurement.

For "important provincial events" the simple W/F formula could be used with windage estimated from charts.

For "minor events" where no fuel measurements could be taken, the basic W/(P x T) formula would have to be used, with chart windage included if thought appropriate, and a flexible attitude to the horse power figure used.

Automotor Journal then tried to rationalise their position by stating that they had never actually proposed eliminating timing, but merely that the use of their simple W/F formula would have avoided delays and enabled the basic results to be announced almost as the last car completed its run. Times and speeds could be declared later for those interested. Throughout the debate *Automotor Journal* never addressed the issues of speed limits and legality.

As an after thought they opined that perhaps the "W" factor, total loaded vehicle weight, should be replaced by a "useful load" factor, made up of body weight plus passengers and luggage.

While the "main event" in the whole debate had been the editorial confrontation between *Automotor Journal* and *The Autocar*, there had, in parallel, been a lively "supporting event"

THE HANDICAP FORMULA DEBATE

in the correspondence columns. The contributions of S.F. Edge and Henry Royce had largely been incorporated into the main event, but many other concerned people expressed their opinions.

It is clear from the wording of many letters that, *Automotor Journal* at least, had distributed copies of their proposal to a selected mailing list and invited comment. Correspondents fell into three identifiable categories, motor manufacturers, academics and club secretaries. The remainder could only be identified as concerned individuals, whether as hill climb competitors or just motorists.

Among the manufacturers, the voices of Napier, Rolls-Royce, Minerva, De Dietrich, New Arrol Johnston, Clement Talbot and Ariel were heard. Daimler, despite being probably the most successful and respected single manufacturer in hill climb events at the time, chose to remain silent.

Mr. L. Turcat from De Dietrich had clearly taken exception to S.F. Edge saying in his original letter that the 60hp De Dietrich should have been called the 104hp De Dietrich, according to his 1hp per 7 cu.ins. rule. He argued strongly, as did many other correspondents, that engine speed had to be factored into the equation. The high speed short stroke engine was generally perceived as a quite different animal to the slow revving long stroke engine. His clever argument was that piston speed was the true limiting factor in engine design and that, for a given engine rotational speed, a long stroke engine generated higher piston speeds than a short stroke engine. Given a 4 inch bore, and a finite limit on piston speed, a short stroke and long stroke engine could therefore be considered equivalent on the basis of swept volume in a given time. The fast short stroke engine would breathe exactly the same amount of air as the slow long stroke engine. On this arithmetic, if instead of 7 cu.ins. you used 2 squ.ins. of piston area, the Napier and the De Dietrich were in fact quite similar at 59hp v. 52hp. Turcat still argued that slow running engines lasted longer, and that the basic W/PxT formula favoured small cars because weight was not directly proportional to power.

A correspondent identified only as "MARINE" echoed the Turcat argument. The 732 cu.ins De Dietrich running at 800rpm was equivalent to the 300 cu.ins. Napier running at 1200rpm in terms of mixture breathed per second. However he concluded by saying that the "reductio ad absurdum" of the argument was to stretch the arithmetic to the limit by saying that a six cylinder engine with one cubic inch cylinders rotating at 15,500rpm would produce the same power as the 60hp Napier. What would he have made of the H16 BRM.

Several correspondents in fact made strong pleas for the small, flexible and light high speed engine as the best way forward for motor car design. Motorists were frightened of high speed engines because cheap and badly made low speed engines quickly broke down if run at higher speeds. They needed to be persuaded that a properly designed and well made high speed engine in fact would wear less and last longer.

Edge's reply to Turcat was another impassioned plea for short stroke high speed engines as the best way forward. He accepted the piston speed constraint, but to reduce tyre wear and improve fuel economy, motor car development must increasingly pursue light weight construction.

Turcat was unrepentant and in turn stated that no engine could run as sweetly at 2000rpm as it did at 1000rpm, and that Edge was only interested in promoting Napier cars. Turcat stoutly defended the long stroke engine.

Fred M. Green took a swipe at S.F. Edge by claiming that the whole issue of under stating horse power was a matter of fashion, and had been started by Edge himself in 1904 when he ran a 20hp car which by his own 7 cu.ins. formula should have been listed as 56hp. That car ran at 1500rpm.

Ernest Arnott of Minerva started by asking whether the prime objective of hill climbs was really commercial or sporting. No one formula could be fair to all cars, and manufacturers would always modify cars to any fixed formula to gain advantage. If really close finishes were the aim then the only way of achieving it was to handicap cars on the basis of past performance. This is what horse racing had always done (and Brooklands would soon do).

Several correspondents made the point that, in hill climbing, gearing was critical. Changing the axle ratio of a car could completely transform its performance. O.D. North proposed that all cars should have two runs, one with driver only and one fully laden. No single axle ratio could be optimum for both runs.

C.R. Garrard of Clement Talbot said that he had since 1898 been advocating the cubic capacity of the engine of a car as a means of classification for competition. However it needed to be related to a ratio of "standard net weight" to capacity, and a "standard thickness of tread" of the tyre. His favoured analogy was to yacht racing where "displacement" and "sail area" were considered the critical factors.

The academics were understandably more concerned with mechanical truths and correct mathematics. Robert Brewer simply stated that the weight, power and resultant speed assumptions behind the *Automotor Journal* "five car scenario" used to justify their own W/F formula were fundamentally wrong.

Mr. G.H. Baillie, a consulting engineer, took this further by saying that rate of fuel consumption did not equate directly to horse power. This assumption favoured slow running engines with large cylinders. Including a weight factor in the formula usually penalised lightweight construction; provided light weight was a result of quality design rather than skimpy construction then it surely should be encouraged. Fuel economy in the specific conditions of hill climbing was much less important than for long distance touring. Cars set up and tuned to win hill climbs would not be optimum for normal touring. Any declaration of true engine efficiency, going right back to the energy content of the fuel, would embarrass the industry.

Mr. H. Linley Byrd, a railway engineer, criticised all the formulae as being far too simplistic. He could not see the point of trying to compare a 6hp car with a 60hp car through a universal efficiency formula; the first requirement therefore was to put the cars in separate classes to compare like with like, but to make sure that chassis price was included. The formula to be used then needed to consider three factors:

1. The energy required to lift the car from the foot of the hill to the top.

2. The friction of the wheels on the road surface. (nb: unmade roads)

3. Wind resistance.

The Byrd formula included the height and length of the hill, the fuel consumed, the cross sectional area of the car, the weight of the car and the time taken. As we shall see later this turned out to be prophetic.

The voice of the local car clubs, who would be stuck with operating any chosen formula, was also heard. Eric Walford, secretary of the Coventry Motor Club was, like most other club correspondents, mainly concerned with the purely practical aspects of organising hill climb

THE HANDICAP FORMULA DEBATE

meetings. His prime concern was the fixing to every car of a fuel measuring device. He argued that, unless somebody like the Motor Union held a stock of the devices to hire out to organising clubs, it just would not happen. He also saw problems with the Roebuck model where no separate fuel taps were incorporated. Continuing the fuel theme, he made a plea for some standardisation of the fuel used; he was aware of such things as picric acid dopes being used at some meetings. He was the only correspondent to raise this crucial issue.

Godfrey Lowe of the Lincolnshire Automobile Club was the only club correspondent to state quite openly that hill climbs should be sporting events and not trade demonstrations. His club did not admit trade entries and the results were not allowed to be used for advertising. His members "went in for a quiet afternoons enjoyment without any undue fuss". "A competition without timing would be poor fun". He thought an over emphasis on fuel consumption would lead to "carburettor freaks" and that the way forward was through an official engine rating scheme and a simple formula.

J.S. Napier of New Arrol Johnson, (nothing to do with Napier cars), took up the club problems with fitting fuel measuring devices but thought the idea was right and should be persisted with. It was also essential to retain timing to maintain the sporting interest. He believed however that manufacturers would pursue quiet and smooth engines over simple efficiency. He supported the engine rating and marking proposal but doubted many manufacturers had the test facilities to carry it out. He believed anyway that most engine makers could calculate horse power accurately if they chose to. It was "simple maths".

Several correspondents, including Chas. Sangster of Ariel Motors, defended the previous hill climb classification system based on chassis price. If in fact hill climbs were primarily a show case for new cars to help buyers choose, then the first criterion in their mind was surely price. The main concern was that manufacturers should actually run cars that were the same as those offered for sale, and a proper system of scrutineering was needed to ensure this. Daimler were held up as an both a successful manufacturer and an example of good practice.

Entwined within the main debate about handicap formulae was this separate but related debate about trade participation in hill climb events. The letter following Edge's in the 14th July issue of *Automotor Journal* was one from Chas. Jarrott, fellow racing driver, one time business partner and friend. In this he lamented the decline of local club hill climbs from "sporting contests" into "nothing more than trade demonstrations". Worse though, he openly accused manufacturers of "entering machines which have either been specially built or specially faked up for the purpose of winning the event".

He therefore proposed that entries to all local club events should only be accepted from members with no trade connections, living within twenty miles of club headquarters, and driving cars genuinely belonging to them. Jarrott campaigned on this issue throughout the summer.

In all the *Automotor Journal* editorial outpourings they had never addressed the issue of trade participation in hill climb events, which were normally organised by private clubs. However, implicit in their belief that the primary purpose of hill climb events was to be a showcase for production cars must surely have been an assumption that the manufacturers would and should participate. The issue of specially prepared, non standard cars, was either not foreseen or ignored.

The Autocar, still looking for strands of argument to differentiate themselves from *Automotor Journal*, took this issue up in an editorial on the 8th September. Under the heading

"Unfairness in Competitions", they attacked the practice of "building special machines for competition purposes". They specifically mentioned bored out engines, high compression ratios, the use of non standard fuels and supplements, gearing too low to be practical in normal motoring, and special lightweight bodies. They contrasted hill climb events with the Tourist Trophy races, where a standard fuel was issued to competitors, and strict scrutineering ensured that all cars were run to standard production specifications.

In a later editorial *The Autocar* proposed that there should be separate classes for trade entries and (non trade) club members. This had become necessary, they argued, as there was evidence of manufacturers joining many regional clubs, often in the name of an unknown employee rather than a known director, solely to get their cars into closed events. Jarrott's "twenty miles from club headquarters" proposal would have closed this loophole in most cases.

By the end of September 1906, as the hill climb season drew to an end, so did the debate and correspondence in the journals about future classification systems, handicap formulae, and bogus trade entries. A huge amount of technical argument, proposal and counter proposal, and comment had been committed to print. Everybody now retired to consider the issues raised and try to work out what to do in 1907. Nowhere would brows have been more deeply furrowed than at the headquarters of the ACGBI.

CHAPTER 3

THE ACGBI HANDICAPPING SYSTEM

On 23rd February 1907 both *Automotor Journal* and *The Autocar* published accounts of a new ACGBI Handicapping System for hill climbs. *Automotor Journal* published a virtually verbatim version of the recently circulated ACGBI pamphlet, whereas *The Autocar* chose to publish notes written by a "very practical Hon. Secretary of a well known automobile club". Both also published some editorial comment. The following is a summary of the original pamphlet, without the mathematics, as published by *Automotor Journal*.

The objective of the handicapping system was to give every car an equal chance of success based on a time allowance which could be calculated and published before the event. This way the results could be announced very soon after the final car had ascended the hill. Part 1 of the pamphlet presented the theoretical basis for the system, and Part 2 dealt with the practical implications of applying it to a real event.

The theoretical basis for the system was that five factors governed the speed of a particular car up a particular hill:

    a. The difference in height between the starting and finishing point, through which the car had to be lifted.

    b. The rolling resistance of the car which had to be overcome. (dependent on the length of the course and not the height)

    c. The resistance of the air to the motion of the car.

    d. The power available at the road wheels.

    e. The running weight of the car.

Fairly well defined mathematical formulae were available to calculate the horse power necessary to overcome **a**, **b** and **c** provided certain generalisations were made, such as the average rolling resistance to be overcome in **b** being 40lb per ton. This would actually vary from course to course according to the road surface conditions but a low figure was selected to match the better surfaces.

The critical factor in the system was the power available at the road wheels. The power at the engine (flywheel) was to be calculated using the ACGBI formula of $D^2n/2$ for maximum power, where D is the diameter of the cylinder in inches and n the number of cylinders. The "assumed efficiency of transmission from the engine to the back wheels should not be less than 66%". The overall formula was therefore taken as $D^2n/3$.

This power model was then tested against actual results from real hill climb events where all the necessary information was available. Since it was a major event which met all the criteria, the 1906 South Harting Hill Climb was chosen as one of a pair with the Henry Edmunds Trophy run at Blackdown Park. The procedure for doing this was to calculate, for specific cars, the "horse power needed" for factors **a**, **b**, and **c**, then back calculate the maximum engine power using the 66% assumption. This was then compared with the engine horse power as calculated from cylinder dimensions using the ACGBI formula.

The results were encouraging. Looking firstly at the winning cars at the two meetings, the differences between the "66% assumption" and the "ACGBI formula" horse powers, the differences were small; for example 49.5hp against 47.5hp. Secondly, where more than one car of the same type competed in the same event, the same calculations were done to see if the differences in the "66% assumption" rated the cars in the same order that the stop watch did in the real event. They did.

With a degree of confidence in the robustness of the mathematics thus established, the model was then used to look at the results data from a wider range of cars which had competed in the two specimen events. The 66% assumed transmission efficiency was made the variable by using the horse power calculated from the formula. The overall range of efficiency found ran from 33.5% to 72%. The differences between cars of the same type ranged from 47.4% to 68.7%. These differences were taken to be measures of inherent differences between car types, the quality of car preparation for the event and driver skill. On this basis the theory was deemed to provide an acceptable basis for a hill climb handicap formula with "still plenty left to chance and skill".

In a real world event it would be necessary to know in advance:

> 1. The height of the hill.
> 2. The length of the hill.
> 3. The running weight of each car.
> 4. The cross sectional area of each car.
> 5. The cylinder dimensions and number of cylinders of each car.

To minimise the mathematical chores before each event it was recommended that each venue should plot two Charts specific to that location. The first, Chart X, would show the relationship between the horse power required to overcome **a** and **b**. The second, Chart Y, would show the relationship between the hp required to overcome wind resistance, **c**, for every 10 square feet of vehicle cross sectional area, and the run time **t** for that particular hill. Specimen Charts for South Harting were included in the pamphlet. (see pages 58-59).

THE ACGBI HANDICAPPING SYSTEM

The procedure then would have been:

1. To calculate 66% of the maximum horse power of each car using the $D^2n/3$ formula.
2. This number was then taken as the power available at the back wheels and assumed equal to the horse power necessary to overcome **a + b + c**.
3. An approximate value of **c** was read from a table by estimating an average speed for that car up the hill.
4. The value of **a + b** was then calculated by subtracting **c** from the answer to 2.
5. The value of **a** was found by reference to Chart X.
6. The run time **t** was then calculated.
7. By reference to Chart Y the assumed value of **c** was checked against the calculated run time and a correction to the run time **t** made if necessary.

This corrected run time then became the time allowance for that car, which was in effect an estimate of the time the car should have taken to climb the hill if the transmission efficiency were in fact 66%, the car had been prepared to the best possible condition, and it had been expertly driven. The method of presenting the results was not specified, but one way would have been to deduct the allowance from the actual time, another way would have been to express the allowance as a percentage of the actual.

The final paragraph of the ACGBI pamphlet stated:

"It will be seen that the method above described is a very simple one, involving the minimum of calculation, whilst it gives the result required in order to arrive at the handicap, viz., time. There should be no difficulty with this method, if the running weights are known, in announcing the result at the close of the meeting".

The notes written by the "very practical Hon. Secretary of a well known Automobile Club", and published in *The Autocar* on the same day as the *Automotor Journal* piece, are best summarised by the following two quotations:

"At the end of three hours gruelling I am afraid I am unable to comprehend the system, if it is to be comprehended".

"If the system is to be taken seriously, I would suggest that it is really necessary that it be explained fully, and examples worked out in which only such figures are used as would ordinarily be known".

The entire one page article was taken up with trying to unravel the mathematics and understand the system, and pointing out that the workload on volunteer club officials, few of

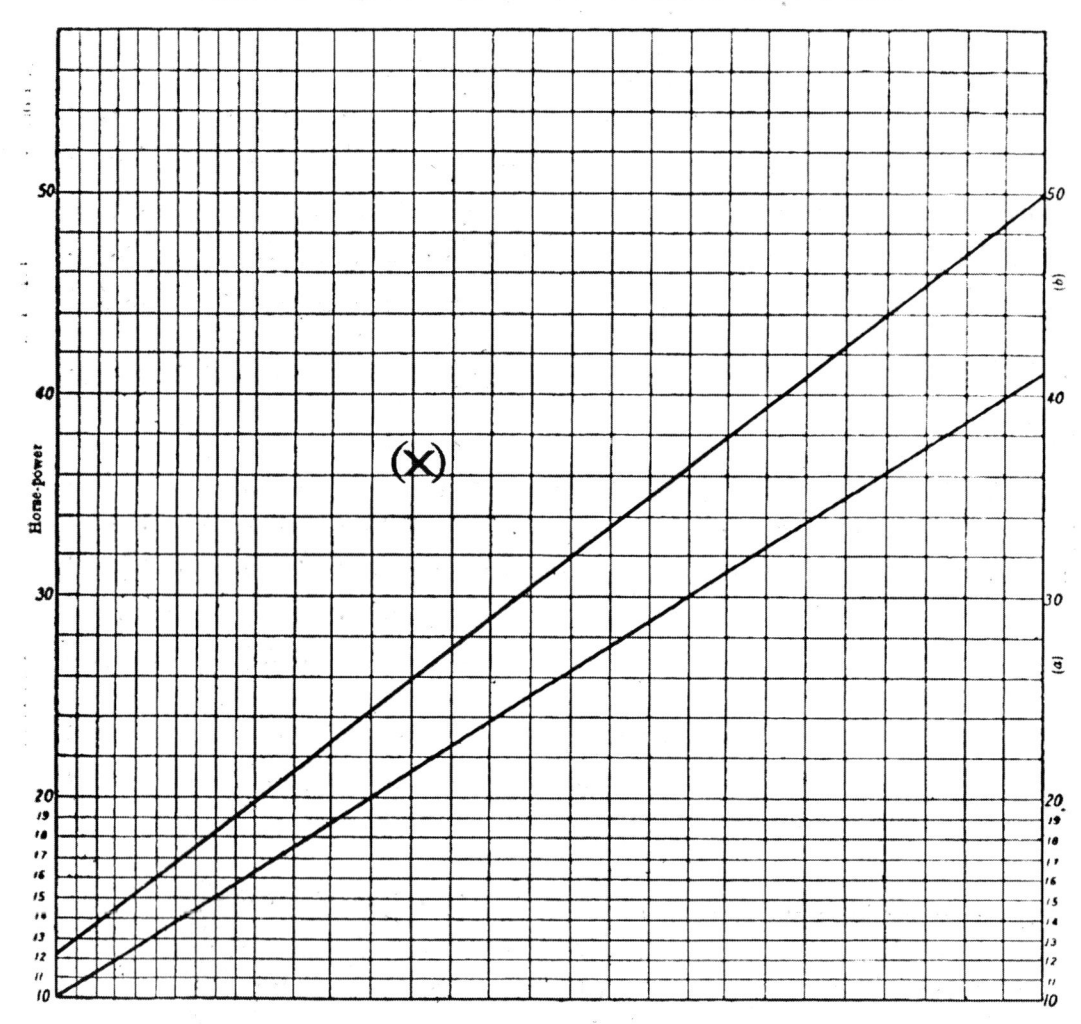

RELATIVE VALUES OF (a) AND (b) FOR SOUTH HARTING HILL.

CHART X.—The use of this chart may be explained by reference to an example already given in the text. The total h.p. available in the first example in Part II is 31·3, which is, as already explained, the sum of $(a) + (b) + (c)$. Assuming (c) tentatively to be 2·5, then $(a) + (b)$ must be equal to 28·8. Find the point on the upper line in the chart which corresponds to 28·8; then the intersection of a vertical line drawn through this point with the lower line will give the value of (a), which is 23·66, and (b) will therefore be equal to the difference between 28·8 and 23·66—viz., 5·14—and, correspondingly, the values of (a) and (b) for other powers can be found; for example, $(a) + (b)$ equals 44, then (a) will be 36·2, and (b) 7·8. By making a chart for each hill, the relative horse-powers for overcoming gravity and road resistance can be ascertained for cars of any horse-power.

THE ACGBI HANDICAPPING SYSTEM

SOUTH HARTING HILL.

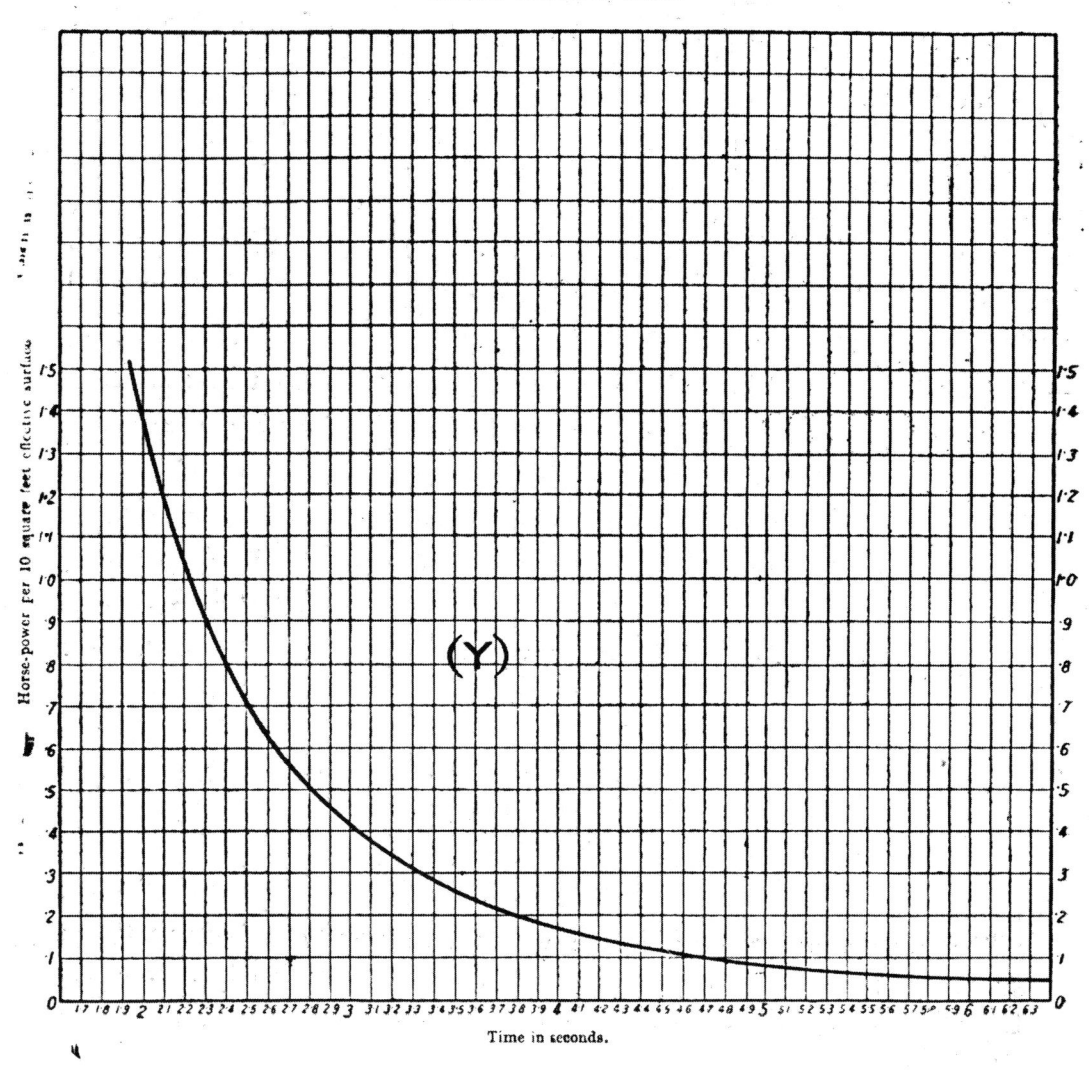

(Chart Y: Horse-power per 10 square feet effective surface vs. Time in seconds)

CHART Y.—The use of Chart Y is to readily ascertain whether the figure assumed for the value of (c) is correct or not; for instance, in the second example in Part II the value of (c) is assumed to be 3·0, but this for that particular hill would correspond with a time of 1·86 m. or thereabouts instead of 2·03 m., and therefore it is obviously too high, as the corresponding value of (c) for 2·03 m. would be 2·6, which, though still a little high, is very approximately correct—2·55 being the correct figure.

THE TWO CHARTS INCLUDED IN THE ACGBI PAMPHLET
FOR SOUTH HARTING HILL.

whom were mathematics graduates, would have been totally impractical and therefore unacceptable. No actual critique of the system on theoretical grounds was even attempted.

The editorial comments in *Automotor Journal* and *The Autocar* were not much more positive. *The Autocar* wrote "when it comes to the ACGBI system, we must say that, in its present form, it is, to a large extent, unworkable". The only way the system could have been made to work, thought *The Autocar*, would have been to employ a professional lecturer to design and operate a study course for club officials, and not let any club operate the system unless they had a team of trained officials who had all passed an examination and thus been effectively "licensed" by the ACGBI.

Automotor Journal had, because of their own role in the affair, to be slightly more diplomatic. While generally welcoming the ACGBI pamphlet, and applauding the enormous amount of work that had obviously been involved, when it came to the detail they were less than happy. Their first problem, not surprisingly, was that the ACGBI system still relied on a horse power formula based solely on piston area. They had been campaigning for months against this concept and had hoisted their own colours on the twin masts of fuel consumption and the laboratory rating of engines. They did however welcome the fact that the ACGBI system had, for the first time, introduced a windage factor. But they bemoaned the fact that it could not be applied to steam cars.

CHAPTER 4

THE YELLOW TROPHY 1907

Within weeks of the Automobile Club of Great Britain and Ireland publishing its handicapping system for hill climb events, King Edward VII granted the club his Royal Seal of Approval and it became the Royal Automobile Club as we know it today. On 13th June 1907 the R.A.C. published a preliminary programme for the South Harting Hill Climbs that were scheduled to be run on Wednesday 10th July; "climbs" in the plural because there were three separate events being held on the same day. The Yellow Trophy was an open competition for cars fitted with internal combustion engines where the value of D^2n was between 45 and 151. This was equivalent to between approximately 22 and 75 maximum horse power under the R.A.C. rating system. To comply with the wishes of *Automotor Journal* the event was also open to steam cars whose engines had been laboratory rated and "found (by the R.A.C.) to be within the limits of corresponding maximum brake horse power of the internal combustion engines".

The R.A.C. described the Yellow Trophy in these terms:

"This Trophy, which has been kindly presented to the CLUB by the proprietors of *The Automotor Journal*, will be offered annually for competition by the ROYAL AUTOMOBILE CLUB, with the object of obtaining data and for testing the effects of the R.A.C. formula for handicapping, and of other formula, if required. The CLUB reserves the right to vary the formula employed each year without consulting the holder of the trophy".

An innovation for the Yellow Trophy was that one third of the entrance fees, three guineas per car, was to be set aside for a sweepstake to boost the prizes for the winners and runners up. Half the total would go to the winner, one third to second place and one sixth to third place. The main prize for the winner was the Trophy, to hold for one year, and the Club's Gold Medal to keep.

Vol. XXI., No. 269. London, July 17, 1907. Price Sixpence.

The CAR ILLUSTRATED.

A JOURNAL OF TRAVEL BY LAND, SEA, AND AIR.

Edited by LORD MONTAGU.

SOUTH HARTING HILL-CLIMB.
A COMPETITOR NEARING THE SUMMIT.
(See page 419.)

THE YELLOW TROPHY – 1907

F. BLAKE DRIVING VISCOUNT INGESTRE'S CLEMENT-TALBOT. (1907)

The other two events were closed events for members of the R.A.C. and the other organising club, the Sussex County A.C., and would be run after lunch. The first was for cars where D^2n was up to 65, and the second for cars where D^2n was below 40. In contrast to the Yellow Trophy, there was no provision for steam cars in the two closed events.

In Class A the previous year a Stanley steamer had posted the fastest time and also won on handicap. A White steam car had not only won the specially staged match race against Dorothy Levitt on her 50hp Napier, but in the process beaten the fastest time of the day set by Manville on his 35hp Daimler. In a letter to *Automotor Journal* dated 22nd June Earl Russell had publicly berated the Committee of the R.A.C., of which he was a member, for being dominated by petrol engine interests and accordingly framing the regulations for South Harting in such a manner as to exclude steam cars from the closed club events. This may explain why he did not appear among the list of R.A.C. officials for the 1907 event. (see Appendix IV)

The Supplementary Regulations covering the three events contained some interesting clauses. Quote:

1. Vehicles must be of a recognised tourist type, furnished with lamps, mudguards, efficient silencer, and proper body, and must carry their full complement of passengers (including the driver), seated in a fair manner, of an average weight of 140lb.

2. Only petroleum, spirit, air and water may be used as fuel.

3. No form of auxiliary exhaust release will be permitted.

THE SCENE AT LIPHOOK STATION WHERE THE COMPETITORS AND THEIR CARS WEIGHED IN. (1907)

4. No car which has taken part in a competition for racing cars in the period 1903-1907 will be eligible.

5. No car carrying a manufacturers' or dealers' general identification mark will be allowed to compete.

The Yellow Trophy was clearly the main event of the day, attracting 43 actual starters out of an initial entry list variously reported as 52, 53 or 54. The two closed events attracted 13 and 10 starters respectively. Many familiar names from the previous two years at South Harting were present, S.F. Edge and his cousin Cecil, Tom Thornycroft, Dorothy Levitt, William Allday, and J.T.C. Moore-Brabazon among them.

In the reporting of the event the contrast between *The Autocar* and *Automotor Journal* was startling if not surprising. The first report published was by *The Autocar*, three days after the event. It was a bare half page, with no illustrations, no mention of its rival journal, and a parting comment to the effect that the handicap results were not available at the time of writing. A week later they published the handicap results with a few pictures. *Automotor Journal*, a full ten days after the event, published a 15 page, lavishly illustrated, self congratulatory report.

For flowery language however *The Car Illustrated*, edited by Lord Montagu, again took the prize. The first sentence of their report read:

> "If it had never done aught else, the annual hill climbing competition at South Harting would have served one useful purpose in introducing automobilists to a panorama of extreme picturesqueness which in all probability they would otherwise have failed to discover".

Motor emphasized the benefit to the local economy of 60 odd competing cars visiting, and mostly staying over the night before. It was estimated that the Petersfield, Liphook and South Harting hotels alone must have taken a total of over £100.00 between them!

Weighing-in, and measuring for windage, was carried out at Liphook Station starting at 8.00am. on the day of the event. The windage measurement required was (the mean width

Though given a handicap rating of over 50 h.p., the

Incomparable

White Steam Car

Won the

Yellow Trophy

At the

South Harting Hill Climb, July 10th, 1907.

Also winning the
Royal Automobile Club's
Gold Medal and Sweepstake

In Third Fastest Time

though carrying over
four cwt. more weight
than the fastest car.

Send for Catalogue to

The White Company,

35, 36, and 37, Kingly Street, Regent Street, London, W.

Telegrams—"Yenisean, London." Telephones—7925 Gerrard, 7926 Gerrard.

Scottish Branch—7, Devon Place, Edinburgh.

F.R.S. BIRCHAM, IRIS, AND OTHER COMPETITORS
ASSEMBLED IN THE THE VILLAGE BEFORE THE EVENT.
(1907)

of the back) x (the height plus one foot), and varied from a minimum of 12.5 sq.ft. for Saunder's Gracile up to 21.6 sq.ft. for Barwick's Daimler. When that was all completed the entire entry was led the ten miles back to South Harting in procession behind the Secretary of the Meeting, Mr. J.W. Orde, in his Daimler.

The weather on this occasion seems to have been fairly kind in that there was a heavy shower just before the start, fine weather all day, and another heavy shower which just caught the last few cars in the afternoon. However it was also recorded that there was a strong wind throughout the day, but nobody commented on what effect this would have had on the windage calculations in the R.A.C. formula. Road conditions were reported as being excellent and that the local authorities had done a lot of good work repairing pot holes and muddy patches.

Another innovation in this Yellow Trophy year was an attempt to measure the "horse power hours" of each car during its run. The theory was that, if it were known how much time each car spent in each gear, it would be possible to work out the total piston displacement during the run and therefore some measure of the "quantity" of horse power developed. The mathematics of doing this were not explained, but the mechanism of collecting the data was that the course was marked with numbered posts every twenty yards and each car was issued with a "scoring" card. One hapless passenger was required to note every gear change the driver made and record on the score card the marker post opposite which the change was made. "This information may well prove to be of considerable utility to the R.A.C., and in addition to that which they obtained in the ordinary course of the event,

THE YELLOW TROPHY – 1907

FREDERICK COLEMAN, WHITE STEAMER, AT THE
START LINE. HE WAS THE YELLOW TROPHY WINNER
WITH A CALCULATED. EFFICIENCY OF 79.10%.
(1907)

and may we hope aid towards arriving at the object for which the Yellow Trophy has been instituted" stated *Automotor Journal*.

The first Yellow Trophy car was called to the start line just after 11.00am and was Mr. Frederic Coleman on his White steam car. He was followed by Mr. W.T. Clifford-Earp on his 60hp Thames and Mr W.H. Phillips on his De Dietrich. Mr. Phillips, however, was apparently delayed by a horse and cart on the way up and was therefore allowed another run in the afternoon. *Motor* thought Harrison on his Ariel-Simplex by far the most dramatic to watch, and that Dorothy Levitt on her Minerva was "the essence of grace and dexterity". The last of the 43 starters did not climb the hill until 12.40pm.

The fastest car up the hill was Cecil Edge on his Napier in 1.860mins., followed by Harrison on his Ariel-Simplex in the almost identical time of 1.867mins. Third was Coleman in his White steamer in 1.927mins. Rather surprisingly *Automotor Journal* published not only real times but actual speeds. The fastest car averaged 33.6mph, and 24 of the 43 cars averaged more than the legal limit of 20mph.

The handicap results gave first place to Coleman in his White steamer, second place to Stokes in his Talbot, and third place to Deacon in his Talbot. Of the six Talbots entered, all by different entrants, five finished in the first seven on handicap.

The method of reporting the results under the R.A.C. Handicapping System was slightly different to the method originally described in the ACGBI pamphlet and probably reflected the *Automotor Journal* obsession with efficiency rather then performance. Rather than work the system right through to time allowances, and then present the results in stop watch

SCENE AT THE START LINE, (1907)

order, the method used went back to the theoretical section of the pamphlet and used the "66% assumption" of transmission efficiency as the variable. The results were therefore expressed as "Per Cent Efficiency". The winner thus achieved 79.10%, the second 72.35%, the third 71.69%, going right down to 14.32% for the Daimler of Bush. The fastest car up the hill, the Napier driven by Cecil Edge, achieved an efficiency of 49.35%, about half way down the list. The other Napier, driven by Newton, achieved 68.75% and was placed 7th. They make an interesting comparison:

	D^2n	Weight	Time	Speed	Efficiency
Cecil Edge	75.00	3,808lbs	1.860	33.6	49.35%
F. Newton	48.00	4,256lbs	2.280	27.4	68.75%

The missing data which would have been interesting is fuel consumption.

The full results, as published in *The Royal Automobile Club Journal* on 18th July, took a complete double page table with no less than fourteen separate columns of data.

The two closed events in the afternoon were straight forward speed events against the clock, and several of the morning Yellow Trophy competitors ran again. In the first event, for cars up to approximately 25hp on the normal R.A.C. rating, the winner, out of 13 starters, was Ramoisy on his Germain in 2mins. 15.4secs. He had been much slower in the morning and finished 15th out of 43 on efficiency. Second was Hutton on a Berliet, who had just beaten Ramoisy in the morning, and third was Rosenheim on an Arrol-Johnston.

In the second closed event, for cars up to a nominal 15hp on the R.A.C. rating, the winner,

THE YELLOW TROPHY – 1907

CLIFFORD EARP ON HIS THAMES. (1907)

out of 10 starters, was J. Lindsay Scott on his Lindsay in 3mins. 36.6secs. Second was Blakemore on a works Alldays in 3mins. 57.4secs., and third Hall on a Singer in 4mins. 18secs.

As a postscript to the 1907 South Harting Hill Climbs there was, two weeks later, a very acrimonious exchange of letters in both *Automotor Journal* and *The Autocar*. It was started by T.H. Woollen, General Manager of Clement-Talbot Ltd., who wished to "strongly protest against the advertisement of S.F. Edge Ltd., which appeared in your last issue, and in which they state that "for efficiency" the 40hp Napier beat a large number of cars at South Harting and Shelsley Walsh, including three Clement-Talbots". Mr. Woollen then quoted the official R.A.C. results at length to prove his point. In *The Autocar* another letter from J.E. Hutton, who drove a Berliet at South Harting, picked up the same point and accused Edge of claiming fastest time at Shelsley Walsh when in fact an 80hp Berliet had that honour. It was also alleged that Edge had similarly misrepresented the results at the 1906 South Harting event.

S.F. Edge replied a week later, saying "we wish always to be correct, but little slips will sometimes appear". He then went on to accuse Daimler of doing the same to him, and Mr Woollen of "splitting hairs". Trying to unravel the data it seems Edge claimed that a Napier had "won South Harting Hill Climb" when it had only won Class D, and that he had miscounted how many Talbots it had beaten. He had also conveniently forgotten to mention how many Talbots had beaten the Napier. It does, however, underline the importance that manufacturers and agents attached to events like South Harting.

What nobody realised in the autumn of 1907 was that there would be no more hill climb events at South Harting for six years, and that the 1907 event would be the first and last event there organised by the R.A.C.

The 6-cylinder NAPIER

LONDON MADE.

continues to beat 4-cylinder cars on both SPEED and EFFICIENCY in open competition.

SOUTH HARTING

Hill Climb, July 10th.

60 h.p. Six-cylinder

NAPIER-FASTEST

beating the following 4-cylinder cars: 3 Daimlers, 3 Berliets, De Dietrich, 2 Iris, 2 Thornycrofts, Germain, 2 Deasys, Maudslay, etc.; and the following 6-cylinder cars: Minerva, 2 Iris, Thames.

SHELSLEY WALSH

Hill Climb, July 13th.

60 h.p. Six-cylinder

NAPIER-FASTEST

in Club Hill Climb, beating the following 4-cylinder cars: 2 Mercedes, 5 Daimlers, 2 Siddeleys, 2 Lanchesters, 5 Ariels, 2 Deasys, Martini, 2 Minervas, Thornycroft, etc.

FOR EFFICIENCY

the 40 h.p. six-cylinder **NAPIER** beat, amongst others, the following 4-cylinder cars:

Berliet,	Mercédès,	5 Daimlers,
3 Clement Talbots,	Rover,	Lanchester,
Austin,	Siddeley,	5 Ariels,
Singer,	Deasy,	Maudslay,
Minerva,	Darracq,	Star,
Swift,	Arrol-Johnston,	Humber, etc.

Four-cylinder Napier Cars must be cleared.   A few 18-22 h.p., and 45 h.p. Four-cylinder Napier Cars at Bargain Prices. Write for Particulars.

S. F. EDGE, LIMITED, 14, NEW BURLINGTON STREET, LONDON, W.

The six-cylinder Napier in Liverpool can be seen and tried at 6, 8, and 10, Slater St. Our representative always in attendance.

A GROUP OF SPECTATORS WITH EARL RUSSELL ON THE FAR LEFT
(1907)

DOROTHY
LEVITT
DRIVING
WARWICK J.
WRIGHT'S
MINERVA.
(1907)

SOUTH HARTING HILL CLIMB 1905-1924

THE AUTOMOTOR JOURNAL

PERCY DEAN DRIVING A SCOUT ABOUT HALF WAY UP THE HILL
WITH VIEWS BACK TO THE START LINE (NEAR THE POND)
AND THE VILLAGE CENTRE BEYOND. (1907)

THE YELLOW TROPHY – 1907

JULY 20, 1907.

The AUTOMOTOR JOURNAL

THE "YELLOW TROPHY" CARS WHICH "WEIGHED OUT," AND THEIR DRIVERS.

White Steamer (1st), Frederic Coleman.

Thames (29th), W. T. Clifford-Earp.

Lorraine-Dietrich (35th), W. H. Phillips.

Brooke (24th), S. W. Humphrey.

Talbot (2nd), W. Stokes.

Deasy (5th), E. W. Lewis.

Scout (31st), J. Percy Dean.

Talbot (7th), G. Day.

Talbot (4th), J. Hedge.

Talbot (6th), Mr. Blake.

1015

SOUTH HARTING HILL CLIMB 1905-1924

JULY 20, 1907. *The* AUTOMOTOR JOURNAL

Daimler (10th), John Goddard. | Minerva (*), D. Citroen. | Napier (23rd), C. Edge.

Napier (6th), F. Newton. | Berliet (12th), A. J. Brooks. | Berliet (11th), J. E. Hutton.

Gracile (20th), C. H. Saunders. | Maudslay (8th), R. H. Verney. | Berliet (8th), W. Watson.

Talbot (3rd), R. E. Deacon. | Deasy (9th), Philip Graham. | Alldays (39th), Claude M. Taylor.
* Did not run.   "Yellow Cover" Copyright Photos.

THE "YELLOW TROPHY" CARS WHICH "WEIGHED OUT," AND DRIVERS.

1017

– 74 –

THE YELLOW TROPHY – 1907

July 20, 1907. *the* AUTOMOTOR JOURNAL

Lindsay (*), H. Pennington.   Ariel-Simplex (17th), A. E. Harrison.   Climax (36th), Cecil H. Lamb.

Climax (15th), Thos. Watson.   De Dion (21st), J. W. Stocks.   De Dion (16th), Walter Munn.

Germain (11th), H. Ramoisy.   Thornycroft (38th), Tom Thornycroft.   Thornycroft (26th), H. Niblett.

Mass (18th), A. F. King.   Iris (25th), A. Earp.   Iris (30th), A. Perman.
* Did not run.   "Yellow Cover" Copyright Photos.

THE "YELLOW TROPHY" CARS WHICH "WEIGHED OUT," AND DRIVERS.

SOUTH HARTING HILL CLIMB 1905-1924

JULY 20, 1907. *The* **AUTOMOTOR** JOURNAL

Iris (19th), F. R. S. Bircham.   Iris (22nd), G. F. J. Knowles.   Minerva (14th), Miss Dorothy Levitt.

Buick (27th), H. H. Sternberg.   Osterfield (37th), Douglas S. Cox.   Cadillac (34th), F. S. Bennett.

Daimler (28th), G. S. Barwick.   Daimler (40th), Oliver Bush.   Talbot (32nd), F. Martin.

Humber (33rd), Arthur E. Gould.   Daimler (13th), Herbert Musker.

"Yellow Cover" Copyright Photos.

* Did not run.

THE "YELLOW TROPHY" CARS WHICH "WEIGHED OUT," AND DRIVERS.

1021

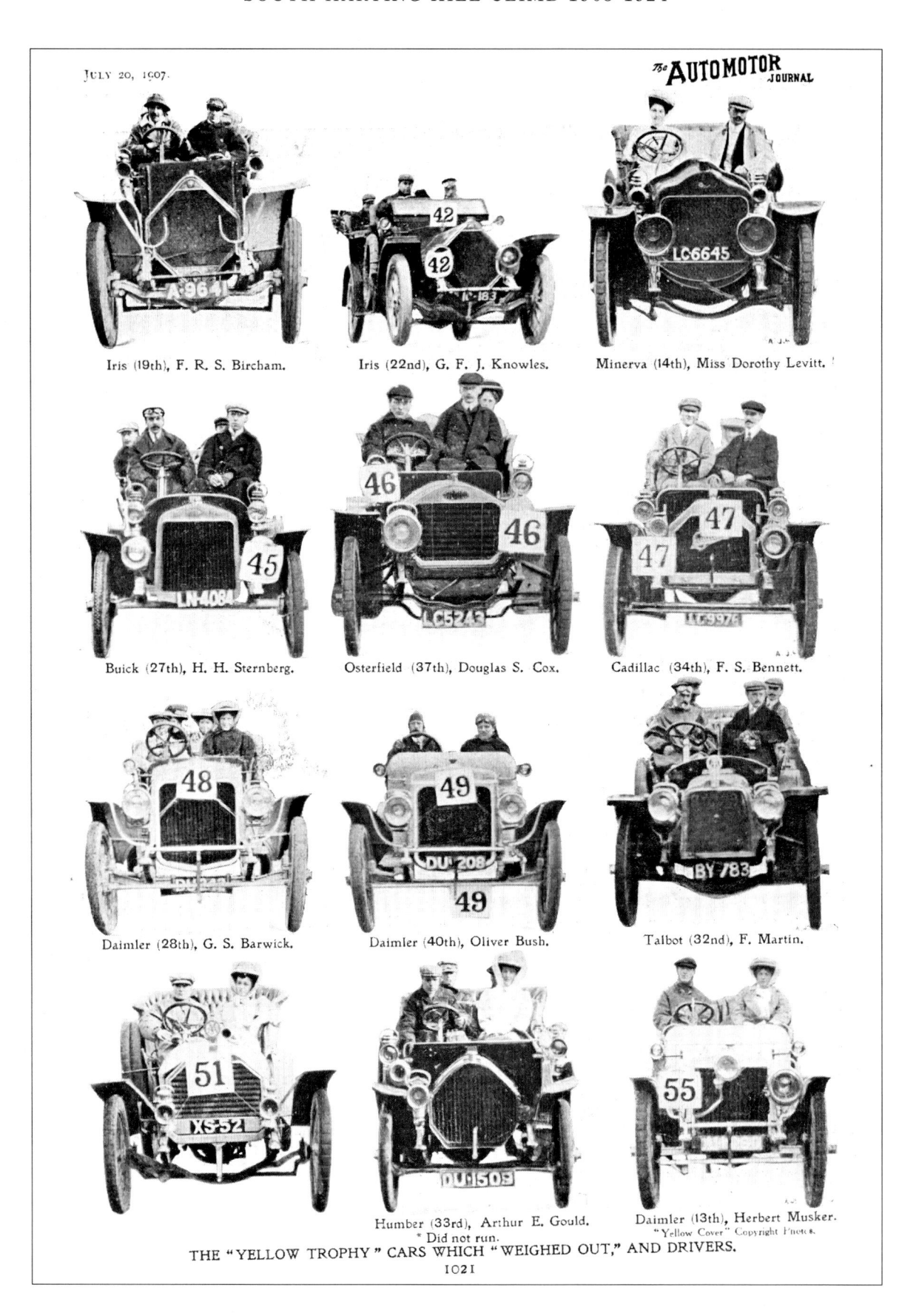

THE YELLOW TROPHY – 1907

J. HEDGE, CLEMENT-TALBOT,
LEAVING THE START.
(1907)

CHAPTER 5

"THE R.A.C. ABOLITION OF HILL-CLIMBS"

The first official sign of future trouble for motoring competitions on public roads was a Parliamentary question in May 1907. Mr. Cathcart Wilson asked the President of the Local Government Board, one Mr. Burns, "if his attention had been called to the Frome's Hill Climb, the speed at which some of the motors were driven, and the consequent injury to a spectator; and if the Government would see that in future competitions on public roads due regard would be paid to the provisions of the law and the safety of the public".

Mr. Burns replied that his attention had indeed been drawn to the case, but that "in practice the administration of the law relating to the use of the highway by motor cars was in the hands of the local police". He had been advised that, in this case, the police had taken precautions to safeguard spectators but that the public were "well aware that the event was taking place". He himself was "not in a position to take action in cases of the kind".

Mr. C. Wason then asked Mr. Burns to consider, in conjunction with the Home Secretary, the advisability of stopping the trials of motors on the public highway altogether. Mr. Burns said he would communicate with the Home Secretary. His own personal view was that, "except under very special conditions, and then early in the morning, no speed or other test trials should take place on the public thoroughfares".

Such a strongly establishment organisation as the R.A.C. could not afford to ignore such a clear signal. On the 28th November 1907, after the hill climb season had finished, the Competitions Committee unanimously resolved, on the motion of the Chairman, Mr. J. Lyons Sampson:-

> *That in view of the annoyance caused locally, and in the interests of the automobile movement generally, the Club shall neither hold nor issue any permits for Open Competitions other than Reliability Trials, nor support any Closed Competitions, on the public highway where a speed in excess of the legal limit is a factor, unless such highway has been closed to ordinary traffic by the authorities, or the competitions are held on the foreshore with the sanction of the authorities.*

"THE R.A.C. ABOLITION OF HILL-CLIMBS"

Given the passion of the formula debate the previous year, and their part in it, the responses of *Automotor Journal* and *The Autocar* were, at first reading, surprising.

Automotor Journal, whose editorial headline forms this chapter heading, appeared to go full circle;

> "We are quite unable to raise a single tear at this decision, since it cannot be truthfully said that the average hill climb of recent times has taught anyone much or has been conspicuously successful as a sporting function".

Within the space of eighteen months they had gone from open condemnation of hill climbs, through an impassioned debate about handicap formulae, to sponsorship of a major event, The Yellow Trophy, and back to condemnation.

The main condemnation now, however, was not the previous technical argument about horse power, efficiency and formulae, but the background issue of trade entries monopolising the open events, often with non standard cars, and thus virtually excluding the private owner from any real chance of success. An extension of this, and relevant to the "annoyance caused locally" cited by the R.A.C., was the assertion that;

> "These events have quite ceased to be the half-day monopolisers of a single stretch of highway that they are supposed to be in theory. In other words, practising for day after day – in some cases for weeks in advance – has been indulged in freely prior to the actual contest, and as a result the R.A.C. and other clubs have on many occasions been inundated with protests from the residents in the neighbourhood".

They also made the shrewd closing comment that;

> "Fresh legislation may crop up in Parliament at no very distant date from now, and that the influence of the Club will then largely depend upon the extent to which they have adhered to the letter, as well as the spirit, of the law as it now exists".

The Autocar also bowed to the inevitable. While sympathising with the smaller organising clubs, they again picked up on the local annoyance factor;

> "The feelings of whole neighbourhoods have been outraged again and again by the wild, indescribable, and irresponsible practising which has taken place up every advertised hill for weeks and weeks before the trial itself. Nor does the annoyance to the neighbourhood end with the trial, because for some time afterwards disappointed competitors turn up with irresponsible journalists aboard to testify to the encompassment of a better performance than accrued to that particular car upon the day".

If the journals were already aware of all these problems, they were never mentioned in their, usually enthusiastic, reports on the meetings.

-79-

SOUTH HARTING HILL CLIMB 1905-1924

The Autocar finished with the same warning of impending legislation;

> "With all the potent possibilities of an adverse majority in the House of Commons, with a motorphobist feeling abroad, as strong and as scathing as ever it has been, automobilists as typified by the Club in the eyes of the world at large cannot afford to engender a further access of bad feelings by conniving at competitions on the public highway".

Their closing comment was that clubs should seek venues on private land, as the Midland A.C. had done at Shelsley Walsh.

Even before the R.A.C. resolution in November, some events had already been abandoned in 1907 because of local antipathy and police hostility. Frome's Hill, inevitably, but also venues such as Birdlip and Kidd's Hill. From the first recorded hill climb in Britain, up Petersham Hill near Richmond in 1899, the popularity of hill climb events had steadily increased reaching some sort of peak in 1907 with well over fifty events being held during the season. After the R.A.C. resolution there should have been no more open events on public roads, although closed events, which did not need an R.A.C. Permit, could proceed with the agreement of the local authority. However, in the face of strong opposition from some clubs who threatened to resign from R.A.C. affiliation, some open events were sanctioned in 1908, provided there was strong support from the local authorities and an assurance that speed limits would not be exceeded !

The overall numbers though did go into decline. The main casualties initially were the premier events, particularly in those areas where police hostility was greatest. Two major losses were the R.A.C. flagship events, South Harting and the Henry Edmunds Trophy. The lowest point was in 1910 when fewer than twenty hill climb events were held, but interest picked up slightly again from 1912 until the outbreak of war. Thus it was not quite the complete "abolition" *Automotor Journal* had predicted.

However this decline should not be seen solely as a result of official and public antipathy to competition on public roads and the R.A.C. resolution on open events. Many things had changed since that first event in 1899. Firstly the cars had grown bigger and faster; from the days when they struggled to climb the hills at all, to the day when the fastest car up South Harting in 1907 averaged over 33mph, well over the legal limit.

Also there was a general slump in car sales and the manufacturers were becoming less interested in expensive participation in competitions every week during the summer. Furthermore, Brooklands had opened in July 1907 and racing per se, and the development of the more overtly sporting cars, was increasingly centred there. For some of the wealthier competitors there was also the more exciting diversion of powered flight.

Meanwhile South Harting reverted to the sleepy village it had been up until 1905.

CHAPTER 6

THE MIDDLE YEARS 1913 AND 1914

1913 – The First Cyclecar Club Event

The *Cyclecar* magazine first appeared on bookshelves on the 27th November 1912, and the inaugural meeting of the Cyclecar Club was held at the Motor Cycle Show at Olympia on the 29th. Social meetings apart, the first major competitive event organised by the new club was an Open Hill-Climb for Cyclecars at South Harting on Saturday 28th June 1913. That was to be followed by a Lobster Supper Week End at the Selsey Hotel, some twenty miles to the south at Selsey Bill.

The Cyclecar Club was affiliated to the Auto-Cycle Union rather than direct to the R.A.C., so the question of R.A.C. Permits did not arise. In fact reading the contemporary reports it is rather as if all the events of six years previously had been air brushed from history, and almost as if the club had just "discovered" the hill at South Harting by chance.

The first mention in *Cyclecar* was in early May 1913:

> "a few members of the Cyclecar Club visited Harting Hill,
> near Petersfield, with a view to determining its suitability
> for the open hill climb on 28th June".

In other words, less than two months before the event, they had not even decided on the venue. This low key, last minute, approach may in part account for the fact that the only other journal apart from *Cyclecar* to report the event was *Motor Cycle*. Throughout four weeks of writing about the event, however, *Cyclecar* only once mentioned that South Harting had ever previously hosted a hill climb. From a modern perspective 1913 and 1907 seem equidistant, but even *The Royal Automobile Club Journal*, acknowledging the event in July 1913, referred to South Harting as:

> "a famous hill in the old days".

SOUTH HARTING HILL CLIMB 1905-1924

VOL. XXVI., No. 584. New Series. No. 131.
REGISTERED AT THE GENERAL POST OFFICE.

July 4, 1913.

THE ROYAL AUTOMOBILE CLUB JOURNAL.
Price Sixpence.

The Royal Automobile Club Journal

SOUTH HARTING AGAIN!

AT THE CYCLECAR CLUB'S OPEN HILL-CLIMB.

Last Saturday the recently-formed Cyclecar Club held a hill-climb on South Harting hill, Hants. South Harting was a famous hill in the old days, and even now is a slope to be treated with respect. Our frontispiece shows Mr. A. P. Bradley on his Duo approaching the steepest pitch.

CYCLECAR

A G.N. AND A DUO ON THE FIRST
STEEP BEND ROUND THE CHALK PIT.
(1913)

Entries were invited in five Classes:

1. Monocars up to 1100cc having three or four wheels.
2. Three wheeled machines carrying one passenger, up to 750cc.*
3. Three wheeled machines carrying one passenger, up to 1100cc.*
4. Four wheeled cyclecars carrying one passenger, up to 750cc.*
5. Four wheeled cyclecars carrying one passenger, up to 1100cc.*

*The passenger and driver to have a combined weight of over 280lbs.

The entrance fee was 10 shillings and 6 pence, reduced to 5 shillings for Cyclecar Club members.

A minimum of three entries were required for a Class to actually run, and four runners must finish before a second place award would be made. A total of twenty nine entries were received, but with none in Class 2. Apart from the Class awards, a silver cup was to be awarded to the lady driver making the best performance, and another to the best performance by a private owner. Trade entries were clearly still an issue. There was also a special award for the best performance against handicap regardless of Class.

SOUTH HARTING HILL CLIMB 1905-1924

SCENES AT THE WEIGHING-IN AT PETERSFIELD STATION. THE CAR
IN THE UPPER PICTURE IS LORD EXMOUTH'S GRAND PRIX G.N., LOLA II. THE CAR IN
THE LOWER PICTURE IS G. HOLZAPFEL'S SINGLE SEAT CARDEN WHICH
SUCCUMBED TO TWO ENGINE FIRES AND FAILED TO COMPLETE THE CLIMB. (1913)

THE MIDDLE YEARS – 1913 AND 1914

CYCLECAR

LIONEL MARTIN DRIVING A SINGER WHICH, DESPITE
BEING THE HEAVIEST CAR IN THE COMPETITION, VERY NEARLY
MADE THE FASTEST TIME OF THE DAY. (1913)

The monocar class was run to handicap formula only, but all other classes were run both to formula and against the clock. The formula used was devised by Dr. A.M. Low and took the form:

$$\frac{W}{(C-K)^2 \, T \, P}$$

Where:
- W = weight
- C = cubic capacity
- K = constant for length of hill (200 for South Harting)
- T = time
- P = constant for gradient of hill (1.75 for South Harting)

This formula would appear to be a distant relative of the R.A.C. Handicap Formula.

The list of entrants and their vehicles was less familiar than the lists at previous South Harting events, but there were some interesting names. H.R. Godfrey had an entry in his G.N. but did not start, A.G.F. Nash in another G.N. did start and won Class 5. Three Morgans were the only entries in Class 4. Lionel Martin was driving his highly tuned Singer. His newly formed company, Bamford & Martin Ltd., were Singer agents and their tuning of the new 10hp car was so successful that Martin was often entered as a works driver.

Weighing-in took place on the Saturday morning at Petersfield Station, followed by lunch at the Dolphin Hotel. The Dolphin had been selected as the headquarters for the Cyclecar Club, the only problem being that nobody had thought to tell the proprietor and the hotel was completely overwhelmed by a combination of club members, motorists and visiting groups, including the Public Schools M.C.C. who were acting as flag marshals for the event.

SOUTH HARTING HILL CLIMB 1905-1924

Many people who could not get into the Dolphin "raided confectioners shops and fed as best they could on lemonade and strawberries and cream".

Cyclecar Club "members came from all parts of the country, scurrying along the dusty roads on their tiny three and four wheelers…Mr. Buckingham had driven his single-cylinder Chota from Coventry the same morning and another competitor had come from Malvern, having been somewhat delayed through sticking in the middle of a river…Glorious weather prevailed".

The first competitor was not due up the hill until 3.00pm, but delays at Petersfield, and the late arrival of the competition numbers for the cyclecars, meant that the first did not leave the start line until 3.23pm. This was A.W. Lambert in his Morgan single seater who went up very rapidly and made fastest time of the day despite one of his front mudguards coming off and hitting him on the head. He was the only finisher in Class 1. W.G. McMinnies (editor of *Cyclecar* magazine) in his GP Morgan could well have recorded a faster time if his near side front tyre had not come off the rim in hard cornering, the inner tube then coming out and blowing up to the size of a football before bursting. He still finished and won Class 4 on time.

A.W. LAMBERT IN HIS SINGLE SEAT MORGAN WAS
THE ONLY FINISHER IN CLASS I, DESPITE LOSING A MUDGUARD
ON THE WAY WHICH STRUCK HIM ON THE HEAD.
(1913)

THE MIDDLE YEARS – 1913 AND 1914

The unluckiest competitor must have been G. Holzapfel in his Carden monocar. Practising the day before the meeting, he had crashed badly and broken both axles. He had worked 24 hours to repair the vehicle and then his carburettor caught fire on the start line because of a sticking inlet valve. Given a second start at the end of the meeting he caught fire again on the first bend. The crowd put out the fire by "covering the engine in gravel".

A.E. Parnacott's tiny four cylinder, 499cc, Cycar arrived at the start covered in advertising messages. This was in breach of the rules and he was told to cover them up, which he did by pasting brown paper over them. Lord Exmouth, in his G.N., failed to finish, having stopped on the second bend because "he could not get his gears in... after attempting to change speed for 100 yards, with much noise from the dog clutches".

> "Mr Lionel Martin found that he could get best results from a hot engine, and ran it with a coat over the radiator until the water boiled. He then tied rags and a handkerchief round the filler cap to stop the water blowing back in his eyes. The tremendous hum of the well tuned engine, and Mr. Martin's marvellous quickness in changing gears, made a great impression on the spectators".

J.F. Buckingham in his Chota won Class 3 in 2mins. 29.4secs., and McMinnies in his GP Morgan won Class 4 in 1min. 43secs. The biggest Class by far was Class 5, which was won by A.G.F. Nash in his G.N. in a time of 1min. 50.8secs. with Lionel Martin in his Singer second. Lambert's ftd was 1min. 33.4secs. The overall winner on formula, by a curiously huge margin, was the single cylinder, 746cc, Chota of J.F. Buckingham. No mention was made in any of the reports about the special awards for lady drivers and private owners.

Motor Cycle did the calculations and published average speeds. The fastest up the hill was A.W. Lambert in the single seater Morgan, burst tyre not withstanding, at 32.2mph. For comparison this is only 1.4mph slower than Cecil Edge in his 60hp Napier in 1907. The winner of Class 3, J.F. Buckingham, recorded 20.5mph, the winner of Class 4, W.G. McMinnies, recorded 29.8mph and A.G.F. Nash, the winner of Class 5, recorded 27.6mph. The slowest cyclecar up the hill, K. Kreitmayer in a Zebra, averaged 9.4mph. Seven out of twenty four starters failed to reach the top of the hill.

The ambivalent attitude of *Cyclecar* magazine, and presumably the Cyclecar Club, towards the police can be summed in two quotations from their report. In the section on the actual hill climb the comment was made that crowding at the start line was controlled with the help of the "local police rendering valuable assistance". Yet later, in the account of the mad scramble down to Selsey Bill for the Lobster Supper Week-End, the following appeared:

> "At first an easy pace was kept, but soon throttles were opened, until the milestones were being passed at a prodigious speed, amid clouds of dust. The bark of the Chota was quite distinctive above the rest, and bears a close resemblance to what one would expect to hear if a large explosion took place in a 6ft. steel pipe. At Chichester speed was slackened, for a timely warning of police traps made it advisable to drop down to the legal limit".

This short, less than well planned, event seems a world away from Earl Russell, the R.A.C. Competitions Committee, separate entrants and drivers, S.F. and Cecil Edge, Dorothy Levitt, Napiers and Daimlers, and tea with Lady Russell afterwards.

SOUTH HARTING HILL CLIMB 1905-1924

THE ROYAL AUTOMOBILE CLUB JOURNAL

THE, BY NOW FAMILIAR, SCENE OF COMPETITORS
QUEUING UP TO REACH THE START LINE. (1914)

THE CAR

NASH VINSON'S WRECKED 25hp TALBOT (1914)

THE MIDDLE YEARS – 1913 AND 1914

S. JONES DRIVING HIS PRINCE HENRY VAUXHALL,
WITH ENTHUSIASTIC PASSENGER, SOON AFTER THE START.
HE WON CLASS III. (1914)

1914 – The Inter Club Meeting

The first of two events, held on successive Saturdays, at South Harting in 1914 was an Inter Club Meeting held on July 11th. The four clubs who jointly organised the event were the Hampshire, West Surrey, Dorset and Kent Automobile Clubs. Not, surprisingly, the Sussex County A.C., who had been involved in three events in earlier years, and in whose home county South Harting lay.

Entries were invited in six classes, up to 10hp, up to 16hp, up to 26hp, over 26hp, an Inter Club team race, and an open class for any car made before 1909. Twenty nine starters were recorded by the four journals that reported the event. However no journal published a complete list of entrants; partial lists have been reconstructed in Appendix III from information in the reports.

All Classes were run on handicap, using the familiar (weight)/(time x horse power) formula. The horse power however was quoted as being calculated by the ratio cc/10. This

– 89 –

was presumably a misprint, and more likely to have been cc/100. No times or speeds were published, except for the fastest time of the day.

The four journals that reported the event were *The Car* and *The Light Car* on the following Wednesday, *The Royal Automobile Club Journal* on the Friday, and *The Autocar* on Saturday July 18th, the same day that the second event, organised by The Cyclecar Club, was to be held. *The Light Car* only reported Class I, for cars up to 16hp, and even then half of the one page report was taken up with a description of the new Bifort car, making its first public appearance. Presumably because it was only a local, closed club event none of the reporting was detailed; the most informative report was that in *The Autocar*. *The Light Car* prefaced their report with the revelation that "in the old days South Harting was a famous battleground for motor cars", referring to events less than ten years previously.

H.F.W. FARQUHARSON DRIVING A 15hp MASS
FOR DORSET A.C. IN THE TEAM RACE.
(1914)

THE MIDDLE YEARS – 1913 AND 1914

A G.N. WAITING FOR THE OFF. (1914)

SOUTH HARTING HILL CLIMB 1905-1924

VOL. XXVIII., No. 638. New Series, No. 185.
REGISTERED AT THE GENERAL POST OFFICE.
July 17, 1914.
THE ROYAL AUTOMOBILE CLUB JOURNAL.
Price Sixpence.

The Royal Automobile Club Journal

A RACING LIMOUSINE.

MR. N. S. HIND'S STREAMLINE BERLIET.

On Saturday last four of the southern automobile clubs held a joint hill-climb at South Harting. In the above illustration Mr. Hind is seen making the fastest time of the day. By the way, visitors to Brooklands on August 3rd may expect to see this limousine taking part in the races, as Mr. Hind has announced his intention of pitting the Berliet against the usual type of single-seated, streamline racing cars.

THE MIDDLE YEARS – 1913 AND 1914

CAPTAIN HEATH CROSSING THE FINISHING LINE
IN HIS 12-20hp BENZ. HE WON CLASS II AND WAS PART OF THE
WINNING HAMPSHIRE AC TEAM IN THE TEAM EVENT.
(1914)

The first competitor was sent up the hill at 1.45pm on a scorching hot summers afternoon. The location for the weighing-in, presumably conducted that morning, was not recorded.

There were three entries in Class I, for cars up to 10hp, two 10hp Bugattis and a 10-12hp Bifort. The latter was a new car, built in Fareham, Hampshire using a French chassis and a Belgian 4 cylinder engine. Mr. R. Van Namens Bugatti carried a polished mahogany body similar to that on his well known Brooklands Berliet. The Bugattis were faster up the hill but the Bifort won on handicap. Mr. H.P. White, driving the Bifort, said that he would have been much quicker if he had had more ballast over the rear axle, as he was scrabbling for grip on the corners. The Bifort already weighed 1,300lbs more than the lighter of the Bugattis.

Class II, for cars up to 16hp, attracted six entries, all of which were reported as "by no means fast" by *The Car*. The winner was Capt. H. Heath on his 12-20hp Benz.

Class III, for cars up to 26hp, attracted nine entries. The winner was S. Jones on a Prince Henry Vauxhall, with another Vauxhall second. Jones had originally been placed last, but somebody then realised that his registration number had been used in the handicap calculation instead of the actual weight of the car.

Class IV, for cars over 26hp, provided the only real drama of the day. Mr. W. Nash Vinson on his 25hp Talbot burst his front near side tyre rounding the first bend at "very high speed"

SOUTH HARTING HILL CLIMB 1905-1924

and plunged into the hedge topped bank. Both driver and mechanic climbed out unhurt and fortunately there were no spectators at that point. The car however was badly damaged. To *The Car* the incident "provided spectators with a thrill", to *The Royal Automobile Club Journal* it was "unwelcome excitement". Had the accident occurred on one of the higher corners the car could have plunged some 500ft. down the steep bank. Class IV was eventually won on handicap by Mr. N.S. Hind in a 25hp Berliet "carrying a handsome egg shaped, all-enclosed, saloon body finished white picked out in black". Other sources refer to the car as the "White Beetle".

This car was also credited with the fastest time of the day at 1min. 42.4secs. This seems an astonishingly quick time for a saloon car and was faster than any time reported at any previous meeting over the full 1833yd. course. The previous fastest known time was 1min. 51.6secs. recorded by Cecil Edge in his Napier in 1907. The apparently faster time by Lambert in his Morgan in the 1913 Cyclecar Club meeting was run over a shorter 1500yd course. The speed of the Berliet probably says something about the relative aerodynamics of it and the Napier.

The inter club team competition was won by the three man Hampshire team comprising Capt. Heath on his Benz, J. Guthlac-Birch on his Clegg-Darracq, and C.E.S. Gillett on his 25-50hp Talbot. The Dorset club were second represented by R. Van Namen on his 10hp Bugatti, N.S. Hind on the 25hp Berliet saloon, and H.F.W. Farquharson on his 15hp Mass.

The final event of the day was Class VI, which attracted five entries and was open to any vehicle built before December 31st 1909. Perhaps in those days of rapidly changing technology, cars of the previous decade were already thought of as "vintage", when events less than ten years previously were already being referred to as "the old days". Mr. R.W. Radclyffe won the class on his 1908 20hp Vauxhall, from Hugh Garnett on his 1909 38.8hp Metallurgique.

At the end of the competition, echoing happenings in "the old days", tea was served in a marquee at the top of the hill, before the prizes were presented.

THE MIDDLE YEARS – 1913 AND 1914

1914 – The Second Cyclecar Club Event

The second hill climb held at South Harting in 1914, just one week after the Inter Club Meeting, was the Cyclecar Club Meeting held on Saturday the 18th July. This was also the second event that the Cyclecar Club had organised at South Harting. This event, however, was altogether bigger, and better organised, than the rather last-minute affair of 1913.

The nature of the event was also different, with more light cars than cyclecars taking part.

Entries were invited in six classes:

1. Standard touring two-seated cyclecars up to 750cc.
2. Standard touring two-seated cyclecars and light cars up to 1100cc.
3. Standard touring two seated light cars exceeding 1100cc. but not exceeding 1500cc.
4. Lady drivers of standard touring two-seated cyclecars or light cars up to 1100cc.
5. Standard touring monocars up to 1100cc.
6. Racing machines up to 1100cc.

The entrance fee was 5 shillings for the first entry and 2 shillings and 6 pence for each subsequent entry. In addition, any three members, on payment of an extra shilling, could

WEIGHING-IN IN PETERSFIELD.
BARTON ADAMSON'S 9hp ADAMSON ON THE WEIGH BRIDGE AND
G. GRIFFITHS PUSHING HIS 8hp MORGAN AWAY AFTER WEIGHING.
(1914)

SOUTH HARTING HILL CLIMB 1905-1924

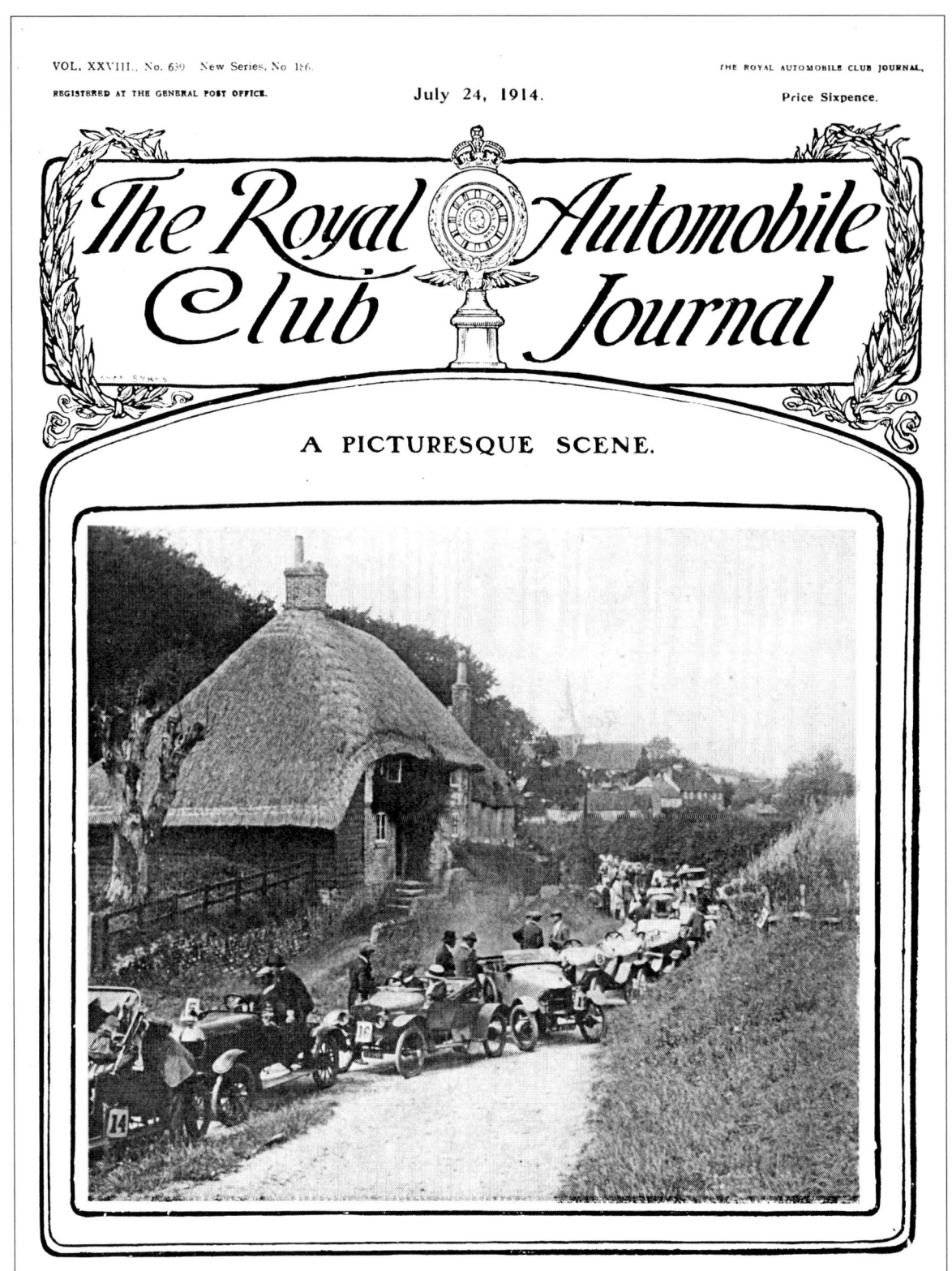

VOL. XXVIII., No. 639 New Series, No 186.
REGISTERED AT THE GENERAL POST OFFICE.
July 24, 1914.
THE ROYAL AUTOMOBILE CLUB JOURNAL.
Price Sixpence.

The Royal Automobile Club Journal

A PICTURESQUE SCENE.

WHICH WILL WIN?
Light Cars and Cyclecars lined up at the foot of South Harting Hill on Saturday last. *(See page 73.)*

THE MIDDLE YEARS – 1913 AND 1914

constitute a team and enter for the team prize. One entry allowed one climb of the hill, and practicing on the day of the event was banned with disqualification as a penalty.

All classes for standard machines had to carry "a passenger in the normal position". Awards were made on time and formula in these classes; Dr. Low had devised a new, somewhat simpler, formula for 1914 which excluded the constants for particular hills used previously. The new formula was:

$$\frac{W}{C^{1.1} \times T^{1.3}}$$

where W, C, and T were weight, capacity and time respectively.

There were three, three driver, team entries comprising G.N., Carden, and A.C. machines. Sixty six entries were received in total, compared to twenty nine the previous year. The special class for lady drivers was claimed as a first.

The Light Car, describing the journey down to Petersfield, was moved to comment that "there are few roads in England having a more billiard table-like surface than that from London to Portsmouth, and it is remarkable for the great length of it which is well tarred."

Weighing-in was conducted on the public weighbridge in Petersfield Square, starting at 11.00am, and a charge of 1 shilling per vehicle was levied. The vehicles were at the same time subject to scrutineering to detect non standard fittings, to comply with the regulations for all standard and touring classes. The competition numbers were hung on the railings in the Square for easy collection by the drivers. After lunch at the Dolphin Hotel, hopefully notified in advance this year, the competitors assembled at the foot of the hill at 1.30pm for a 2.00pm start. *The Light Car and Cyclecar* observed that "interested villagers had gathered, naming the machines, asking where were the heroes of last years climb, who, when they appeared were received with cheers".

The precise location of the start and finish lines, and the actual length of the course, were not officially recorded. One journal quoted a length but this is not consistent with the pictures published and the times recorded. The only event at South Harting that had published a precise course map was the very first one in 1905, and this was the course length that was now quoted, even though the start line was clearly in a different place. This makes accurate comparisons of times between events impossible.

The first car up the hill at 2.00pm was H.D. Leno in his 9hp Charronette in Class II. This was because Class I had been scratched due to there being only one entrant. There were twenty seven entries in Class II, which was generally reported as "uneventful". Dr. Colvert-Glauert in his G.N. was estimated to have rounded the first bend at some 45mph, whereas the touring cars in general only "crawled round". Godfrey's G.N. looked even faster, despite persistent misfiring. G. Griffith's Morgan was expected to be fastest in the Class but he failed to finish because "such was the compression that he blew a cylinder clean off". Messrs. Noble and Scott, both in 10hp A.C., scratched under protest because the scrutineers had deemed their cars not to be standard. Their defence was that they were "standard sports models". Scott did in fact climb the hill.

The results were a clean sweep for G.N. with Nash, Godfrey and Thomas in the first three places. Nash's time was 1min. 51secs., and only three starters out of twenty seven failed to complete the climb. The winners on formula were W.R. Morris and L. Davies, both driving Morris Oxfords. Nash was third.

SOUTH HARTING HILL CLIMB 1905-1924

MISS NAN HENRY DRIVING AN 8hp G.W.K. TO FINISH THIRD
IN CLASS IV. THE RETURN ROAD TO THE FOOT OF THE HILL IS
ON THE RIGHT OF THE PICTURE.
(1914)

There were only six entries in Class III for standard touring cars between 1100cc and 1500cc. Four were Calcotts and the other two Bugattis. D. Cohen in an 8hp Bugatti was first up the hill and the eventual winner in a time of 2mins. 55.2secs. N.S. Hind in the other Bugatti failed to finish, and Calcotts took second, third and fourth places. J. Coop who finished fourth "drove in a bowler hat and changed down too late" on the first bend. Cohen in his Bugatti also won on formula and was awarded the Torkington Trophy.

Class IV, for lady drivers in standard machines, attracted six entries. Miss Adyce Price driving a 8.3hp Mathis stopped on the first corner because of "too much oil or too little petrol". However, having re-pressurised the petrol tank she re-started and finished the course. Miss Portwine in an A.C., with her father as passenger, made a good start but missed a gear and stopped further up the hill, she restarted however and still managed second place on time. Only Mrs. Warren-Lambert, sharing her husband's 9.8hp Warren-Lambert car, and Miss Henry in an 8hp G.W.K. achieved clean ascents, with Mrs. Warren-Lambert posting the fastest time of 2mins. 52.4secs. However the order was reversed on formula with Miss Henry taking the honours. Miss Kent in a Humberette did not start, and Miss Douglas in an 8hp de P failed.

THE MIDDLE YEARS – 1913 AND 1914

The "de P" was made in south London from 1914-1916. The name derived from L.F. de Peyrecave who, having worked for DUO Cyclecars, then took them over. The de P had engines by Dorman and shaft drive.

Class V for standard touring monocars provided the only real excitement of the day. There were six entries, three Cardens, two Morgans and an Aviette, and a great dual between Carden and Morgan was expected. The dual however did not materialize as the Morgans were reclassified as racing machines and moved to Class VI.

The excitement was provided by A.M.N. Holzapfel in his 5hp Carden. In the Cyclecar Club event the previous year he had crashed badly in practice the day before the event, stayed up all night repairing the car, only to have the engine catch fire twice on successive attempts to climb the hill. This year he overcooked it on the first bend, swerved violently, bounced off the bank and rolled several times before coming to rest upside down. He was lucky to suffer no serious injuries, and even the car was not badly damaged. Not a man you would choose as a chauffeur, although he was apparently the financial backer behind Carden Engineering. It was nevertheless a good day for Carden with W.E. Humphries winning the Class in 1min. 29.4secs., and J.V. Carden himself coming second. The same result prevailed on formula.

The prime event of the day was Class VI for racing machines. This attracted twenty entries, although several were cars which had already competed in earlier Classes for standard machines, including A.M.N. Holzapfel in his 5hp Carden. G.L. Holzapfel, presumably brother or son, was entered in an 8hp Carden. A new racing air-cooled G.N., designed for the cyclecar race in the Isle of Man, McMinnies's grand prix winning Morgan, and an 8hp Carden were also entered.

The most polished driving performance in the Class was reported to be J.W. Leno in his 6hp Baby Peugeot, but the time was not fast enough to figure in the first four. J.F. Buckingham, in his 12hp Buckingham with a brand new engine, failed when a spark plug blew out. W.D. Hawkes in his 10hp Victor also failed. John Valentine Carden in his 8hp Carden was the star performer however, making a "sensational ascent skidding twice right across the road". His time of 1min. 25secs. was the fastest of the day. Humphries in a 5hp Carden was third with Nash in his G.N. between the two Cardens. Despite this result, Nash was accused of being over cautious and using the cut out continually.

Although hardly a "light car", an Alpine Eagle 40/50hp Rolls-Royce, driven by works driver James Radley, provided a diversion for the crowd by doing an impressive demonstration run.

The days results based on times were announced over tea back at the Dolphin Hotel. The formula results were not available until a few days later. Since neither the A.C. Team or the Carden Team had finished complete, the Team Prize was awarded to the G.N. Team.

According to *The Royal Automobile Club Journal*, competitors were scheduled to leave Petersfield at 6.30pm for a weekend of festivities at Selsey. Whereas *The Cyclecar* magazine had made much of the Lobster Weekend at Selsey after the meeting in 1913, including a virtual road race to get there, the same magazine, now renamed *Light Car and Cyclecar*, did not mention it at all this year. Perhaps the Light Car element had a sobering influence on the more rowdy Cyclecar folk.

Within three months of this Cyclecar Club event the country was on a war footing, and South Harting Hill would not echo to the sound of competitive motoring again for five years. By that time many things would have changed.

SOUTH HARTING HILL CLIMB 1905-1924

**WAITING FOR THE RESULTS OUTSIDE
THE DOLPHIN HOTEL IN PETERSFIELD.
(1914)**

**MRS WARREN-LAMBERT DRIVING HER 9.8hp WARREN-LAMBERT
TO WIN CLASS IV FOR LADY DRIVERS.
(1914)**

THE MIDDLE YEARS – 1913 AND 1914

20   The Light Car and Cyclecar   27TH JULY, 1914.

Bugatti

The Light Car De Luxe

The Light Car De Luxe

WINNER OF THE TORKINGTON TROPHY

at the South Harting Hill Climb, organised by the Cyclecar Club and run off on July the 18th. Mr. D. Cohen drove his 8 h.p. Bugatti to any easy victory and, as mentioned in our headline, won the trophy presented for the best performance put up by a standard touring light car of more than 1,100 c.c. and less than 1,500 c.c. The car was privately owned and was an absolute standard touring model.

If you want a light car that is built like a gun, and can be depended upon to give many years highly efficient service at a small running cost, yet priced at quite a moderate figure, drop us a line and arrange for a trial run or, even better, call at our showrooms.

For catalogue and complete details write to—

Charles Jarrott & Letts, Ltd.
(Sole Concessionnaires)

West End Showroom: 45, Gt. Marlboro' St., London, W.
'Grams: "Jemidar, London."   'Phones: 2363 Gerrard (3 lines).
Service Depot Address: 50, Page St., Westminster.
'Phone: 7240 Victoria.   'Grams: "Chassilets, S'west, London."

A Bugatti with a special boat body which attracted considerable attention at South Harting.

– 101 –

CHAPTER 7

THE POST WAR YEARS 1919 to 1924

1919 – The First Junior Car Club Meeting

The last hill climb held at South Harting before the 1914-18 war was organised by the Cyclecar Club. That meeting attracted more light cars than cyclecars and the club was already feeling uncomfortable with its name. At its first committee meeting after the war name change was the main topic of discussion, and at the first post war general meeting on 1st March 1919 the name was changed to the Junior Car Club. The first competitive event organised by the renamed club, and one of the very first motoring events of any sort after the war, was the South Harting Hill Climb held on Saturday the 21st June 1919.

This was to be a closed club event with entries invited in eight classes, defined in *Light Car and Cyclecar* as follows:

Class 1	Standard three wheeled cyclecars, with engines not exceeding 1100cc. A passenger must be carried in the normal position in addition to the driver. Awards on time and formula according to the number of entries received.
Class 2	Standard touring two-seated light cars and cyclecars with engines not exceeding 1100cc. A passenger must be carried in the normal position in addition to the driver. Awards on time and formula.
Class 3	Standard touring two-seated light cars and cyclecars with engines not exceeding 1500cc. A passenger must be carried in the normal position in addition to the driver. Awards on time and formula.
Class 4	Standard four-seated light cars, engine limit 1500cc, three passengers to be carried in addition to the driver. Awards on time and formula.

THE POST WAR YEARS 1919 TO 1924

Class 5   Lady drivers in standard touring two-seated and four-seated light cars and cyclecars, with engines not exceeding 1500cc. A passenger must be carried in the normal position in addition to the driver. Awards on time and formula. Lady drivers only are eligible for this class.

Class 6   Non-standard, or racing, class for three wheeled cyclecars cars up to 1100cc. Awards on time only.

Class 7   Non-standard, or racing, class for light cars or cyclecars up to 1100cc. Awards on time only.

Class 8   Non-standard, or racing, class for light cars or cyclecars up to 1500cc.

In addition to the foregoing classes and awards, any three members by paying an extra 5s. each may constitute a team and enter for the team prize, which will be awarded if there are not fewer than three teams entered. The winning team will be that in which the sum of the three figures of merit gained by its respective members is the highest. The entrance fee is 7s. 6d. for a single entry in one event and 12s. 6d. for entries in two events, with the exception of the racing classes, for which each entrance fee is 10s. 6d.

The meeting attracted a total of 32 event entries, compared to 65 at the last pre war meeting. The formula to be used was the same formula, derived by Dr. Low, as in 1914.

Competitors were required to report to the weighing-in station at Midhurst Station by 11am on the Saturday, where all vehicles in the Standard classes would also be scrutineered. Drivers and passengers were also to be weighed. No practice was allowed on competition day, the penalty for which was disqualification.

For some unexplained reason there were no telephones up the hill and timing was to be carried out by timekeepers at the start and finish with "synchronised watches". Quite how this was done to an apparent accuracy of 0.06secs. is unclear.

The first car up the hill at 2.30pm, in glorious sunshine, was F.J. Findon in his 8hp Morgan. Since he was the only entrant in Class 1 he could not technically receive an award, but he nevertheless put up the fastest time of the day for any standard car at 2mins. 3.0secs.

The lack of any organised competitive motoring for five years meant that many of the entrants were inexperienced, or simply out of practice. Comments were made in the reports that as many as 80% of the starters in all classes made poor starts, being slow off the line and changing up too quickly. The notable exceptions were the older, experienced drivers such as Godfrey, Frazer-Nash, Stead and Bedford, who all did proper racing starts.

Class 2, for standard two seaters up to 1100cc, "did not produce much excitement with most of the competitors touring up". J.H. Wadham in his Baby Peugeot "did some stout climbing in clouds of smoke". The best performance in the class was by Capt. A.G. Frazer-Nash in his 10hp G.N., with a time of 2mins. 25.2secs. The winner on formula was W. Wadham in his 9.5hp Standard.

Class 3 for standard two seaters up to 1500cc provided some better sport, but was still marred by poor starting. Stead in his A.C. made the most impressive climb, and proved to be fastest with a time of 2mins. 18.6secs. He also won the class on formula. "Brownsort toured up chatting with his passenger" and made the slowest ascent. H.R. White in his Bifort was hampered by a car coming down the hill but made a good recovery and finished well.

Classes 4 and 5 produced only one completed climb each. Class 4 for standard four seaters up to 1500cc was a walkover for J.T. Wood in his 10.8hp G.W.K., who had just finished second in Class 3. This friction drive car was one of the few brand new 1919 vehicles on display at South Harting and had only been completed on the morning of the event.

The only clean climb in Class 5, for lady drivers, was that by Miss J.A. Hill, driving Noble's A.C., in her very first event. The other entrant was Mrs. Frazer-Nash whose over head inlet valve G.N. suffered a broken cotter that allowed a valve to fall into the cylinder.

Class 6 for non standard three wheeled cyclecars up to 1100cc produced only two entries, both 8hp Morgans. The drivers were Major A.C. Hardy and F.G. Layzell, and Hardy is credited with the faster time, but there was a suspected misprint in the published results since the much slower Layzell on a similar car was listed as winning on formula. No awards were made to non standard cars for performance against formula, but the results were published anyway.

Class 7, for non standard light cars and cyclecars up to 1100cc, generated five entries and "provided some thrills". Godfrey and Frazer-Nash were the stars of the day. Frazer-Nash in his G.N. made fastest time of the day with 1min. 20.8secs. and "had to cut out on every corner to get round", but still did a broadside skid coming out of the last corner. Godfrey in his G.N. Vitesse was reported to "be doing at least 30mph on the 1 in 9 gradient at the top". Capt. J.S. Coats in his Singer made an excellent start and "roared up the hill" to win the class on formula. This Singer racing car was built for the Light Car T.T. that was to have been held in the autumn of 1914.

The final class of the day was Class 8 for non standard light cars and cyclecars up to 1500cc, which generated nine entries, including Godfrey, Frazer-Nash and Coates fresh from Class 7. New cars seen however were the Hillman Speed Model, one of the first of the post war generation of sporting light cars, and two silver coloured A.C. competition specials which "seemed somewhat out of place, since they were really just ordinary chassis with special bodies, not, as is more usual, special chassis with ordinary bodies".

Frazer-Nash was not able to better his performance in Class 7 since he broke a chain on his G.N. while changing up. McCulloch, in one of the A.C.'s, made a run but was disqualified for being caught practicing on competition day. Both the Hillman and the Chiribiri were thought to be over geared, although G. Bedford on the Hillman finished second on time and first on formula. H.R. Godfrey in his G.N. Vitesse made the fastest run at 1min. 35secs., faster than his previous run but not fast enough to beat Frazer-Nash for fastest time of the day.

Note: Archie Frazer-Nash was variously referred to in the reports as Nash and Frazer-Nash. Before the war he was mainly known as Archie Nash, and after the war as Archie Frazer-Nash.

THE POST WAR YEARS 1919 TO 1924

C.A.S. PETO ON THE 10hp ERIC-CAMPBELL
(1919)

SOUTH HARTING HILL CLIMB 1905-1924

CAPT. J.T. WOOD DRIVING THE NEW 4 CYLINDER G.W.K.
(1919)

THE POST WAR YEARS 1919 TO 1924

G.C. STEAD ON THE 10hp A.C. WELL ON THE WAY TO WINNING CLASS III.
(1919)

SOUTH HARTING HILL CLIMB 1905-1924

SPECTATORS PARKED ON HARTING DOWN.
(1919)

H.D. LENO DRIVING HIS 8hp CHARRONETTE
IN CLASS 2. HE FINISHED FIFTH ON TIME
AND SECOND ON FORMULA. (1919)

LAT PHOTOGRAPHIC

G. BEDFORD DRIVING A "NON-STANDARD" 11.9hp HILLMAN IN CLASS 8.
HE CAME SECOND ON TIME BUT FIRST ON FORMULA. (1919)

LAT PHOTOGRAPHIC

SOUTH HARTING HILL CLIMB 1905-1924

J.H. WADHAM NEAR THE TOP OF THE HILL
ON HIS 7.5hp BABY PEUGEOT.
(1919)

THE POST WAR YEARS 1919 TO 1924

CAPT. J.S. COATS DRIVING THE RACING SINGER WHICH WAS
ORIGINALLY BUILT FOR THE 1914 TT RACE IN THE ISLE OF MAN.
(1919)

SOUTH HARTING HILL CLIMB 1905-1924

W.D. HAWKES AT THE START ON HIS MORGAN.
HE WAS THE ONLY RUNNER IN CLASS 1 BUT FAILED TO
FINISH IN THE 1100cc RACING CLASS.
(1920)

A PEACEFUL SCENE
IN THE PADDOCK.
(1920)

THE POST WAR YEARS 1919 TO 1924

1920 – The Second Junior Car Club Meeting

Light Car and Cyclecar, in announcing the meeting to be held on Saturday, 24th July 1920, stated that;

> "probably the most important competition organised purely for light cars and cyclecars is the South Harting Hill-Climb...This fixture was first instituted in order to demonstrate the fact that light cars and cyclecars could climb steep hills, but owing to the general improvement which has take place in design and construction, this event is becoming more and more a test of fast hill climbing."

This highlights both the importance of South Harting as a venue, and the developing trend for hill climb events to move away from the simple trade demonstrations that they were up until 1913, to the more overtly sporting events that started at South Harting in 1914 with the introduction of racing classes.

Entries were invited this year in nine classes, the first eight of which were the same as the previous year except for Class 6, which was now for standard monocars rather than non standard three wheeled cyclecars. The new class, Class 9, was for "Sporting cars, catalogued as such, having engines not exceeding 1500cc. A passenger to be carried. Awards on time."

"Cars in Classes 2,3,4,5 must have lamps, full sized wings, running boards, horn, screen and hood...Entrants are reminded that specially light pistons or connecting rods, special camshafts, gears (or aluminium pistons if such are not standard), special carburettors, or

LAT PHOTOGRAPHIC

SOUTH HARTING HILL CLIMB 1905-1924

A.E. BARRETT ON HIS 10hp G.N.
DRIVING TO SIXTH PLACE IN CLASS 2.
(1920)

THE POST WAR YEARS 1919 TO 1924

other non standard parts will not be allowed, while the full touring equipment shown in the catalogue must be carried. Entries should be sent as early as possible to Mr. S.C.H. Davis, 42, Mecklenburgh Square, W.C.1."

The meeting attracted 71 event entries, compared to 32 in 1919. Discounting multiple entries, there were 49 separate cars. Among the familiar names were a few notable new ones, such as The Hon. Victor Bruce in a 10hp A.C., Capt. N. Macklin in a 10hp Silver Hawk and Miss Violet Cordery in another Silver Hawk. The Silver Hawk was made by Noel Campbell Macklin, after he ended his connection with the Eric-Campbell. Miss Meeking continued the tradition of Dorothy Levitt from earlier years and was a lone lady entrant in Class 3, as well as competing in Class 5 for Lady Drivers.

Another new name was E.A. Tamplin in an 8hp Tamplin. Edward Tamplin had been an agent for Carden cyclecars, but in 1919 he was granted a licence to manufacture them under his own name. The bodies were reportedly made of fibre board impregnated with linseed oil.

MAJOR WARREN-LAMBERT DRIVING HIS 10hp WARREN-LAMBERT
TO SECOND PLACE IN CLASS 3.
(1920)

SOUTH HARTING HILL CLIMB 1905-1924

MRS HATTON (NÉE PORTWINE) TOOK THE PLACE OF A. NOBLE
IN HIS 10hp A.C. IN CLASS 3 BUT ONLY FINISHED 19th OUT OF 20 STARTERS.
(1920)

THE POST WAR YEARS 1919 TO 1924

In 1919 the 1100cc touring class had attracted the largest entry, but the general trend to bigger engines meant that the 1500cc class became the biggest in 1920.

There was to be no practising on Sundays since "the police, although agreeable to the holding of the event are very much averse to practising by noisy cars." The weather on the Friday had been very wet and the officials were concerned as to whether the meeting would be able to take place, however Saturday dawned dry and sunny and continued the South Harting tradition of fine weather.

Weighing-in and scrutineering were held between 10am and 1pm on the Saturday at Midhurst Station; S.C.H. Davis and Major Bale were in charge of the weighbridge. *The Autocar* made much of the intensity of the scrutineering, describing it as an "inquisition based on Torquemada". There were four scrutineers, including Lionel Martin, under Chief Scrutineer Hugh McConnell, and competitors were required to sign a declaration that their machines were completely standard. Some drivers were reportedly "removed to the weighbridge almost in tears." Some illegal devices were removed and some cars were switched to other classes.

On the day A. Noble did not appear, his A.C. was therefore driven by Mr. Portwine's daughter, "to whom heartiest congratulations on her recent marriage" were offered. *Light Car and Cyclecar* reported that "resources at South Harting are somewhat limited, and,

E.A. TAMPLIN ON HIS 8hp TAMPLIN IN CLASS 3.
HE WAS PLACED SIXTH OUT OF TWENTY STARTERS (1920)

SOUTH HARTING HILL CLIMB 1905-1924

VIOLET CORDERY DRIVING HER 10hp SILVER HAWK IN CLASS 5.
SHE PUT UP THE FASTEST TIME BUT WAS DISQUALIFIED AS THE
CAR WAS DEEMED A RACING CAR. (1920)

THE POST WAR YEARS 1919 TO 1924

therefore, the club has been unable to make any arrangements for lunches, tea, etc."

After weighing-in and scrutineering at Midhurst the cars proceeded to the paddock at South Harting. This comprised some fields at the foot of the hill made available by sympathetic locals of whom the only one named was a Mr. Alan Taylor.

The course in 1920 was slightly shorter than in previous years since the finish line had been brought back to coincide with the entrance to the return road, thus cars were able to return to South Harting village immediately after their climb rather than wait for the course to be closed to return in batches. It had also been to decided to allow cars to start their climb before the last car had actually crossed the finish line, a strategy that would speed proceedings up but needed precise marshalling. The course was quoted as ¾ mile instead of the 1833 yards of the original full course.

The formula used was not published, but since it was attributed to Dr. A.M. Low, no longer referred to as Major, it can only be assumed that it was the same as the previous year.

The meeting was scheduled to start at 2.30pm, but the timekeepers were delayed and the first car did not go up the hill until 2.45pm. That first car was W.D. Hawkes in his 1100cc, eight valved, GP Morgan, and in a repeat of what happened in 1919, he was the only starter in Class 1. The other entrant, H.J. Fisher in a 6hp Reindeer, did not appear.

Class 2, for touring two-seaters up to 1100cc, attracted 10 entries, "but did not provide any thrills, as the speeds of the machines did not call for any stunt work on the bends, the only exception being the Tamplin, which the driver skidded slightly to get round."

S. Watson in a 10hp Deemster "faced the starter wearing an expression of intense Pelmanism," but made a good climb after a slow start. Marchant in the Bleriot-Whippet was reported fastest up the lower slopes, but was stopped because of a jammed kick starter. Major Empson in his Lawrence-Jackson "toured up", but Finch in the G.N. was "fast and steady."

Frazer-Nash was due to appear in Class 2 in the standard G.N. but did not. *Light Car and Cyclecar* found out later however that, just before the start, he had "discovered he was devoid of a clutch spring...so he tied a piece of rope to the clutch pedal and kept a strong pull on the rope as the car ascended the hill". Having missed his turn in Class 2, he was allowed to run later with Class 3. His time was still counted in Class 2, and he still came fifth.

E.R.R. Starr, driving Major Baskerville Cosway's 10hp Deemster, made a good climb but on returning to the paddock he damaged the front axle. This robbed Miss Adyce Price of a drive in Class 5 as she had been entered in this car.

"Tamplin went well, his passenger leaning in on the bends", and recorded the fastest time at 1min. 40.2secs. Watson (Deemster) was second and Finch (G.N.) third. On formula it was Watson, Phillips (Deemster) and Finch.

Class 3, for touring two-seaters up to 1500cc, carrying a passenger seated beside the driver, attracted the biggest field of the day with twenty three entries. The biggest disaster of the day beset the Hon. Victor Bruce in his A.C. His "engine suddenly collapsed as he was about to start. There was a nasty thud, and in a few seconds the roadway under the car was covered in water." W.D. Hawkes (Horstmann) was also a non starter.

The Deemsters again impressed. "Phillips made even the savants lift an eyebrow by the way his little Deemster smoothly and quietly simply devoured the gradient and slid over the finishing line in great style."

Marchant in the Bleriot-Whippet, who had not completed his climb in Class 2, ran again and surprised and impressed everybody with a fine showing. R.E.H. Allen in his 10hp Bugatti

– 119 –

SOUTH HARTING HILL CLIMB 1905-1924

KAYE DON ON THE SINGLE SEAT TAMPLIN WINNING CLASS 6.
(1920)

had difficulty maintaining petrol feed pressure, despite frantic efforts by his passenger, and misfired all the way up. Herrington in his 9.5hp Hurtu completely enveloped the crowd in a smoke screen.

It was the Deemsters day, with Phillips fastest in 1min. 38.0secs., and Watson third in 1min. 42.2secs. They were separated by Warren-Lambert, driving a car bearing his name, in 1min. 40.0secs. On formula the result was Phillips, Watson, Finch (G.N.), compared to Watson, Phillips, Finch in Class 2.

Class 4, for four seat touring cars up to 1500cc, carrying three passengers, was "purely a demonstration of G.W.K.'s", with the entry comprising six identical 10.8hp cars. Not

THE POST WAR YEARS 1919 TO 1924

surprisingly the times were all very similar, but D.H. Owen Edmunds was fastest at 2mins. 11.8secs., with R.A. Pope second and Stevenson third. Predictably the results on formula were the same.

Mr Pope was particularly congratulated as he had only recently had one leg amputated. This success may have prompted GWK to produce an "all hand control" car for the disabled soon after.

Class 5 was for lady drivers in touring cars up to 1500cc. There were seven entries of which five actually appeared at the start line. Mrs. Hawkes in the Horstmann and Miss Adyce Price in the Deemster were the non starters.

Violet Cordery drove her Silver Hawk up the hill without any identifying numbers. The car had been deemed not to be a touring car by the scrutineers, and therefore not eligible for an award, but they let her make the climb anyway. She was reported as having climbed "in masterly fashion, although the spectators appeared alarmed at her skids." Her time of 1min. 37secs. would have won the class.

Mrs. Frazer-Nash drove the standard G.N. up the hill only one second slower than her husband had in Class 3; he had presumably in the meantime fitted a proper clutch spring. Miss Meeking improved on her time in Class 3, but Mrs. Warren-Lambert won the Class in 1min. 49.2secs. Mrs. Frazer-Nash was second and Miss Meeking third. The results on formula were the same.

Class 6 was for monocars, sold and used as single seaters, up to 1100cc. It only attracted four entries, three A.V.'s and one Tamplin, and Major Empson in one of the A.V.'s was a non starter. Davenport in an 8hp A.V. "provided us with something akin to the exploits of a cinema hero and his wonderful pluck was warmly applauded on all sides". He allowed his nearside wheels to get into a twelve inch deep rut on the inside of a right hand bend, but rather than slow down to get out of it, he kept his foot down and, at an alarming angle, followed the rut all the way round the bend, miraculously emerging out without crashing.

The fastest climb was made by Don in his 8hp Tamplin. "The way in which he took the bend on his narrow tracked machine made one fear for the safety of the driver. He came round in a series of skids, which he corrected very skilfully." His time was 1min. 27.0secs. Second was Davenport in 1min. 34.0secs. and third Scofield in his 654cc A.V.

Class 7 for 1100cc racing cars attracted only four entries, of which only three started; Major Empson's 8hp A.V. was not ready in time. The most dramatic of the three runs was Hawkes in his Morgan. He was making a fast run when "with a detonation which drowned even its own piercing exhaust note the near side cylinder flew clean off. It cavorted ungainly up in the air some 10 or 12 feet with a length of exhaust pipe making it appear like some horrible form of deadly grenade." Luckily he managed to stop safely and there were no injuries. He never did find the piston, which either ended up as shrapnel or in the pocket of a souvenir hunter.

Frazer-Nash made a spectacular climb to win Class 7 in Kim I, with a time of 1min. 4.6secs., fastest time of the day. The only other completed climb was Godfrey in his G.N. Vitesse in a time of 1min. 12.6secs.

The second racing car class, Class 8, was for cars up to 1500cc. There were six entries but Hawkes (Morgan), and de Lapalud (J.L.), were non starters. The numbers were boosted back to six however because the Silver Hawk entries in Class 9 had been deemed by the scrutineers to be racing cars.

There is considerable confusion in the reports surrounding the Silver Hawk entries and the results they achieved. In the original *Light Car and Cyclecar* entry list there were six event entries; Macklin in Classes 8 and 9, Bradley, Field and Bray in Class 9, and the Entry No.36 duplicated by Violet Cordery in Class 5 and Bray in Class 9. The team entry was given as Macklin, Bradley and Bray. The scrutineers then deemed the Silver Hawk to be a racing car, although Violet Cordery was still allowed to run unofficially in Class 5, and Bradley in Class 9. *The Autocar* and *Motor* both credited Field with third place in Class 8, whereas *Light Car and Cyclecar* gave third place to Macklin and fourth place to Bradley. To complete the confusion both *The Autocar* and *Motor* report that, by the time Class 8 was run, Bradley and Field were sharing the "only one car available", which "was quite hawkish but utterly devoid of silver." It is not clear which car that was, or what had happened to the others. Apart from being credited with third place in Class 9 by *Light Car and Cyclecar*, Macklin was not mentioned at all in any report.

There was no confusion however about the winners. There was a repetition of Class 7 with Frazer-Nash first and Godfrey second, although neither could better their previous times.

The final class of the day was Class 9 for sporting cars up to 1500cc. This had originally attracted nine entries but, with the four Silver Hawks moved to Class 8, and Warren-Lambert, Hawkes and Marshall non starters, only two cars actually made official climbs. Gilmore-Ellis in his 8.7hp G.N., Green Bug, made the fastest time at 1min. 15.8secs., and Godfrey was runner up in 1min. 18.6secs. in his G.N.

Of the eight Team entries, four were unable to present a complete set of results to the judges. In the No.1 A.C. Team, The Hon. Victor Bruce blew his engine up, In the No.2 A.C. Team, A. Noble did not appear, in the No.4 G.W.K. Team, E.A. Falconer was not reported at all, nor was A. Bray in the Silver Hawk Team. The clear winners were the G.N. Team, with the Deemster Team second, and the No.3 G.W.K. Team third. The only other team to complete were the Warren-Lambert Team.

There was still apparently some sensitivity about reporting actual times. The *Motor* quoted all times as "x + mins. secs.", where "x" was the fastest time of the day, which was not actually reported. Neither *The Autocar* or *Light Car and Cyclecar* were bothered by such political correctness and published real times. A quick calculation based on the published data shows that Frazer-Nash's fastest time of the day represented an average speed of some 41.8mph.

The meeting was closed at 4.30pm., which, since the start had been delayed until 2.45pm and some 51 cars had faced the starter, was a tribute to the slickness of the organisation. Twenty five Junior Car Club members and friends then proceeded to Chichester, as there was not sufficient accommodation available at the traditional Selsey venue. On Sunday morning they drove to Bognor for lunch at the Royal Hotel, then back to London, stopping only for tea on the way at "The Woodlands", Elstead, the home of H.P. McConnell, the long standing Chief Scrutineer of the club.

THE POST WAR YEARS 1919 TO 1924

ARCHIE FRAZER-NASH MADE FASTEST TIME
OF THE DAY ON HIS RACING G.N. "KIM 1".
(1920)

LEON CUSHMAN'S 11.3hp BUGATTI ON THE WEIGHBRIDGE AT MIDHURST.
(1921)

1921 – The Third Junior Car Club Meeting

"Tomorrow, Saturday, is South Harting day" proclaimed *Light Car and Cyclecar* in its issue of 18th June 1921. Entries had been invited in nine Classes, which were essentially the same as the previous year but with two small differences. Class 3 was now for touring two-seaters between 1100cc and 1500cc rather than simply up to 1500cc, which was presumably to stop people running Class 2 cars again in Class 3, and Class 6 was now specifically for Tamplin, A.V. and Carden machines. A strong entry of 87 had been attracted, compared to 71 in 1920 and 32 in 1919. Among the new names in the entry list was one R. Mays in a 9.8hp Hillman in Class 9. Among the new marques of car seen for the first time at South Harting were Aston-Martin, Alvis and Lagonda.

Lionel Martin had last driven at South Harting in 1913 in a Singer, when Bamford and Martin Ltd were Singer agents. He now reappeared with both "Coal Scuttle", the first car ever registered as an Aston-Martin in 1915, and the later production prototype, AM 270. Two other drivers were entered, Jack Addis, the works foreman, and one W.M. Thomas, editor of *Light Car*, and later better known as Sir Miles Thomas, Chairman of B.O.A.C.

Indicative of increasing concerns about crowd control and spectator safety at events held on public roads was a plea in *Light Car and Cyclecar* for any of its readers attending South

THE POST WAR YEARS 1919 TO 1924

Harting to "congregate on the inside of the bends". No such clear message had previously been published.

Weighing-in was again to be held at Midhurst Station on the Saturday morning. The Chief Scrutineer was Hugh McConnell, who concluded that several of the cars in Class 3 were not "standard" and promptly removed them to the Sports or Racing Classes. One had a "special carburettor" and another "special oiling arrangements". All cars in Classes 3, 4, and 5 were supposed to compete with "complete standard equipment". At least four cars in Class 9 for sports cars were also removed to the racing Classes, including R. Mays' Hillman, and the Little Greg entered by H.R. Wilding, the General Manager of the British Gregoire Agency Ltd. Mr. Wilding was so incensed he wrote to *Light Car and Cyclecar* the next week to complain. "The car I entered is in every way standard with the exception of the fact that it has aluminium pistons in place of the ordinary cast iron pattern, and an aluminium sports-type body in place of the standard body." He clearly thought he could have won Class 9.

The Little Greg was a renamed French Hinstin cyclecar, a streamlined version of which did well at Le Mans. "Conspicuous in the station yard were the Gregoire and the racing Charron-Laycock. Two examples of the former appeared; a standard model with comfortable touring body, and a "sports" with streamlined, all aluminium, bucket seated body, which looked good enough for anything". The latter was presumably Wilding's Little Greg. *Light Car and Cyclecar* continued: "The Charron-Laycock only emerged from the works the day before the event and was tested in the wee sma' hours of Saturday morning. A noticeable feature of this car was the lengths of aeroplane "elastic" by means of which the springing of the car was stiffened up."

The elastic shock absorbers on the racing Charron-Laycock, which made its debut at South Harting.

SOUTH HARTING HILL CLIMB 1905-1924

**H.P. TALLEMACHE, 11.9hp LAGONDA,
AND R.A. POPE, 10hp GWK, ON THE START LINE.**
(1921)

On the day the Deemster team did not appear, and Lionel Martin was not well enough to drive. Jack Addis therefore drove Coal Scuttle and W.M. Thomas drove AM 270. The only entrant in Class 1, A.E. Hartfell in a 10hp Morgan, was transferred to Class 2.

After weighing-in and scrutineering the competitors assembled at the paddock at the foot of the hill, where they all had allocated places. The paddock was one of two fields lent by local residents for the event. The second field was a car park for spectators, and was donated by a Mr. E. W. Wild.

The formula used was probably the Dr. A.M. Low formula used in 1919, and presumably also in 1920. The precise formula used however is in doubt since the factors varying the terms C (for cubic capacity) and T (for time) were given as powers in 1919 but simple multipliers for 1921. Probably a typographical error by a non mathematical typesetter.

Earl Russell reappeared at this event as a marshal. His name had not been mentioned in the South Harting reports since 1906. In 1907 he had berated the R.A.C. committee for being dominated by petrol engine interests and discriminating against steam cars in the South

THE POST WAR YEARS 1919 TO 1924

Harting regulations; his name did not appear in the list of R.A.C. committee members or event officials that year. It is not clear whether he was now present as a member of the Junior Car Club, a representative of the R.A.C., or just an influential local resident.

"Hardly had the last luncheon basket disappeared (for everybody seemed to have decided to picnic on the wonderful slopes beside the hill) when, heralded by much flag waving and megaphone work, the first car came up." The crowd was estimated at one thousand people.

Light Car and Cyclecar this year again reported the times in the form "x + Mins.Secs.", where "x" was the fastest time of the day. *Automotor Journal*, however, still could not be bothered with such political correctness and published the actual times of the class winners. The results given in Appendix III are the complete results taken directly from the original Junior Car Club Events Sub Committee minutes.

VIOLA MEEKING DRIVING HER 11.8hp A.C. TO THIRD PLACE IN CLASS 5 FOR LADY DRIVERS.
(1921)

ALFRED MOSS DRIVING HIS 8.7hp G.N.
TO THIRD PLACE IN CLASS 2.
(1921)

The starter, Mr. S.C. Westall, sent the first car up at 2.30pm. In the absence of the Deemsters, Class 2 was between six G.N.'s, three Cardens, one Tamplin, the standard Little Greg and the Morgan transferred from Class 1. In a Class without any drama, Edward Tamplin put up the fastest time at 90.2secs., Frazer-Nash in his G.N. was second fastest, but won on formula.

Third on time and second on formula, on another G.N., was one A.E. Moss; a young Alfred Moss, later to be father of Sir Stirling. This was very early in his motor sport career, before his later circuit racing activities at Brooklands and Indianapolis. Competing at the latter was his great personal ambition and in 1924, as part of the Barber-Warnock Ford team, he came in 16th.

Class 3, for touring two-seaters from 1100cc to 1500cc, had attracted 22 entries. It also attracted the attention of the scrutineer, and between the cars he transferred to the sports and racing classes, and non-starters, only 13 cars actually presented themselves at the start line. Gear changing was again the main distinction between successful climbs and the

THE POST WAR YEARS 1919 TO 1924

M.W.M. THOMAS DRIVING THE 11hp ASTON-MARTIN IN THE SPORTING CAR
CLASS IN WHICH HE FINISHED SECOND ON BOTH TIME AND FORMULA.
HIS PASSENGER WAS MRS LIONEL MARTIN.
(1921)

F. HARRIS DRIVING HIS 10.8hp FOUR SEAT G.W.K.
TO SECOND PLACE ON FORMULA IN CLASS 4.
(1921)

SOUTH HARTING HILL CLIMB 1905-1924

W. HARRIS, 8.9hp MARLBOROUGH, CROSSING THE FINISHING LINE
IN CLASS 8 FOR RACING CARS UP TO 1500cc. HE FINISHED NINTH, HAVING
BEEN "PROMOTED" FROM THE SPORTING CAR CLASS.
(1921)

remainder. "C.E. Maney in his 11.8hp A.C. actually hung on to top gear until he reached the quarry when, however, he had to make a fairly rapid change right down to bottom gear."

"Misfortune overtook Maitland Keddie (10/30 Alvis), the engine developing a sudden derangement which caused the car to come to stop and then run backwards." *Automotor Journal* said it was a broken valve; *The Autocar* said it was a timing wheel which had "worked slack on its shaft"; *Motor* said the cause was a "sooted plug, a burnt exhaust valve and a starter pinion that jumped into mesh with the flywheel, all at once".

A curt note appeared in the *Motor* for 29th June: "We learn from T.G. John Ltd., manufacturers of the Alvis car, that the trouble that beset Mr. Keddie's Alvis on South Harting Hill was entirely ascribable to faulty sparking plugs (the type used were not those

– 130 –

fitted as standard) and not to any of the variety of reasons given by Mr. Keddie."

The most impressive performance was by W.G. Hedges in his 10/30 Alvis and he indeed won the Class in a time of 94.8secs. He also won on formula. Second fastest was Stead in his A.C., despite carburettor trouble.

Class 4, for four-seated touring cars up to 1500cc, carrying three passengers, was predictably the slowest Class of the day by a significant margin. It attracted eight entries, mainly A.C. and G.W.K., with a lone Lagonda and a Warren-Lambert. "D.A. Parsons, 11.8hp A.C., was fast but sure, while the performance of F. Harris (10.8hp G.W.K.), who is without a left arm and a right leg, was a fine demonstration of what a maimed driver can do in a hill-climb." F.M. Harding, in another G.W.K. boiled and misfired. D.L. Underwood in his 11.8hp A.C. recorded the fastest time in the Class at 124.8secs., he also won on formula. G.F. Reeve in another A.C. was second fastest.

Class 5 for lady drivers attracted only four entrants, one of whom, Miss Keddie on a 10/30 Alvis, was a non starter for obvious reasons. Mrs. Warren-Lambert in a 10hp Warren-Lambert was skilful but Miss Viola Meeking, in Stead's A.C., suffered a blocked jet on the first bend. It cleared, however, and she did reach the top of the hill. By far the best climb was by Mrs. Frazer-Nash in her 8.7hp G.N. who was "apparently not at all disconcerted by the skidding of her machine." She was comfortably the fastest at 102.0secs. *Automotor Journal* reported that no awards could be made on formula because "none of the ladies thought of weighing-in," although *Light Car and Cyclecar* credited Mrs. Frazer-Nash with a formula win.

Class 6 for Tamplin, A.V., and Carden machines only attracted five entries, three Carden and one each of Tamplin and A.V. "Capt. J.V. Carden was noticeably slower and appeared to be suffering from a slipping clutch." Edward Tamplin was the fastest at 87.2secs., some 3secs. faster than his winning run in Class 2. W.F. Davenport in the A.V. was second and V.G. Loyd in a Carden third.

"Spectators who had been sitting at ease on the near side bank then made tracks for safety on the other side of the road or stood up in preparation for a precipitous exit through the hedge, for Class 7 was the first of the racing Classes – and the modern hill-climb spectator knows a thing or two." *Light Car and Cyclecar.*

Class 7, for racing cars up to 1100cc, originally attracted only four entries, three G.N., and the lone Morgan of W.D. Hawkes. This was however swelled by the scrutineer by two cars, the lightweight Little Greg driven by H.R. Wilding and J.V. Carden in a Carden.

The first car up was G.L. Hawkins in a G.N. who "slithering from side to side shot towards the summit at what appeared to be twice the speed of anything that had gone before". H.R. Godfrey in the old belt driven Bluebottle was spectacular but not as fast as Hawkins. The highlight of the meeting was Frazer-Nash in the G.N., Kim II. Needing to use the cut-out for some three seconds to get round the first two bends, the car "leapt into sight…lashing its tail like an angry fish." Capt. A. Frazer-Nash won the Class with a time of 70.0secs., with G.N. cars also finishing second and third.

Class 8, for racing cars up to 1500cc, attracted eleven entries including three straight from Class 7. It also gained one entry from Class 9, R. Mays in his 9.8hp Hillman. In 1921 Raymond Mays was a student at Cambridge and his father had bought him a Hillman Speed Model. His fellow undergraduate, Amherst Villiers, helped him tune and convert the car into a successful hill-climb and race car which he christened Quicksilver. It is not clear from any report just how far that conversion had gone by June 1921. Clearly too far for Hugh

McConnell, the Chief Scrutineer. In the event, "R. Mays (Hillman) was not as fast as might have been expected, and his gears apparently did not suit the hill." He would, however, have been second on time in Class 9 if the scrutineers had left him there.

W.M.W. Thomas handled the prototype Aston-Martin "with remarkable skill", and was in fact second only to Frazer-Nash and Kim II. "Nash's performance this time was even more sensational than his first ascent. He seemed to have absolutely no fear, and the little racing car often appeared to be travelling almost broadside on, as it surmounted the formidable gradient and took the "S bends faster than an express train."

Frazer-Nash beat his own time in Class 7, and set fastest time of the day, at 69.8secs. Thomas was second with 75.0secs., and Cushman was third fastest driving a bare Bugatti chassis fitted with a bucket seat.

From an original nineteen entries in Class 9, for sporting cars up to 1500cc, four had been moved by the scrutineer into the racing Classes, and one, A. Hester in a Deemster, did not start. Many of the remaining fourteen cars had already appeared in other Classes. Lefrere, driving Cushman's yellow bodied competition Bugatti, managed third fastest time on paper but was disqualified because he had removed the hood, which had been in place on the weighbridge during scrutineering.

"W.M.W. Thomas in the Aston-Martin, with Mrs. Lionel Martin as passenger, provided the spectators with quite as sensational a performance as in the previous class." Carrying a passenger however cost him nearly ten seconds, and he again came second to a G.N., this time G.L. Hawkins with a time of 81.2secs. Jack Addis in Coal Scuttle came third. The first three places on formula were the same.

The last car up the hill at 5.00pm was E.de W.S. Colver in his G.N., but he failed due to a burnt out magneto. A total of sixty five cars had climbed the hill that afternoon in what was generally agreed to have been a well organised and successful meeting in the traditional South Harting good weather. The officials then retired to the Coach and Horses to work out the results.

"With their customary enthusiasm the local police rendered active assistance throughout the trial, and their courtesy and hard work deserve every acknowledgement." So commented *The Light Car and Cyclecar*, *The Autocar* however reported that those Junior Car Club members "whose duty called them back to London when all the debris had been collected were suddenly reminded of sterner things by being halted and searched by armed police".

That evening another, more fortunate, party of London members joined with members from the newly formed South Western Centre at a formal dinner at the Queens Hotel, Southsea. Mr. G. W. Lucas was in the chair and Lieut.-Colonel Chas. R. Jarrott was the guest speaker. There was clearly disappointment, and some embarrassment, that only forty people had turned up, whereas the room had been set for twice as many.

Many speakers criticised the membership for not supporting the function better. However Capt. A. Frazer-Nash, responding to his award as Champion of the Day, while echoing the disappointment, thought it unfair to "pitch into" those who were there on account of those who were not.

Chas. Jarrott, rather ambiguously, said that he had been "astonished at the wonderful organisation" of the event at South Harting, and then proceeded to regale the audience with anecdotes of his early motoring experiences.

THE POST WAR YEARS 1919 TO 1924

1922 – The Fourth Junior Car Club Meeting

The most obvious difference between the 1922 South Harting Hill Climb and any previous event was the time of year. Every previous event had been held in either June or July, but the 1922 event was held on Saturday 10th September. No reason for this change is evident from the record.

Another significant change was in the style of the reporting. Only two years previously *Light Car and Cyclecar*, as mouthpiece for the Junior Car Club, had given full details of the Class regulations, a full list of entrants with competition numbers, and full results for all competitors including non starters. By 1922 the details of entrants and results in the published reports had shrunk to simply reporting the first three places in each class. This despite eulogies about it being the "annual classic event of its nature". Worse still, there was some confusion and disagreement between the various journals on results. Thankfully the *Junior Car Club Gazette* did list the full results, but still did not list non starters, failures or "promotions" between classes.

Entries were invited in nine classes, which were broadly as in 1921 with three exceptions. The class for touring three-wheelers, and the special class for Tamplin, Carden and A.V. machines were dropped, and in their place were classes for disabled drivers and private owners. Details, such as how many passengers had to be carried in the touring four-seater class, were not mentioned so we must assume them to be the same as in 1921. No report made any mention of the formula used, so again we must assume it was the same as the previous year.

COMPETITORS ASSEMBLED AT MIDHURST STATION FOR THE WEIGHING-IN.
(1922)

SOUTH HARTING HILL CLIMB 1905-1924

The Light Car and Cyclecar

Founded 1912 — The only Small Car Journal

4D
Vol. XX, No. 512
Sept. 16, 1922
Registered at the GPO as a Newspaper

AT SOUTH HARTING.
The hill-climbing contest held by the Junior Car Club at South Harting is recognised as the classic small car event of this nature of the season. The above photograph gives a vivid impression of the scene on Saturday last.

THE POST WAR YEARS 1919 TO 1924

A.E. BULL, 8hp AMILCAR, WITH EYES FIXED ON THE STARTER.
(1922)

The inclusion of a class for "private owners" is intriguing. *Light Car and Cyclecar* commented that it was a "special class for private owners who have "unstandardised" their cars to the extent of fitting such minor improvements as extra air inlets, ignition controls, shock absorbers and so forth". The implication is that, although not explicitly mentioned, the "standard" car classes, which were so heavily scrutineered, were still composed mainly of factory sponsored cars.

Although no actual numbers were quoted, *Motor* reported that entries were down on previous years, but that the crowds were the biggest ever seen, "some of whom came in motor coaches", the weather ideal and the event the most successful yet. Given the previous caveats, there are records of 55 event entries which, when discounted for multiple entries, equates to 45 separate cars. The high, in 1921, had been 87 event entries.

New names among the entries included Captain Donald M.K. Marendaz in a Marseal. The Marseal (or more correctly in 1922, Marseel) was a car produced by Marendaz, and his partner Seelhaft, up to 1925. When that company was closed down he launched the Marendaz Special.

Another new name was H.K. Moir in a works Aston-Martin. Bertie Kensington Moir had been recruited by Lionel Martin from the Zenith carburettor company, where he had acquired considerable knowledge of engine tuning. The driving skills and pit management experience he then gained with Aston-Martin were later put to good use as driver and team manager for Bentley.

Raymond Mays was clearly dissatisfied with his lack of success in 1921 in his Amherst Villiers tuned Hillman Speed Model. He reappeared at South Harting this year with a brand

SOUTH HARTING HILL CLIMB 1905-1924

VIOLA MEEKING DRIVING HER 11.8hp A.C. TO WIN THE
SPORTING CAR DIVISION OF CLASS 5 FOR LADY DRIVERS.
(1922)

new Brescia Bugatti, "liberally daubed with vermilion paint", which he had christened Cordon Rouge.

Weighing-in and scrutineering were again based at Midhurst railway station under the control of Hugh McConnell. While there were still some disputes, the *Motor* reported that fewer cars than previously were transferred to other classes, which they said "shows that the modern competition entrant has acquired a better understanding of official definitions". This charitable view ignored the fact a special class had been set up for "unstandardised" cars. *The Autocar* acknowledged this "loophole" and reported the actual number of cars "promoted" as two, but they were not named.

THE POST WAR YEARS 1919 TO 1924

**H.J.C. SMITH DRIVING THE "200 MILE" ERIC-CAMPBELL
TO FINISH THIRD IN CLASS 9.
(1922)**

The Autocar were very complimentary about the South Harting event and the Junior Car Club in general, saying that it was "in its way, a more interesting event than are the majority of such competitions. It is a very cheery affair, at which most of the competition drivers of the small car world meet each other for an afternoon's sport, banter and merriment".

Despite this general air of approval *The Autocar* sounded a prophetic note of warning that South Harting "hill was becoming too easy as cars improve".

Light Car and Cyclecar advised all spectators that "to follow such an event intelligently it is preferable if the visitor be present throughout the proceedings which in the present instance start soon after 10.00am in Midhurst, where the weighing-in and scrutineering

SOUTH HARTING HILL CLIMB 1905-1924

takes place. Here the various competing cars may be viewed at close quarters, and their appearances familiarised". They advised, however, to either have lunch in Midhurst or take a picnic, as South Harting village could not cope with the "diminutive invasion".

The scheduled start time was 2.30pm, but the *Motor* thought that future meetings should start at 2.00pm "as some impatience was being manifested by those – and they formed the majority – who had arrived in good time". *Light Car and Cyclecar* reported that, at the appointed start time, "one or two officials dashed up and down the hill (incidentally, might one ask, why do quite a number of the leading lights of the Junior Car Club, which caters solely for small car owners, run cars which are well outside the 1½-litre limit ?)".

The first car up the hill was the G.N. of R.W.B. Billinghurst in the 1100cc standard two-seater touring car class, which had attracted eight entries. A new name was the Lewis driven by A.J. Graham-Wigan, "an interesting cyclecar, equipped with a water cooled MAG engine,

F.M. LUTHER DRIVING THE NEW 1500CC AUSTRO-DAIMLER
RACING CAR TO FINISH FIFTH IN CLASS 9.
(1922)

THE POST WAR YEARS 1919 TO 1924

LEON CUSHMAN DRIVING HIS BRESCIA BUGATTI TO SECOND PLACE IN CLASS 9 BEHIND RAYMOND MAYS.
(1922)

SOUTH HARTING HILL CLIMB 1905-1924

ARCHIE FRAZER-NASH DRIVING HIS 8.7hp G.N. "KIM II" TO
WIN CLASS 8 FOR RACING CARS UP TO 1100cc.
(1922)

Opperman 3-speed gearbox, and what looked suspiciously like a Ford back axle". With a polished aluminium two seat body, it survived less than a year in a very competitive light car market.

J.F. Slaughter in his 8hp Talbot "appeared to glide up the hill without effort or fuss…but made third fastest time…a very creditable performance". However the "star performers" in their Morgans were Holmes and Parsley. Parsley's car was J.A.P. engined, but the faster, by 3.2secs. in a time of 88.8secs., was Holmes' ohv pushrod Anzani engined car. On formula however it was Talbot's day, with Slaughter first and Hawkes second. A.E. Bull in his Amilcar was third.

Four of the starters in Class 1 ran again in Class 2, for standard two-seater touring cars up to 1500cc. None however, including both winning Morgans, could make any impression on the bigger engined cars. There were nine starters in Class 2. Billinghurst in his G.N. oiled a plug, but W.H. Oates " made one of the most workmanlike and clean climbs of the day with his speckless, highly polished Lagonda". He was not fast enough however to make the first three.

"Klaxoning his way up the hill in no uncertain manner…Hedges (in his 10/30 Alvis) was obviously fastest". He won on both time and formula and made a "most impressive climb". His time was 82.8secs. E.G. Lefrere, London sales manager for Jarrott and Lett, the Bugatti

THE POST WAR YEARS 1919 TO 1924

**RAYMOND MAYS DRIVING HIS BRESCIA BUGATTI
CORDON ROUGE IN CLASS 7.
(1922)**

distributors, could only manage second, with Linsley in another Bugatti third. They were also second and third on handicap.

Soon after the last car in Class 2 had ascended, Vaughan Knight paraded up the hill in his GWK with a blackboard attached to the back on which were written the provisional results, including both the winners and their times in Class 1. Autocar praised the organisers for their efficiency and commented that "class after class went up without pause and with the minimum of interference from casual traffic". At the end of the meeting the full results, on time and formula, were available from the club H.Q. in the village almost by the time the last competitor had returned to the paddock.

Class 3 was for 1500cc four-seaters, carrying three passengers, and attracted only five entries. It "naturally provided few thrills". The lone lady driver, Miss Viola Meeking in her A.C., spoilt a good ascent with a bad gear change but still came third on both time and formula.

"S.C. Westall (11.9hp Albert) with five up was out for formula not speed" but was unsuccessful. D. Chinery in a similar car but "boasting a fine saloon body, toured up easily" and came second on time and formula.

The clear class winner, however, was again Hedges in his Alvis. Although his time was 23.6secs. slower than in Class 2, because of carrying extra passengers, he was still nearly forty seconds faster than Chinery in the Albert saloon. He also won on formula.

Class 4, for private owners with "unstandardised" cars, attracted seven entries, including two possible "promotions". R. D'Oyley Hughes suffered a cracked cylinder head, and Maney in his Enfield-Allday had to contend with a broken throttle linkage. Alvis again made a good showing with Pollard and Bennett being second and third on time and first and second on formula.

The fastest time however was posted by A.R. Linsley in his Bugatti, "again cutting in and out with a rising and falling droning note from the engine, suggestive of a gargantuan, if rather lazy, bee". He had previously been third in Class 2, but now managed to better his time by nearly two seconds and win Class 4 in 85.4secs. He also come third on formula.

Miss Viola Meeking had already driven her A.C. up the hill in Class 3 and achieved third place on time and formula. She was now one of only four starters in Class 5, for lady drivers in standard touring cars up to 1500cc. Without the penalty of three passengers she now knocked over a minute off her time and won the class easily from Mrs. W.D. Hawkes in her Talbot in a time of 77.0secs. *The Junior Car Club Gazette*, however, sub divided Class 5 into "sporting cars" and "touring cars" and credited Mrs. Hawkes with winning the touring cars division with a time of 101.8secs. Mrs. Frazer-Nash was overall third in her G.N.

In fact at this point in the proceedings Miss Meeking's time was the fastest of the day and she drove in a "manner any professional competitor might be proud of, especially at the start". The fourth lady driver, Mrs. F.N. Pickett in her G.N., "appeared to be handicapped by being unfamiliar with the ground".

Class 6, for disabled drivers, attracted only two entries. F. Harris in his G.W.K. had competed in the 1500cc, four-seat touring car class in 1921 and put up a creditable performance despite being without an arm and a leg. This had presumably prompted the establishment of a special class this year.

"Fielden kept his "good" foot on the accelerator and climbed well, Harris, in removing his only arm (from the steering wheel) on the first bend to change gear, almost charged the bank". Fielden in his G.N. was the fastest in a time of 124secs., but Harris was only three seconds slower.

In Class 7, for sporting cars up to 1500cc, there are records of only seven cars presenting themselves at the start line. However the reports talk of "many non-starters"; how many original entries there were was not recorded.

Raymond Mays' new Brescia Bugatti had caused some controversy during scrutineering, but since it was a standard catalogued model it was allowed to remain in the "sporting car class". Hawkins new ohc engined G.N.-Vitesse was similarly allowed.

W.G.H. Hedges, driving his 10/30 Alvis again, continued to impress. He "travelled better than ever in its third climb" and recorded a time of 80.4secs. to give him third place on time and first on formula. S.H. Newsome in another 10/30 Alvis, described in *"The Vintage Alvis"* as being modified by shortening the chassis and "altering the car beyond recognition", went well until two cylinders cut out. The Hon. V.A. Bruce in his 75mph sports model A.C. had clutch slip at the start and was not placed.

It was Raymond Mays appearance at South Harting for the first time in Cordon Rouge that set the crowd alight. "An ear-splitting, clear-cut roar, a dead silent slither round the first two bends, with foot off the accelerator, then Mays hove into sight of the natural grand-stand at the quarry and, jabbing his foot hard down, seemed to hurl the Bugatti at the 1 in 8 section. A blue haze, a cloud of dust, the patter of falling stones, and he was out of sight. The crowd

W.G.H. HEDGES DRIVING HIS 10/30 ALVIS. HE WON AWARDS
IN THREE SEPARATE CLASSES
(1922)

sighed". His time was 64.2secs., and he beat the second man, Hawkins in his G.N.-Vitesse by 11.4secs. On formula Hawkins was second and Mays third.

Only three cars presented themselves at the start of Class 8 for racing cars up to 1100cc, two G.N. and one Morgan. Despite a choked jet on the higher reaches, Frazer-Nash in Kim II still made the fastest time at 62.2secs. He was very closely followed by Hawkes in the venerable Morgan, Land Crab, in 62.4secs., "which proves it still cares little for pimples like South Harting". Picket in the ex 200 Mile Race G.N. was a distant third.

The final group of the day was Class 9 for racing cars between 1100cc and 1500cc. which attracted ten starters, including Mays fresh from his win in Class 8. Kensington Moir in the works Aston-Martin had stripped a timing gear on the Friday and had arrived at South Harting very late; his luck did not improve and he suffered a misfire on his run. McCulloch's A.B.C. Sports lost time at the start with clutch slip.

Frazer-Nash, this time in the 1219cc, 200 Mile Race, G.N. suffered another blocked jet and failed to finish. Third place went to H.J.C. Smith in his Eric Campbell in 69.2secs. First and second places was between the Bugattis of Mays and Cushman. Mays in Cordon Rouge, now stripped of mudguards and lamps, came out on top beating the works driver by 5.2secs., although Cushman had lost time with a bad skid near the quarry. Mays recorded the first ever sub-minute time at South Harting of 59.8secs. The previous fastest time had been 64.6secs in 1920 by Frazer-Nash in Kim I. Assuming the course was still the shorter ¾ mile course first used in 1920, then Mays average speed was some 45mph.

In his autobiography, *Split Seconds*, Mays said;

> *"This was the best thing I had ever done, and how excited I felt when crowds of people gathered round the car, firing off questions and clamouring for my autograph. Among those who spoke to me for the first time was S.C.H. Davis of the Autocar. He was, of course, a big noise in the racing world and his words of encouragement and advice I valued".*

This was clearly a very successful meeting. There were no reports of continuing weekend celebrations at Southsea, Chichester or Selsey as in previous years, but perhaps this only reflected the changing journalistic approach seen in the general reporting. While Raymond Mays in Cordon Rouge, and the first sub-minute climb, provided the high drama for the day, the superb performance by W.G.H. Hedges in his 10/30 Alvis is perhaps more significant. He had won Classes 2 and 3 on both time and formula and won Class 7 on formula and was third on time.

THE POST WAR YEARS 1919 TO 1924

1923 – The Fifth Junior Car Club Meeting

For 1923 the South Harting Hill Climb reverted to its traditional timing of late July. The reporting also returned to near normality with a proper listing of classes and entries, except that cars were defined by make only with no model or hp figures given. Caution prevailed however in reporting the results. No actual times were recorded in any journal; in the motoring press the winner of each class was credited with a "zero" time, and the differential recorded for second and third. In the *Junior Car Club Gazette* the "zero" for all competitors was taken as the fastest time of the day. The only clue given to actual times was that the fastest time of the day was slower than the previous year.

The first mention of the event in the press was in *The Light Car and Cyclecar* for June 1st, when they reminded intending entrants that, to comply with the R.A.C. closed competition rules, they must be members of the Junior Car Club and have their names "inscribed on the club roll prior to June 23rd."

Entries were invited in nine classes:

Class 1	Standard touring cars with two-seater bodies and engines not exceeding 1100cc.
Class 2	Standard touring cars with two-seater bodies and engines not exceeding 1500cc.
Class 3	Standard touring cars with four-seater bodies and engines not exceeding 1500cc.
Class 4	Bona fide private owners driving touring cars with engines not exceeding 1500cc.
Class 5	Lady members driving cars with engines not exceeding 1500cc.
Class 6	Disabled drivers in cars with engines not exceeding 1500cc.
Class 7	Standard sporting cars with engines not exceeding 1500cc; fully equipped.
Class 8	Racing cars with engines not exceeding 1100cc.
Class 9	Racing cars with engines between 1100cc and 1500cc.

A total of 82 event entries were received, but none in Class 3 which was therefore abandoned.

Several new faces and cars featured in the entry list. Among the lady members were The Lady Belper in an A.C., Ivy Cummings in a Frazer Nash and Miss W.M. Pink in an Aston-Martin. Winifred Pink was the Secretary of the Ladies Motor Club and had bought the prototype Aston-Martin, AM 270, from Lionel Martin. Rebuilt with wire wheels and four wheel brakes, this was its first competitive outing driven by Miss Pink and she was entered in three separate classes.

Also driving an Aston-Martin was G.E.T. Eyston making his first visit to South Harting. George Eyston had been very impressed by Kensington Moir driving the streamlined Aston-Martin at Brooklands in the 200 Mile Race in 1922. He later bought the complete Brooklands car, and an Aston-Martin Grand Prix chassis which had been driven in the French Grand Prix

JOHN MARTIN / A. B. DEMAUS

G.E.T. EYSTON DRIVING HIS ALCOHOL FUELLED ASTON-MARTIN
TO FINISH FOURTH IN CLASS 9 FOR RACING CARS UP TO 1500cc.
(1923)

JOHN WHEELEY / ALVIS OWNERS CLUB

C.M. HARVEY ON ALVIS "RACING CAR No1" HP 6161.
THIS PICTURE WAS TAKEN A FORTNIGHT AFTER THE SOUTH HARTING
MEETING AT WEST HARLING HEATH NEAR THETFORD.
(1923)

at Strasbourg. It was the Brooklands engine in the Grand Prix chassis he had brought to South Harting.

The Grand Prix chassis has been reported as the one driven at Strasbourg by Count Zborowski, but according to Brian Demaus, (who later owned that car), it was the second car, driven by Clive Gallop, that Eyston bought. The confusion arose because, when both cars were back at the works in late 1922, the original registration numbers were, perhaps accidentally, transposed. The Zborowski car was bought by Bobby Morgan, of whom more later.

Another new face (and car) at South Harting was Major Cyril Maurice Harvey, who was the chief competition driver and Service Manager for Alvis. He was at the wheel of HP 6161, described as "a special 12/50 intended for freak hill climbs and sprints" in Peter Hull's definitive Alvis history. "It had a much drilled chassis and nothing much behind the driver except a bolster tank". It was the first so-called racing car built after Smith-Clarke joined the firm in 1922 and it was listed as "Racing Car No.1", despite Harvey's earlier efforts in France and at Brooklands in a 10/30. The car did not win its class on this occasion and was reportedly completely "wrecked", but rebuilt with a new engine, soon after this meeting.

Also making their first appearance at South Harting were E.C. Gordon England and his Austin Seven. He had bought the ex works car raced by Captain Arthur Waite, Herbert Austin's son-in-law, rebodied it at the family coachbuilding business, and then extensively developed the engine before embarking on a successful competition season.

S.F. Edge had not appeared at South Harting since the Yellow Trophy in 1907. He now re-appeared in the list of entries, in the 1500cc racing car class, with an A.C.. However the reports of the event indicate that the car was actually driven on the day by J.A. Joyce. Selwyn Frances Edge, by then aged 53, had joined the board of Autocarriers Ltd. in 1921. When Weller and Portwine resigned in 1922, he took control of the company as chairman and managing director and changed the name to A.C. Cars Ltd. He then actively promoted the sporting heritage of A.C. with a campaign of record breaking and competition.

Other makes of car not seen previously at South Harting were Riley (probably a Redwing), Salmson and Cooper. This Cooper, however, was made in Coventry in 1922/1923 only, but even then had a Coventry Climax engine. It also had a Moss gearbox and Wrigley axle.

Weighing-in and scrutineering were again carried out at Midhurst Station Yard on the Saturday morning, but this year the South Harting record for fine weather was broken and it rained heavily throughout proceedings at Midhurst. Relatively few cars, however, were reportedly "promoted" into either the sporting or racing classes.

Although the rain had almost stopped by the 2.30pm start time, the surface of the hill was badly affected, being wet, loose and "extremely dangerous". For the faster cars towards the end of the meeting this would cause some spectacular incidents.

After the cars in each class had completed their runs, a motor cycle climbed the hill with a sign proclaiming "FINISH", followed a few seconds later by the Hon. Victor Bruce in his car with a passenger carrying a blackboard showing the results of that class on time.

One innovation at this 1923 event was that the last two classes, the racing classes, were run twice, the faster of the two times counting. The only problem was nobody had told the spectators, so that, on their second run, some competitors founds streams of people walking down the hill. The fact had not even been mentioned in the programme.

Another pointer to the changing nature of the event was that most of the reports focussed very heavily on the racing classes and gave only passing mention to the standard car classes at the end of the reports. *Light Car and Cyclecar* went as far as to say that "by comparison with the racing classes the touring events were dull and long drawn out."

It was also recorded for the first time at a South Harting meeting that significant delays were caused by normal traffic ascending the hill. This reached a point where the traffic had to be held at the bottom of the hill and then allowed up in batches.

In Class 1, for standard two-seat touring cars up to 1100cc, only five out of the ten entries presented themselves at the start line. H.W. Holmes in his Morgan then oiled a plug so that only four cars actually crossed the finish line. *Motor* nevertheless commented that "it is very noticeable how small cars have improved in speed. Houghton's Tamplin, which won Class 1, was astonishingly fast, and so was the little 8hp Gwynne that ran second, and easily won on formula." A.J. Dixon in his Singer was third on both time and formula. Another Gwynne was second on formula.

Nineteen entries were reported for Class 2, for standard touring cars up to 1500cc, but only sixteen actually started. Frazer-Nash was one of the non starters. King and Oates in their Lagondas were "very steady", the Cooper "was not very fast on the steep portion, but could be heard accelerating well on the last stretch." Hedges Alvis "made a good fast climb; but White's A.B.C. appeared to be over geared. A.R. Simmins (Talbot-Darracq) made a good showing for so small a car, and changed down for the steep portion. Miss Pink, on the Aston-Martin, took the bend steadily, but did not lose time by it".

The fastest in the class was Cushman in his Bugatti, with Noble on the Deemster second by 3.0 seconds. Miss Pink was third, 5.4 seconds behind the Bugatti.

Class 3 having been cancelled due to lack of entries, the next Class up the hill was Class 4, for private owners in touring cars up to 1500cc. Out of the six entries five started. The fastest was Pollard in his Alvis, with Linsley in his Bugatti only 0.8 seconds behind. A distant 19.6 seconds behind was White in his A.B.C. "Goossens (Eric Campbell) was apparently under geared on first gear and hung on to second until he almost stopped."

Class 5, for "lady members" driving cars up to 1500cc, attracted four entries but only two actually started. The Frazer Nashes of Ivy Cummings and Mrs Frazer-Nash were non starters. Miss Pink in her Aston-Martin proved too fast for The Lady Belper in her A.C. by a margin of 5.8 seconds. The result on formula was the same.

There were again only two starters in Class 6 for disabled drivers in cars up to 1500cc. Pope in his G.W.K. was much too quick for Fielden in his G.N. by a margin of 24.6 seconds.

Class 7 for standard sporting cars up to 1500cc attracted fifteen entries. Miss Pink again made a fast climb but on this occasion could manage no better than fourth on time, but she won the class on formula. "A.R. Simmins (Wolseley) was evidently unsuitably geared, for between the chalk-pit corner and the summit he was heard to drop to first and go back to second three distinct times." He fared better however in his Talbot-Darracq, which he drove in the same Class.

C.M. Harvey's aluminium bodied Alvis, with its piercing exhaust note "provided the big thrill in this class with much wheelspin combined with considerable speed." He just beat Hall on the "small four" Frazer Nash by 0.2 seconds with Cushman's Bugatti 1.6 seconds behind. Miss Pink was only 3.0 seconds behind in the Aston-Martin. B.E. Lewis on a four cylinder Frazer Nash was going well when fuel starvation caused a bad misfire.

The racing classes provided the real excitement of the day. In Class 8, for racing cars up to 1100cc, Gordon England in his Austin Seven however disappointed, trailing smoke caused by a bad misfire. Formilli, in his 6.9hp New Carden, "a tiny monocar fitted with an air cooled

THE POST WAR YEARS 1919 TO 1924

J.A. JOYCE DRIVING THE 100mph A.C., HAD A DRAMATIC ACCIDENT
ON HIS FIRST RUN AND DAMAGED THE CAR, BUT IT WAS REPAIRED IN TIME
AND MADE A SECOND RUN LESS THAN 5 SECONDS SLOWER
THAN HALL'S FASTEST TIME OF THE DAY.
(1923)

ARCHIE FRAZER-NASH, DRIVING A HYBRID KIM/MOWGLI G.N.,
SEEN PASSING THE DAMAGED A.C. ON HIS WAY TO
SECOND FASTEST TIME OF THE DAY.
(1923)

SOUTH HARTING HILL CLIMB 1905-1924

E.R. HALL HANDLED HIS 11.9hp BUGATTI WITH SUFFICIENT SKILL
TO BOTH WIN THE 1500cc CLASS AND MAKE FASTEST TIME OF THE DAY.
(1923)

twin cylinder two stroke set around the back axle...devoured the gradient without noise or apparent effort."

But the honours went to J.A. Hall in the new four cylinder Frazer Nash who "impressed by reason of his speed, silence and road holding qualities." Second by a margin of 3.2 seconds was Eaton in a G.N., an old touring car fitted with a Vitesse engine. Wilson Jones in his Salmson "with bulbous cigar like body was awe inspiring and apparently much faster on his second run", was a further 2.2 seconds behind in third place.

The real drama however was held back for Class 9, for racing cars up to 1500cc. There were several lurid descriptions of the accident which befell J.A. Joyce driving the 100mph A.C., entered by S.F. Edge, on its first run. The following is the version that appeared in *Motor*:

> "To understand what happened one must describe the hill. From the start there is a stretch of about 200 yards of easy gradient to a fork in the road, where competitors swing sharp to the left; this is followed by a sharp bend to the right, the road here being very loose, and then a series of easier bends until the last straight, steep stretch to the finish is reached. It was at the fork that Joyce lost control. His front wheels skidded, and he narrowly missed the signpost in the centre. His wheels ran along the grassy bank, then missed a deep gully, and the car shot at terrific speed clean across to the other side of the road, and into the hedge. Here the car straightened up and, and commenced ploughing a way along the top of the hedge, his near side wheels high up in the air, and then, with the engine still running, he crashed onto the road again. And still he kept going, the spectators cheering and shouting: "Go on !" Alas, a near-side back tyre burst, and

he stopped. The front springing seemed twisted, a wheel was splayed out, and the starting handle was bent under the axle, but the car sustained no serious injury, and was able to make a second – and much more sedate – attempt later on, which only shows what a racing car will stand. We should say, however, that this car, with a narrower rear track than the front, is not suitable for hill climbing, and would be very prone to skid."

This comment seems a bit harsh as, on his second run, Joyce managed sixth place only 4.8 seconds slower than the fastest time of the day. S.F. Edge's response to this comment is not recorded!

There is more. *Motor* then reported another incident:

"Another alarming skid was provided by B.H. Austin, who is a disabled driver with a double amputation, driving an 11.4hp Bugatti in the racing class, for on the first bend he shot across the road into the gutter, and hit the bank. For a moment it looked as if he would turn over, but he righted the car, and careered on, skidding all over the road, and even on the last straight stretch he was slewing round from side to side."

Raymond Mays, who had set the fastest time the previous year in his Bugatti, Cordon Rouge, this year had the misfortune to shed a key in the rear axle just before the start of the event. His mechanic made desperate attempts to remedy the problem but to no avail. He was therefore a non starter.

Honours on the day went to E.R. Hall in his 11.9hp Bugatti. Hall was an amateur driver who had never seen the hill before. He had towed the Bugatti the 250 miles from Huddersfield behind a 10hp Wolseley, packed in sacking to keep the dust out. He climbed the hill superbly, fighting skid after skid, to make fastest time of the day.

He beat Archie Frazer-Nash, driving a Kim/Mowgli combination, by only 0.4 seconds. Frazer-Nash had excessive wheelspin at the start and then struggled to control it all the way up. *The Autocar* commented that "these larger racing cars were, in fact, too fast for the hill, especially in its loose condition, and the rise and fall of the exhaust notes told how the drivers were having to cut out."

In third place, only one second behind Hall, was C.M. Harvey on the Alvis, HP 6161. "All the way up he fought the swaying racer, wrenching the wheel first one way then another. His cornering was absolutely hair raising, and with the sole exception of Hall, (he) probably kept his foot down more continuously than any other driver of a fast car."

Eyston, on his alcohol fuelled Aston-Martin was very fast but "looked anxious". He finished fourth in front of Cushman in his Bugatti and Joyce in his A.C.. Lionel Martin was in the list of entrants prior to the event but no report of the meeting mentions him. Only 4.8 seconds covered the first six cars.

Altogether a rather mixed bag of a meeting, what with the wet weather, Raymond Mays being a non starter, and the escalation of normal traffic causing interruptions to proceedings. High drama apart, the day surely belonged to Winifred Pink who, with her newly acquired Aston-Martin, was in the points in all three classes she entered.

SOUTH HARTING HILL CLIMB 1905-1924

R. G. OATS DRIVING HIS SCARLET 2-LITRE ANSALDO MADE TWO CLIMBS IN THE IDENTICAL TIME OF 31.0 SECONDS. HE WON THE 3-LITRE SPORTS CAR CLASS AND WAS SECOND IN THE 2-LITRE RACING CAR CLASS.
(1924)

1924 – The Surbiton Motor Club Meeting

The Surbiton Motor Club had previously held an annual hill climb event at Kop, but this year, in conjunction with the Ealing Motor Club, and for reasons not reported, they moved the venue to South Harting. The meeting was held on Saturday 31st May and had classes for motor cycles as well as cars.

The course used was different from all previously reported events at South Harting. All the other organising clubs, from 1905 on, had marked out a course of approximately one mile running from the present B2146, taking the left fork just south of the village, up the B2141 towards Chichester. Surbiton MC chose a course of approximately half a mile in length, using the same starting point but taking the right fork, a continuation of the B2146, towards West Marden and Emsworth.

This event also differed from previous events in two other ways. Firstly a short flying start was allowed, which led to a secondary competition to see who could recruit the strongest team of push starters. Electric timing was also used for the first time, triggered by the breaking of a thread across the start and finish lines. Actual times were reported, which were around the 30 second mark. There were no awards on formula.

Car entries were invited in nine classes numbered from 19 to 27; classes 1 to 18 were for motor cycles. The car classes were:

> 19. 1100cc Racing Cars
> 20. 1500cc Touring and Sports Cars
> 21. 1500cc Racing Cars
> 22. 2000cc Touring and Sports Cars
> 23. 2000cc Racing Cars
> 24. 3000cc Touring and Sports cars
> 25. 3000cc Racing Cars
> 26. Unlimited cc Touring and Sports Cars
> 27. Unlimited cc Racing Cars

Unlike previous Junior Car Club meetings at South Harting, there were no classes for lady drivers, disabled drivers or private owners. No list of entries was published before the event, nor was any scrutineering or weighing-in before the event reported.

The Autocar described the course as having "a gradual and very awkward bend about a quarter of the way up, of S shape and banked the wrong way. To add to this difficulty, it rained just enough to make the surface really tricky, and the run from the start to the bend was long enough to allow the cars to approach it at high speed. It was, therefore, a fine course to test the skill of the drivers."

Among the notable names not seen at South Harting before was Dario Resta, trying out the new 1924, 2-litre, supercharged Grand Prix Sunbeam, and Humphrey Cook in the 3-litre TT Vauxhall. It was obviously acceptable in 1924, at least to Surbiton Motor Club, to run a 2-litre supercharged car against normally aspirated 2-litre cars in the same class.

In the absence of Raymond Mays, Bugatti fortunes were in the hands of the works driver Leon Cushman and B.S. Marshall. Leon Cushman had brought both a 1452cc sports car and a 1496cc racer, and "emphasized the already plain difference between his four seater and the racer by smoking a pipe in the first, but looking really grim in the second."

The motor cycle classes opened the event at 1.00pm and gave "a lifelike imitation of what the Rodeo at Wembley will be like, three of the first four riders coming to grief in sensational manner, luckily without serious injury."

"The worst crash of all was that of V.W. Derrington, who executed a triple somersault in the air, all arms and legs, finally coming to earth in a crumpled heap. His crash helmet saved him from absolute disaster, but he had to be carried down the hill, and the crowd was amazed when, later on, he appeared at the wheel of a Salmson."

"Owing to the casualties in the motor-cycling section the classes devoted to these vehicles took a long time to run off, and it seemed that the car section would not be completed before lighting up time, but actually the four wheeled cars were despatched with remarkable celerity, and the event terminated at 6.00pm."

One contributor to this "remarkable celerity" was the driver of the 30-98 Vauxhall which carried the results announcement board up the hill at the end of each class. He "so enjoyed the corners that hardly anyone could read the notices on the board."

Normal traffic was also evidently an increasing problem for events held on public roads since "the good tempered crowd…were also cheering the drivers of a nondescript collection of non competing vehicles which ascended and descended the hill."

The first car up the hill in the 1100cc class was J.P. Dingle in his Austin Seven, which was "streamlined to the nth degree", he made "a very pretty climb, holding the road beautifully on the bend."

"It was for Miss Ivy Cummings, however, to provide the first thrill. Down through the trees one heard the bark of the exhaust from her Frazer Nash, saw the tiny red-winged projectile leap like an arrow across a pool of sunshine, arrive "all-out" at the bend, skid just where its mistress wanted it to skid, and tear up to the summit. This, for cool nerve and perfect judgement, would be difficult to beat. Nor was this the most exciting of this dashing girl-drivers climbs." Phew !

By contrast Wilson Jones in his "200 Mile Race" Salmson was "tame", although his time was only two seconds slower than Ivy Cummings, who was fastest in 31.4 secs. Wilson Jones was second and Dingle third, one second behind the Salmson.

In the 1500cc classes all the drama was in Class 21 for Racing cars. In Class 20 for Touring and Sports Cars, Vic Derrington was clearly not fully recovered from his earlier crash in the motor cycle classes and was reported as being "cautious". Ewen and Stewart, both in standard Victory model Palladiums, "swept round at a speed which clearly proved the capabilities of the Palladium." Joyce in his A.C. "purred up with hardly a suggestion of a cut-out." "B.S. Marshall, in his famous black Bugatti, played for caution on his first ascent, but afterwards improved and on his third attempt handled his car with skill, rounding the bend in a series of short, sharp sideslips, which were instantly and cleverly corrected."

This multiple entry was a feature of the meeting. In fact the winner of Class 20, Leon Cushman in his sports Bugatti, entered his two cars for all classes in which they were eligible and was placed in all six of them. We also know that R.G. Oates, in a scarlet Ansaldo, made several runs, but only the two in which he was placed were reported.

In Class 21, for 1500cc racing cars, Ivy Cummings in the same 1086cc Frazer Nash again took the honours but did not provide the drama. "This time she profited by her experience, taxing her machine to the uttermost" to beat her previous time in Class 19 by nearly two

THE POST WAR YEARS 1919 TO 1924

IVY CUMMINGS WON BOTH CLASS 19 FOR 1100cc RACING CARS AND
CLASS 21 FOR 1500cc RACING CARS ON HER 1086cc FRAZER NASH. IN THE PROCESS
SHE BECAME THE THIRD FASTEST DRIVER OF THE DAY.
(1924)

SOUTH HARTING HILL CLIMB 1905-1924

IVY CUMMINGS DRIVING THE 5 LITRE BUGATTI.
NO TIME WAS REPORTED FOR THIS RUN.
(1924)

BOBBY MORGAN FIGHTING THE FIRST OF A SERIES OF SKIDS ON
HIS ASTON-MARTIN WHICH LED TO A SPECTACULAR CRASH.
(1924)

THE POST WAR YEARS 1919 TO 1924

seconds. Second was Joyce in the racing A.C. and third Leon Cushman in his racing Bugatti.

The drama, however, was provided by Bobby Morgan in his newly acquired Aston-Martin. He had been persuaded to enter this basically unsuitable car by Kaye Don, who was under the impression that the usual mile course up the B2141 was going to be used. This was the car, with its long tail and locked rear axle, driven by Count Zborowski in the 1922 French Grand Prix. Later, with a different engine, it became known as Green Pea.

> "With a mighty roar R.C. Morgan swept towards the corner. He kept his accelerator pedal hard down, refusing to ease it a fraction as he approached the bend. There followed four hair-raising broadside skids, to correct which the driver had to pull over his steering wheel to the full extent of its lock, and cheers had already broken from the lips of the spectators when Nemesis overtook him. In correcting the last wild swerve the tail of the machine slithered right round, the off-side rear tyre went off with a sharp report and, entirely out of control, the car charged the bank, literally bouncing off, then proceeded up the hill for several yards in a backward direction before coming to rest."

Morgan walked away unhurt, but he had to pay Bamford and Martin Ltd. the sum of £65.19s.6d., plus £28.8s.11d. for parts, to repair the car. In a letter to Bobby Morgan, reflecting the hard times he was suffering, Lionel Martin stated that "as the amount is such a large one, and we, as you know are running on our private means, I should be very much obliged if you would let us have your cheque when you collect your car."

Class 22, for 2-litre road cars, was nothing more than a re-run of Class 20, for 1500cc road cars, and produced the same result. Leon Cushman in his Bugatti followed by Kaye Don in the Darracq and Ewen in his Palladium.

Class 23, for 2-litre racing cars, brought out the supercharged Grand Prix Sunbeam. "The star performance of the day was made by Dario Resta, on the little Grand Prix 2-litre Sunbeam, a performance beautifully exemplifying the real art of driving, and so finished that the car was exceedingly deceptive. Not only did it hold the road so well that its cornering lacked the wild sensation of the others, but the peculiar thin whine of the supercharged engine was in marked contrast to the roar of the others."

Dario Resta proceeded to win Classes 23, 25 and 27, for 2-litre, 3-litre and unlimited capacity racing cars respectively, in progressively faster times culminating in the fastest time of the day of 25.8secs. The only other car to break 30.0 seconds was Humphrey Cook in the 3-litre TT Vauxhall, who finished second in both the 3-litre and unlimited capacity racing classes. Leon Cushman and Cyril Paul in Bugatti and Beardmore respectively were equal third in the 3-litre racing car class, and Joyce in the racing A.C. was credited with third place in the unlimited racing car class.

Ivy Cummings made another heroic drive in a 5-litre Bugatti in Class 26, the unlimited road car class, but no time was reported. The only time recorded for Class 26 was B.S. Marshall in his 1496cc Bugatti at 34.8secs.

This closed club event had more than its fair share of drama, and was an undoubted crowd pleaser. Even *Light Car and Cyclecar*, whose primary allegiance was to the Junior Car Club, was moved to say that the meeting would "long be remembered as one of the most exciting that has ever been run off; in fact it would be safe to assert that there never has been an afternoon providing a greater number of sensations or better exhibitions of driving skill."

THE AFTERMATH OF BOBBY MORGAN'S CRASH ON HIS ASTON-MARTIN.
(1924)

THE POST WAR YEARS 1919 TO 1924

HUMPHRY COOK IN THE 3-LITRE TT VAUXHALL WAS THE ONLY
OTHER CAR IN CLASS 25 TO BREAK 30 SECONDS. HE WAS ALSO SECOND TO
THE SUNBEAM IN CLASS 27 FOR UNLIMITED RACING CARS.
(1924)

left
DARIO RESTA ON THE GRAND PRIX
2-LITRE SUNBEAM IN CLASS 25. HE MADE
FASTEST TIME OF THE DAY. THE LEFT FORK IN
THE BACKGROUND IS THE COURSE USED BY
ALL OTHER MEETINGS AT SOUTH HARTING.
(1924)

SOUTH HARTING

Junior Car Club's
Annual Hill Climb
Saturday, July 26th

FIVE FIRSTS
SIX SECONDS
and
FOUR THIRDS

out of ten events

WON ON

"BP"

The British Petrol

British Petroleum Co. Ltd. Britannic House, Moorgate, E.C.2
Distributing Organization of the
ANGLO-PERSIAN OIL CO. LTD.

Support those who support us.

THE POST WAR YEARS 1919 TO 1924

1924 – The Sixth Junior Car Club Meeting

The sixth annual meeting of the Junior Car Club at South Harting was held on Saturday 26th July 1924. Entries were invited in eight classes, with the total number of entries received announced the week prior to the event but not individually named. No entries were received for the 1100cc touring or sports car classes, perhaps indicating that cars in general were getting bigger, so the actual programme was as follows:

Class 1	Standard 2-seat touring cars up to 1500cc	11 entries
Class 2	Touring cars up to 1500cc	15 entries
Class 3	Sports cars up to 1500cc	11 entries
Class 4	Standard sports cars up to 1500cc	11 entries
Class 5	Racing cars up to 1100cc	9 entries
Class 6	Racing cars 1101cc to 1500cc	10 entries

This is a total of 67 event entries, but the meeting reports only identified 63 starters. The meaning of the qualification "standard", in the absence of the qualification "private owner" as applied in previous years, is not entirely clear from the reports. There were no separate classes for lady drivers or disabled drivers, as there had been in previous years, but both entered with success in the general classes.

Scrutineering and weighing-in began, as usual, at 10.00am at Midhurst Station. Several

DORIS HEATH DRIVING HER FOUR SEAT 12hp DARRACQ,
SECURED THIRD PLACE IN CLASS 4, WHICH WAS WON BY HER
BROTHER HAROLD IN ANOTHER DARRACQ.
(1924)

SOUTH HARTING HILL CLIMB 1905-1924

WINIFRED PINK, DRIVING ASTON-MARTIN AM270,
WON CLASS 1 AND CLASS 2, WAS SECOND IN CLASS 3
AND FOURTH IN CLASS 4
(1924)

THE POST WAR YEARS 1919 TO 1924

J.P. DINGLE DRIVING AN AUSTIN SEVEN IN THE 1100cc RACING CAR CLASS.
THE THREE SIMILAR CARS IN THE CLASS WERE ALL OVER
11 SECONDS OFF THE PACE COMPARED TO THE CLASS WINNER
J.A. HALL IN FRAZER NASH "KIM II".
(1924)

cars were "promoted", including A.Y. Jackson's Alvis from sports to racing, Mrs. Dykes' Alvis from touring to sports, and Simmins' Talbot-Simmins from sports to racing. The 12hp Darracq of Harold Heath attracted the scrutineers attention and there was much argument about whether it should be "promoted" from the sports to the racing classes; this was presumably not unconnected with the fact that the same car had recently won the Presidents Cup at Shelsley Walsh. It was eventually allowed to remain in the standard sports class, which it proceeded to win.

The proceedings at Midhurst in general were sufficiently controversial to generate a heated correspondence in *The Autocar* in the following weeks. There were no particularly noteworthy new cars or drivers at this meeting, but both Raymond Mays and Miss Pink were back to whet the appetites of the spectators, in remembrance of their spectacular previous performances. Mays in particular was determined to hold on to, or preferably beat, his existing course record and had brought both Cordon Bleu and Cordon Rouge Bugattis to South Harting. Both were entered in the same 1500cc racing class, rather than one in the sporting class. Making doubly sure of ultimate honours was clearly more important than the number of awards.

The R.A.C. had recently issued a warning to clubs organising hill climbs where weighing-in was conducted at a separate location, to ensure close surveillance of the cars as they travelled from the weighbridge to the hill. The Junior Car Club were reportedly unaware of this warning, but must have been conscious of the problem since the competing cars were

D.E. CALDER DRIVING A HORSTMANN IN CLASS 2
FOR 1500cc TOURING CARS.
(1924)

THE POST WAR YEARS 1919 TO 1924

escorted front and rear, in three separate convoys, the six miles from Midhurst Station to South Harting. The course to be used was the traditional left fork up the B2141.

> "The hill itself was in a treacherous condition, for, owing to char-a-bancs traffic, the surface had been churned up; in fact on the famous Quarry Bend it was loose even for pedestrianism. In view of the anticipated high speeds the course, some seven eighths of a mile in length, was marshalled from top to bottom, whilst, in addition, a fanfare of Sparton horns, supplied by Alfred Graham and Co., heralded the starting of every car."
>
> Light Car and Cyclecar.

The Autocar, in contrast, commented that:

> "Actually the hill does not lend itself to very high speeds, but the bends – left, right, left, right – about half way up, provided more than enough thrills for the hundreds of spectators."

No actual times were reported in the individual classes, they were all relative to the fastest time in class, although *Light Car and Cyclecar* did publish the fastest time of the day, which was 57.2secs. For a course of 7/8ths of a mile this represents an **average** speed of 55.1mph from a standing start.

As in previous years the national journals only published the provisional class winners and places. It is necessary to refer to the *Junior Car Club Gazette* to obtain the final results in detail, although even they this year only published relative actual times.

There are considerable discrepancies between the "provisional results" and the "final results", presumably mainly due to the resolution of objections in the interim. Fortunately none of these discrepancies involve any of the class winners. There are also some ambiguities in the *Gazette* results which makes it difficult to present any complete "definitive" results. The *Gazette* only published completed runs, and gave no details of non starters of failures. The acronym "n.r." in the results tables in Appendix III is used where the national journals reported a run but nobody reported an outcome. It stands for "not reported".

> "As a rule the standard touring classes are uninteresting, but on Saturday there were some extraordinarily fast cars, there being no fewer than five Aston-Martins in the first class." *Light Car and Cyclecar.*

Class 1 was for Standard Two-Seat Touring Cars up to 1500cc. A.R. Linsley in his Bugatti, with Raymond Mays as passenger, "took the first corner, which leads into what is virtually a double S bend, too fast, skidded broadside, ripped off a tyre, and came to rest with the nose of the car in the hedge. No damage was done."

It was however an Aston-Martin benefit, Lionel Martin's cars taking five places out of the first six. Miss Pink was the clear winner by a margin of over five seconds from second man Calder in a Horstman, who was in turn another five seconds clear of the third man, A.A. Pollard.

Class 2, for Touring Cars up to 1500cc, was largely a re-run of Class 1. Aston-Martins again dominated taking the first three places on time, with Miss Pink again the clear winner by a margin of over seven seconds from H.S. Eaton. She also won on formula. The only competitor to upset the Aston-Martin clean sweep was A.H. Ely in his Talbot Eight, who took second place on formula.

Linsley, having changed the wheel on his Bugatti, was again in trouble. Although he started very fast, with more dramatic skids, he developed carburettor trouble on the way up and stopped 150 yards from the finish, although the *Junior Car Club Gazette* still credited him with a time.

In the reports of Class 2 and Class 3 both *The Autocar*, and *Light Car and Cyclecar*, used the expression "private owners", who had been in separate classes in previous years, but no mention was made of this in either the pre-meeting announcements or the results. The logic seems to have been that the "Standard" Classes, 1 and 4, were mainly for factory entered cars in standard trim, whereas Classes 2 and 3, where some modification was presumably allowed, were for private owners only. Private owners could run in the Standard Classes, provided their car qualified, but not vice versa. In earlier years it had been usual to publish the regulations, at least in summary.

Miss Pink made her third appearance in Class 3 but, despite improving on her previous times, only managed equal second with Jackson in his 12hp Alvis. Linsley also ran again but still suffered from wheelspin, however he managed fourth place on time. It was left to the disabled driver, B.H. Austin, in his 11.9hp Bugatti, to put up the best time in class by a margin of 3.2 seconds.

Miss Pink made her fourth and final run leading off in Class 4, for Standard Sports Cars up to 1500cc., but on this occasion she was not placed. "The first thrill was provided by Harold Heath on a red 1.5-litre Darracq, on which he had won the President's Cup at Shelsley Walsh. He was very fast and controlled the car excellently as it skidded the bends. His sister, Miss Doris Heath, on a grey four seater Darracq was also very good." "Mrs. Dykes (Alvis) seemed to be in earnest conversation with her passenger."

Harold Heath was fastest with his sister Doris third, they were separated by B.H. Austin on his Bugatti. Less than three seconds covered the first three. A.D. Makins on another Darracq won on formula with Alvis second and third.

The two remaining classes were for racing cars and, as in 1923, competitors in these classes were allowed two runs, with the fastest time counting. This reflected a continuing trend for hill climbs to become more overtly sporting events rather than simply trade demonstrations. However the lessons of 1923 had not been learnt, and many spectators began streaming down the hill after the first run under the impression that the meeting was over. There was no mention in the press, or in the programme, that there would be two runs.

"With a considerable amount of extra hooting the Sparton battery announced the beginning of the classes for racing cars, and the crowds stood well back from the bends in anticipation of some exciting corner work". As if on cue it started to rain gently.

Class 5 was for racing cars up to 1100cc capacity and ten cars faced the starter for the first run, including the "promoted" Talbot-Simmins. B.H. Davenport on his 2 cylinder Frazer Nash almost came to a halt due a fuel feed problem, but "J.P. Dingle's Austin appeared to have unlimited power, but to be too light for the rough going." "B.E. Lewis on his Frazer Nash "Rodeo Special" was fast and skidded considerably; and H.S. Eaton on a Gwynne-cum-Frazer Nash slithered round the corners and gave a fine display of driving. He was followed by "Kim II", Capt. Frazer-Nash's old and famous mount, which is now owned and was driven by J.A.

J.A. HALL DRIVING G.N. "KIM II" ON HIS SECOND RUN HAD A DRAMATIC SKID,
ILLUSTRATED BY THIS PICTURE FROM *THE LIGHT CAR AND CYCLECAR*.
ON HIS FIRST RUN HE HAD WON CLASS 5 FOR 1100cc RACING CARS.
(1924)

HAROLD HEATH WINNING THE 1500cc STANDARD SPORTS
CAR CLASS DRIVING HIS 12hp DARRACQ HAVING NARROWLY AVOIDED
"PROMOTION" TO THE RACING CAR CLASS.
(1924)

Hall. With a staccato bark the little projectile simply hurtled up the gradient, the driver correcting skid upon skid in very skilful fashion."

The "Gwynne-cum-Frazer Nash" had been described in the programme of the Bexhill Speed Trials as a Gwynne Eight. It was in fact a new single seat racing car built by H.S. Eaton with a 1496cc Gwynne engine in a chassis largely derived from a 1922 G.N. and was making its first appearance at South Harting.

In Class 6, for racing cars up to 1500cc, E.R. Hall drove "Bunny", which was the first Aston Martin ever to race abroad in September 1921. Although clearly now outclassed, Archie Frazer-Nash still had style. "Undoubtedly one of the finest climbs was that made by A.G. Frazer-Nash (Frazer Nash), who hugged the inside edges of the bends even to within an inch or two of the dangerous gully at the Quarry Bend, and shot quietly to the top of the hill almost as though he were running on lines."

However the day belonged to Raymond Mays. As he later wrote:

> *"I was most anxious to defend my record, and to beat it if possible. As zero hour arrived, rain began to fall and our hearts missed a beat. However, "Cordon Bleu's" engine felt in terrific form, and I was determined that she should put up a good show at her first appearance at the hill. The starter's flag fell and "Cordon Bleu" left the mark like a shot from a gun, rapidly attaining 6400 revs in every gear - and never had such an exhaust note been heard. She literally screamed up the hill, and in spite of the wet road – thanks to the Bugattis road-holding on corners and straights alike – made fastest time of the day and broke my own record by 2.6 seconds."*

He did not mention that, when he went up again in Cordon Rouge, he "narrowly escaped disaster owing to a slight derangement in the steering."

Once the spectators streaming down the hill, thinking the meeting was over, had been halted most competitors in Classes 5 and 6 made second runs. It is not clear from the reports which ones did not, nor is it always clear whether the fastest times were recorded on the first or second runs. However most of the real drama of the day seems to have occurred during these second runs of the racing classes. "In the 1100cc class B.E. Lewis (Frazer Nash "Rodeo Special") shed a rear near-side tyre at the Quarry Bend, but finished at nearly 50mph on the rim and with the inner tube flapping vigorously round the axle. Eaton (Gwynne) "packed up" with a broken valve spring, whilst Hall, on "Kim II", supplied the biggest sensation of the day by sliding right across the road at the Quarry Bend, mounting the grass bank, brushing through the hedge, leaping into the air as the car struck a hillock, and only by remarkable coolness keeping his machine on four wheels and pulling up."

At the end of all the drama, honours in the 1100cc class went to J.A. Hall on Kim II, followed by Lewis and Davenport, also both on Frazer Nashes. In the 1500cc class Mays made fastest time of the day and set a new course record. Second was E.R. Hall on "Bunny", and third J.A. Joyce on the A.C.

As the organisers, competitors and spectators made their way home after an excellent day's sport, little did they realise that Raymond Mays' new course record of 57.2 seconds would stand in perpetuity. They had just witnessed the last ever hill-climb event that would be held at South Harting.

Postscript: In the three weeks following the 1924 Junior Car Club meeting at South

THE POST WAR YEARS 1919 TO 1924

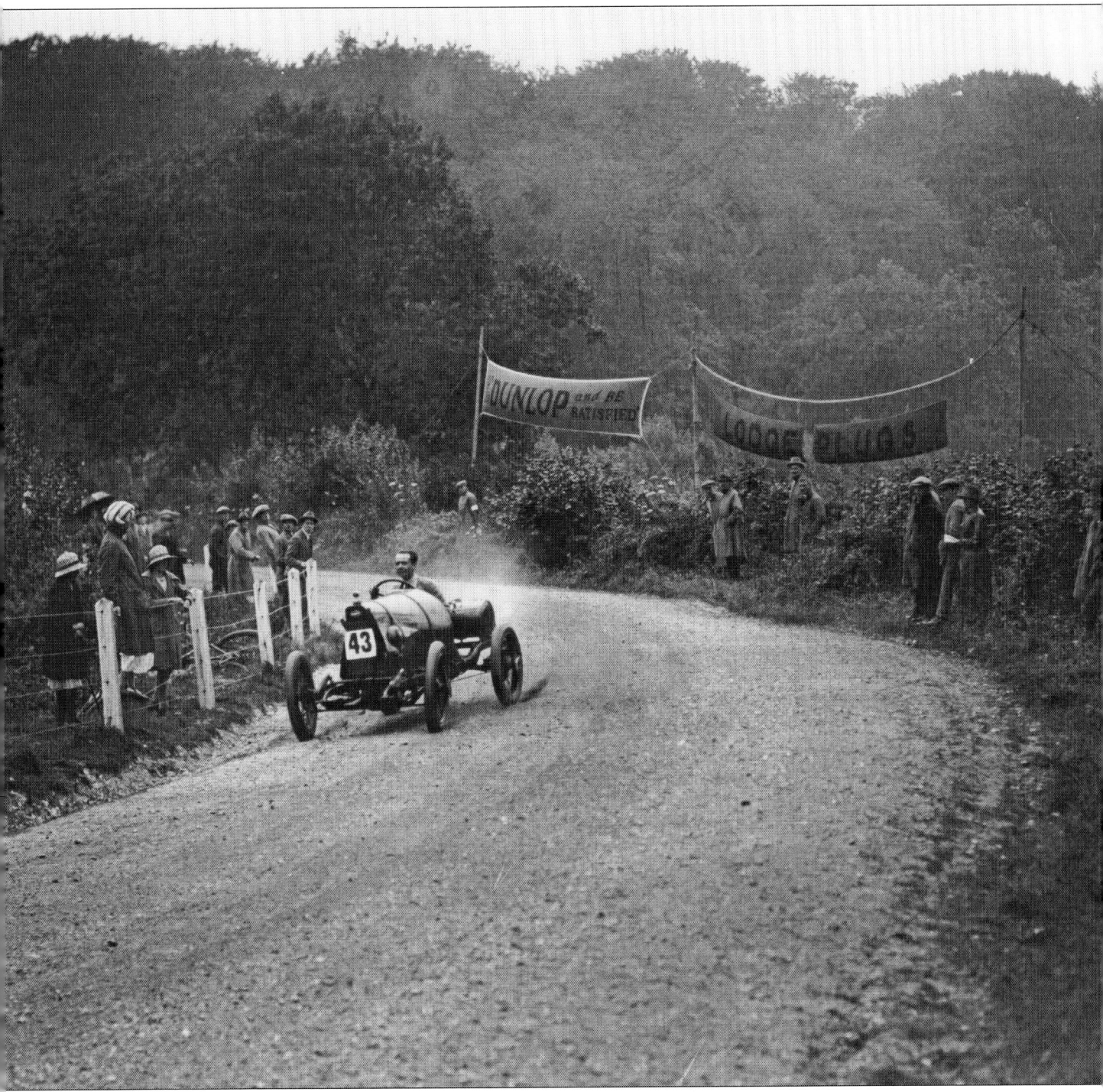

RAYMOND MAYS, DRIVING HIS BUGATTI CORDON BLEU,
MADE FASTEST TIME OF THE DAY IN 57.2 SECONDS, A RECORD
WHICH NOW STANDS IN PERPETUITY.
(1924)

Harting there was some correspondence in *The Autocar* about the scrutineering at Midhurst Station. On August 8th a letter from A.E.F. in Hove protested about the "most unfair discrimination against certain competitors" by the Junior Car Club scrutineers. In particular he picked out several Alvis cars, and the Talbot-Simmins sports cars. Alvis touring cars were "promoted" to the sports classes, and Alvis sports cars to the racing classes. The Talbot-Simmins was entered in the standard sporting class but was "promoted" to the racing class.

The argument used by A.E.F. in all cases was that the cars were standard cars, entered in the appropriate classes according to their manufacturers descriptions. This was in compliance with the regulations which stated that "a sporting car will be considered to be one which is either described or advertised as such by the manufacturers."

The Talbot-Simmins was in fact a much modified Talbot Eight engineered by Simmins Garage (Winchester) Ltd. The engine was bored out to 1000cc, the head was fitted with larger valves and double springs, the connecting rods were lightened and the little end bearings were pressure lubricated. A special light weight two seat body was fitted. The tyres were Pirelli racing cords. Driven by A.R. Simmins one of these cars had recently taken first place on time and formula in two hill climb events. Similar cars were offered for sale, with a choice of gear ratios, for £350.00.

Copy of this letter had been passed to the Junior Car Club and a response from the Secretary, A. Percy Bradley, was printed alongside the original letter in *The Autocar*. He declined to debate individual cases and effectively said that the Club had implicit faith in its scrutineers, "and naturally takes no notice whatever of any accusations of bias which may come to its notice." The regulation quoted by A.E.F. actually continued "...as such by the manufacturers *or falls into that category in the opinion of the scrutineers.*" The regulations extended this even further by adding that, even if a manufacturer had advertised a model for sale, but that in the event *"...no machines, or very few machines, have been sold to the public, the entrant is warned that there is the probability that the machine in question will be called upon to run either in the sporting or racing classes."*

The following week another letter, this time from C.W.D. Chinery, who had "competed in numerous trials and competitions", agreed that standards of scrutineering, and "wangling" on the part of the drivers, was a general problem throughout the country, but that the Junior Car Club was an exception in that "the rules and regulations…are always most explicit, and the scrutineers careful and exacting."

On the 22nd August the Alvis Car and Engineering Company Ltd. rose to the defence of its customers, and explained that the confusion had arisen from a misunderstanding by the Junior Car Club of which Alvis cars had overhead valve engines as a standard option. The Junior Car Club had not allowed Alvis touring cars fitted with ohv engines to run in the touring car classes, on the basis that most such cars were fitted with side valve engines, and that the side valve engines must therefore be "standard". In fact over 60 Alvis touring cars had been sold fitted with the new ohv engine, and the Junior Car Club had been told about this before the event. In any case, the Alvis side valve engine had for some two years been of 1598cc capacity and therefore not eligible for Junior Car Club events.

Alvis sports models with ohv engines had been made to run in the racing classes. The Alvis letter concluded; "While we take it as a compliment that the Junior Car Club officials consider our cars to be in a class above our competitors, we do not consider their classification to have been fair or reasonable on this occasion."

THE POST WAR YEARS 1919 TO 1924

A.H. ELY IN HIS TALBOT EIGHT CROSSES THE FINISHING LINE
TO TAKE SECOND PLACE ON FORMULA IN CLASS 2
FOR 1500cc TOURING CARS. HE WAS FOURTH ON TIME.
(1924)

CHAPTER 8

THE END OF THE ROAD 1925 AND KOP HILL

Back in 1907 the R.A.C. Competitions Committee had resolved to stop issuing permits for open hill climb events, and also to stop supporting closed events, which were held on public roads. This was mainly as a result of a question being asked in Parliament about an accident at Frome's Hill Climb. The primary reason cited in the Competitions Committee resolution was "the annoyance caused locally", but the clear concern was that Parliament would probably soon legislate against these events, which were operating in a legal vacuum, and the R.A.C. did not want to be seen as the sanctioning body.

In the event the "ban" was less than complete and some events did go ahead with R.A.C. blessing provided the organisers could demonstrate support from the police and local authority, and that adequate measures had been taken to prevent nuisance to local residents and to control the spectators. However by the time motor sport started up again after the First World War, memories had dimmed and a degree of laxity seems to have crept into the managing of events held on public roads. These were mainly closed events organised by clubs other than the R.A.C..

In March 1925 the R.A.C. felt sufficiently concerned to issue a Manifesto to all concerned with organising, and competing in, speed based events held on public roads. This included the organisers of closed events as well as open events, since by that time they also needed an R.A.C. permit. The Manifesto was drafted under six headings and the following extracts will convey the essence of the message. Although not complete, the actual words are direct quotations:

"Public Support
While the law remains as is, hill climbs and speed trials on the road can only be held by enlisting the support of the public generally and, in particular, of the police and local

authorities. There are indications that this support may be withheld in the future. This change of attitude is largely due to the behaviour of certain competitors who, in spite of rules and regulations, cause annoyance by practising before the event.

Safety of Spectators

The first consideration of all organisers should be the safety of the public. Permits will be withheld in all cases where it appears that organisers pay insufficient attention to this vital matter.

Observance of Rules

Much discontent amongst competitors has been caused in certain cases by the lax observance of R.A.C. rules by organisers and stewards. The reason for such laxity by local stewards is either a desire to give the public "a good show", or to treat leniently some popular competitor who would be prevented from competing if the rules were strictly enforced. There is also the desire to swell the list of competitors by admitting late entries, permitting a driver to drive more than one car in one class, or starting classes or competitors out of programme order.

Classification of Cars

Another cause of dissatisfaction is the attempted classification of cars by means of rules into racing, sports and touring classes. After exhaustive study the R.A.C. Competitions Committee concluded that it was not possible, and that classification should be made by scrutineers before the start, and that their decisions should be final and without appeal. This must however be clearly stated in the original prospectus and the supplementary regulations for the meeting.

Weighing at Hill Climbs

It is quite useless to weigh cars before a hill climb unless the cars are kept under strict official observation until the commencement of the competition. No open permit will be granted unless the supplementary regulations are considered satisfactory in regard to this matter.

Permits

No open permit will be granted unless the application, accompanied by a draft of the proposed regulations and entry form, is received at least one month before the date of the meeting. For closed meetings the period is ten days before.

Timing

No automatic apparatus may be used for timing open events unless it has been approved by the R.A.C.. At the present time the only apparatus approved by the R.A.C. is the apparatus owned by the club itself, and this apparatus is only allowed to be used for world and international class record attempts. For all other events there must be an official timekeeper at the start and the finish, even if the two points are connected by telephone. The R.A.C. considers it undesirable that the times achieved at hill climbs should be published."

Kop Hill

The next hill climb event, held only days after the issue of this Manifesto, was the Essex MC event at Kop Hill, near Princes Risborough in Buckinghamshire. It was a combined motor cycle and car event and attracted such notables as Henry Segrave in a Grand Prix Sunbeam.

The strong entry list of over 200 had attracted huge crowds, who congregated on the fast bends where any drama was most likely to be played out. One of the early motor cycle entries, T.R. Alchin, lost control at high speed and the riderless machine narrowly missed the crowds before coming to rest. Later in the meeting, the inexperienced F.W. Giveen in the ex-Raymond Mays Bugatti, Cordon Bleu, lost control on a fast right hand bend towards the top of the hill, careered over the grass bank, regained the road and disappeared over the brow of the hill. Luckily it was fairly late in the day and the crowds had thinned a little; only one spectator was hit, and he suffered a broken leg. As *The Autocar* commented it could so easily have been an "appalling catastrophe". The R.A.C. Steward immediately abandoned the meeting.

Viscount Curzon, who had been a spectator at Kop Hill, in a letter to *The Autocar* immediately after the event "sound(ed) a serious note of warning". Commenting on the "very large numbers of spectators" he noted that "little or nothing appeared to be done to control their movements. Entirely careless of their own safety or that of the competitors, they were able to crowd on to the course at almost any point...About 5.15pm a very large number of spectators, whether due to the cold or a desire to find their cars and get away, descended the hill, walking down the road, in spite of the fact that some of the fastest cars were then actually being started. The crowd hardly bothered to get out of the way, and at the first bend were actually still standing in the roadway when some of the cars were passing. The officials at the starting point and the cars themselves were completely hemmed in by the crowd. I saw in all only two policemen and three gentlemen wearing official badges, who were doing their best, but were obviously quite helpless, as their appeals to the sporting instincts of the crowd were ignored."

A few weeks after the events at Kop Hill, Wycombe Rural District Council asked the Buckinghamshire police authorities to stop the use of Kop Hill for motor trials. Other police authorities had already banned speed events on public roads in Worcestershire, Warwickshire and Staffordshire.

The legal position surrounding the organisation of speed events on public roads had become untenable. *Motor* reminded its readers that it had been "laid down by a learned Judge in the High Court that, in the absence of any clear statutory provision, the police have no right to restrict the use of the highway by any one of his Majesties subjects." They could, however, enforce the speed limit. This still stood at 20mph while some of the faster cars were capable of reaching nearly 90mph at the top of Kop Hill. In the early days of hill climb events the main interest was whether the cars would get up the hill at all, now it was more "will they get round the bend." Organising clubs were required by the conditions of the R.A.C. permits to ensure spectator safety, something for which they had no legal basis to work on. On the 2nd of April 1925, a joint statement from the R.A.C. and the A.C.U. imposed a total ban on the issue of permits for speed events held on public roads.

One irony in the situation was that a solution was already at hand; there was a bill before Parliament to allow the closure of public roads for motor racing. After the events surrounding Kop Hill the bill was quietly dropped, and the law remained thus until special permission was given to hold the Birmingham Super Prix in 1986.

THE END OF THE ROAD – 1925 AND KOP HILL

The future of competitive motor sport in Britain now lay entirely with the use of private land, where admission charges could be made and some authority imposed over spectator behaviour. Brooklands had already shown the way for circuit racing, and Shelsley Walsh for hill climbs. *The Autocar* reported on 31st July "that a group of well-known Midland motorists have secured from the landlord rights to hold a series of hill-climbs on the hill during 1926, and clubs will be able to secure from this group the use of this hill for a limited number of climbs. The hill is to be put and kept in perfect condition, both from the competitor's and the spectator's standpoints, and, as there is sure to be a scramble for the use of it, early application is essential."

Even at this low point in the history of motor sport however, the British sense of humour prevailed. *Motor* published the following satirical piece on 14th April 1925;

Safety First !

Too late for inclusion in a recent issue we noticed that the annual hill-climb of the Popanbang M.C. is announced to take place on April 1st, 1926, at Stop Hill, near Pinches Wizzborough. The event is supported by the R.A.C., A.C.U, A.A., B.B.C., G.P.O. and G.W.R., but should any of these bodies alter their minds and ban the climb the competitors will be informed after the meeting.

The regulations state that the start will take place some time during the afternoon near the foot of the hill, and in the event of any competitors reaching the summit the official results will be announced in the Show Number of The Motor. In order to prevent the possibility of errors occurring the timing will be done by the competitors themselves, who may use their own watches, signalling or electrical apparatus. Spectators will be required to wear crash helmets and to come fully armed and insured, and no spectator will be allowed to remain near the course unless he carries an R.A.C. permit certifying that he can be relied upon not to get run over. Permits, price 10s. 6d. each, will be obtainable on the hill or at any bookstall.

The order of starting will depend on how the starter feels after lunch. Competitors may start with their engines running, but should they lose control of their cars and go off prematurely the handicapper will make due allowances. Except in Class 2, competitors must provide their own formulas, which they may declare after the event. In order to allow ample time for complaints to be investigated, protests in quadruplicate should reach the club at least one hour before the time of the start.

The Classes will be divided as follows:-

Class 1a   Motor perambulators, nurses driving.

Class 1b   Ditto, occupant driving.

Class 2   Motor mowing machines, any capacity. Competitors in this event will run in pairs on the edges of the road, the following formula having been specially defined by Prof. I.M. Slow: $D \times G$ over $T \times C$. where D equals the distance covered in yards, G grass cut in blades, T time taken in hours and C capacity of the box. Note: - The formula may have to be altered at the last moment owing to the state of the undergrowth and fairways.

SOUTH HARTING HILL CLIMB 1905-1924

Class 3 Racing cars of 1500cc. Only vehicles which have lapped Brooklands at 140mph are eligible to compete in this event. Every car must be equipped with overhead camshafts, supercharger, front-wheel drive and four-wheeled brakes. Wireless and washing accommodation optional.

Class 4 For touring cars complete with caravans and full complement of furniture.

Class 5 All comers of any capacity including tanks, steamrollers, Lorries, motorbuses and taxicabs, the full complement of passengers being carried. Tickets will be issued during the run, which will provide an ideal means of viewing the hill.

At the conclusion of every Class officials will parade the hill on cars kindly lent by Messrs. F.S. Ledge, Trionel Trapson and others.

The Hon. Sec. will be pleased to see gentlemen of the Press during the morning of the event. Signed biographies of the competitors and a fully illustrated description of what is expected to take place during the event will be available.

The ideals of Safety First and the S.P.C.A. are ensured by the bolstering and padding of all dangerous bends and corners on the course, and a special regulation which requires all cars to be fitted with an approved type of bumper and wheel guard.

South Harting Hill Climb

APPENDIX I

Schedule of Events held
1904 to 1924

1.	1904	October	The Portsmouth Trials. Organised by a group of Naval Officers and partly held near South Harting.
2.	1905	10th June	Automobile Club of Great Britain & Ireland (ACGBI) & Sussex County AC meeting.
3.	1906	23rd June	ACGBI & Sussex County AC meeting.
4.	1907	10th July	R.A.C. & Sussex County AC meeting
5.	1913	28th June	Cyclecar Club meeting.
6.	1914	11th July	Hampshire, West Surrey, Dorset & Kent A.C.'s meeting.
7.	1914	18th July	Cyclecar Club meeting.
8.	1919	21st June	Junior Car Club meeting.
9.	1920	24th July	Junior Car Club meeting.
10.	1921	19th June	Junior Car Club meeting.
11.	1922	9th September	Junior Car Club meeting.
12.	1923	28th July	Junior Car Club meeting.
13.	1924	31st May	Surbiton MC & Ealing MC meeting. (used right hand hill B2146)
14.	1924	26th July	Junior Car Club meeting.

South Harting Hill Climb

APPENDIX II

Contemporary Reports Found

Journal \ Year / Event	19'04 / 1	05 / 2	06 / 3	07 / 4	13 / 5	14 / 6	14 / 7	19 / 8	20 / 9	21 / 10	22 / 11	23 / 12	24 / 13	24 / 14
The Car (Illustrated)	X	X	X	X		X								
The Autocar	X	X	X	X		X		X	X	X	X	X	X	X
Motoring Illustrated	X	X	X											
Automobile Club Journal	X	X	X											
The Motor	X			X				X	X	X	X	X	X	X
The Motor-Car Journal		X	X											
The Automotor Journal		X	X	X						X				
The Royal Automobile Club Journal				X	X	X	X							
The Cyclecar					X									
The Motor Cycle					X									
The Light Car						X	X							
The Light Car and Cyclecar								X	X	X	X	X	X	X
The Junior Car Club Gazette											X	X		X

South Harting Hill Climb

APPENDIX III

Tables of Entries and Results

1904
Motor Car Trials at Portsmouth
Entries

Car	Owner/Driver	No. Cyls.	Wt. Cwt.	Final Drive	Petrol Tank
4½hp Oldsmobile (1902)	Capt. Sir R.K. Arbuthnot, R.N.	1	9½	Chain	3 gln.
5hp Oldsmobile (1904)	Lieut. D. Lane, R.N.	1	8	Chain	3 gln.
5hp Humberette	Lieut. H.G. Vereker, R.N.	1			
5hp Humberette	Com. E.P. Grant, R.N.	1	8	Live Axle	3 gln.
6½hp Humberette	Professor Dykes	1	10	Live Axle	3 gln.
6½hp Lancaster	Lieut. C.D. Burke, R.N.	1			
10hp M.M.C.	Mr. F.T. Jane	2	17	Chain	8-10 gln.
10hp Renault	Mr. A. Langdale	2	16	Live Axle	6 gln.
10hp Panhard	Mr. A. Cave	4			
12hp Panhard	Capt. R. Neeld, R.N.	4			
12hp Sunbeam	Capt. Sir R.K. Arbuthnot, R.N.	4	19½	Chain	6-7 gln.
12-14hp Dennis	Com. H. Blackett, R.N.	2		Live Axle Worm Drive	6 gln.
20hp Dennis	Lieut. F.C. Halahan, R.N.	4	25½	Live Axle Worm Drive	9 gln.
16-20hp Elswick	Lieut. A.N. Loxley, R.N.	4		Live Axle	12-14 gln.
40hp Mercedes	Mr. J.D. Siddeley	4	25	Chain	24 gln.

1904 – Motor Car Trials at Portsmouth – Fuel Consumption Trial Results

Car	No. Pass.	Time up Portsdown mins. secs.	Speed (Gear)	Stops	Petrol Pints	mpg
6½hp Humberette	2	3 42	2nd	Nil	2½	70
5hp Oldsmobile	2	5 30	1st	Nil	4	45
10hp M.M.C.	4	4 0	2nd	Nil	4	45
4½hp Oldsmobile	2	7 12	1st	Nil	5	36
5hp Humberette (Com. E.P. Grant, R.N.)	2	6 0.	1st	Nil	6	30
10hp Renault	4	3 0	2nd	Nil	8	22.5
12hp Sunbeam	4	3 41	2nd	Nil	9½	19
20hp Dennis	5	3 0	2nd	16min., puncture	11	16.4
16-20hp Elswick	5	3 0	2nd	Nil	15	12.3
40hp Mercedes	5	2 19	2nd	Nil	16	11.3
12-14hp Dennis	4	5 0	1st	5min., fuel supply blocked	n/a	n/a

1904 – Motor Car Trials at Portsmouth – South Harting Hill Climb Results

Car	Owner/Driver	No. Pass.	Time mins. secs.	Remarks
40hp Mercedes	Mr. J. D. Siddeley	5	1 5.6	Trouble with ignition before starting.
10hp Renault	Mr. A. Langdale	4	2 24.8	
12hp Sunbeam	Capt. Sir R.K. Arbuthnot, R.N.	4	2 37	Climbed the steep hill 5 up.
6½hp Humberette	Professor Dykes	2	2 37.6	Climbed both steep hills south of Harting.
10hp Panhard	Mr. A. Cave	4	2 56.6	
10hp M.M.C.	Mr. F.T. Jane	4	3 7	
6½hp Lancaster	Lieut. C.D. Burke, R.N.	2	3 10.8	Climbed both steep hills.
20hp Dennis	Lieut. F.C. Halahan, R.N.	4	3 20.6	Stopped on hill, carburettor trouble.
12hp Panhard	Capt. R. Neeld, R.N.	4	3 24	
5hp Oldsmobile	Lieut. D. Lane, R.N.	2	3 31.2	
5hp Humberette	Com. E.P. Grant, R.N.	2	4 7	
12hp Dennis	Com. H. Blackett, R.N.	4	4 16.8	Stopped on hill, petrol supply failed.
5hp Humberette	Lieut. H.G. Vereker, R.N.	2	4 59	
16-20hp Elswick	Lieut. A.N. Loxley, R.N.	4		Broken gearshaft at start.
4½hp Oldsmobile	Capt. Sir R.K. Arbuthnot, R.N.	2	-	Cylinder head joint gave out, lost all water.

APPENDIX III TABLES OF ENTRIES AND RESULTS

1905 – The First ACGBI Event – Starters in CLASS A

For cars the list price of which is £150.00 and not more then £350.00

No	Car	Entrant	Driver
2.	12-14hp Leader	Mr. Malcolm McCraith	Mr. Malcolm McCraith
6.	8-10hp Coventry Humber	Mr. F.W. Adams	Mr. Louis Coatalen
7.	14hp Minerva	Mr. Herbert Ashby	Mr. Herbert Ashby
8.	8hp James and Browne	Mr. T.B. Browne	Mr. C.L. Cattell
9.	8hp Alldays	Mr. William Alldays	Mr. E.J. Blakemore
10.	12hp Leader	Col. C.W. Wilson	Mr. T.H. Shaw
11.	10hp De Dion Bouton	Mr. Walter Munn	Mr. Walter Munn
12.	8hp De Dion	Mr. J.W. Stocks	Miss Dorothy Levitt
13.	10-12hp Peugeot	Mr. W. S. Cutler	Mr. W.S. Cutler
14.	10hp Speedwell	Mr. J.W.H. Dew	Mr. J.W.H. Dew

1905 – The First ACGBI Event – Starters in CLASS B

For cars the chassis price of which is £300.00 and not more than £500.00

No.	Car	Entrant	Driver
15.	12-16hp Spyker	Mr. F.F. Wellington	Mr. C. Machin
16.	15hp Orleans	The Hon. C.S. Rolls	Mr. C. Johnson
17.	13 bhp Dixi	Mrs. Evelyn Bennett-Stanford	Capt. John Bennett-Stanford
18.	15hp Darracq	Mr. A. Rawlinson	Mr. A. Rawlinson
19.	20hp M.M.C.	Major F. Johnson	Major F. Johnson
21.	15hp White (steam)	Mr. Frederick Coleman	Mr. C.E. Stent
22.	15hp White (steam)	Mr. Frederick Coleman	Mr. Frederick Coleman
23.	15hp Whitlock-Aster	Mr. W. Hacker-Arnold	Mr. Claude Clench
25.	16-20hp Beeston-Humber	Mr. Thomas Chas. Pullinger	Mr. C.H. Cooper
26.	12hp Sunbeam	Capt. Sir R.K. Arbuthnot, R.N.	Capt. Sir R.K. Arbuthnot, R.N.
27.	12-14hp Climax	Mr. Joseph Mayfield	Mr. Joseph Mayfield
28.	20-22hp Whitlock-Aster	Mr. W. Hacker Arnold	Mr. O.F. Massingberd Mundy
30.	15hp White (steam)	Mr. G.C. Ashton Jonson	Mr. Ernest Algar
31.	12hp Mors	Mr. E. Cremieu-Javal	Miss Dorothy Levitt
32.	14hp Hallamshire	Mr. Frank Churchill	Mr. S.R. Churchill

1905 – The First ACGBI Event – Starters in CLASS C

For cars the chassis price of which is over £500.00 and not more than £850.00

No.	Car	Entrant	Driver
33.	18-24hp B.A.C.S.	Mr. F.F. Wellington	Mr. F.F. Wellington
34.	24hp Thornycroft	Mr. Tom Thornycroft	Mr. Tom Thornycroft
35.	30hp Daimler	Mr. J.M. Gorham	Mr. J.M. Gorham
36.	40hp Berliet	Mr. J. Ernest Hutton	Mr. L.C. Rawlence
37.	30hp Daimler	Mrs. Herbert Lloyd	Mr. Andrew Fraser
38.	18hp Peugeot	Mr. W. Harold Tribe	Mr. M.F. Mieville
39.	30hp Daimler	Mr. Percy Martin	Mr. Percy Martin
40.	30hp Daimler	Mr. E.M.C. Instone	Mr. E.M.C. Instone
44.	30hp Daimler	Mr. E. Manville	Mr. E. Manville
46.	24hp Wolseley	Mr. Chas. J.P. Cave	Mr. J Hurton
47.	24hp Thornycroft	Mr. G.V. Baxendale	Mr. G.V. Baxendale
48.	16hp Florentia	Lieut. R. St. J. Willans	Mr. J. Morgan Donne
49.	24hp Rochet-Schneider	Lieut. R. St. J. Willans	Mr. J.H. Novis

1905 – The First ACGBI Event – Results for CLASSES A, B, C

	Car	Entrant	Driver
CLASS A			
First Prize	8-10hp Coventry-Humber	Mr. F. W. Adams	Mr. Louis Coatalen
Second Prize	10hp Speedwell	Mr. J.W.H. Drew	Mr. J.W.H. Drew
CLASS B			
First Prize	16-20hp Humber	Mr. T.C. Pullinger	Mr. T.C. Pullinger
Second Prize	13hp Dixi	Mrs. Evelyn Bennett-Stanford	Capt. John Bennett-Stanford
CLASS C			
First Prize	30hp Daimler	Mr. E. Manville	Mr. E. Manville
Second Prize	30hp Daimler	Mr. E.M.C. Instone	Mr. E.M.C. Instone

APPENDIX III TABLES OF ENTRIES AND RESULTS

1905 – The First ACGBI Event – The Gold Medal Handicap Results

Order	Marks	Class	Car	Entrant
1	176.8	B	13 bhp Dixi	Mrs. E. Bennett-Stanford
2	176.5	C	18hp Peugeot	Mr. W. Harold Tribe
3	169.1	A	8-10hp Coventry-Humber	Mr. J.W. Adams
4	165.6	B	12-16hp Spyker	Mr. F.F. Wellington
5	164.3	B	12-14hp Climax	Mr. Joseph Mayfield
6	162.4	B	16-20hp Beeston-Humber	Mr. Thomas Chas. Pullinger
7	161.2	B	12hp Mors	Mr. E. Cremieu-Javal
8	160.7	B	15hp Orleans	The Hon. C.S. Rolls
=	160.7	C	16hp Florentia	Lieut. R. St. J. Willans
9	160.0	C	30hp Daimler	Mr. E. Manville
10	159.9	A	10hp De Dion	Mr. Walter Munn
11	159.6	B	15hp Whitlock-Aster	Mr. W Hacker Arnold
=	159.6	C	24hp Thornycroft	Mr. Tom Thornycroft
12	159.3	B	20hp M.M.C.	Major. F. Johnson
13	159.0	A	10hp Speedwell	Mr. J.W.H. Dew
14	158.5	C	24hp Rochet-Schneider	Lieut. R. St. J. Willans
15	158.0	A	8hp James and Browne	Mr. T.B. Browne
16	156.1	A	10-12hp Peugeot	Mr. W.S. Cutler
17	155.5	B	15hp White (steam)	Mr. Frederick Coleman
18	154.3	B	20-22hp Whitlock-Aster	Mr. W. Hacker Arnold
19	152.2	C	18-24hp B.A.C.S.	Mr. F.F. Wellington
20	150.7	A	8hp Alldays	Mr. William Alldays
21	150.1	C	30hp Daimler	Mr. E.M.C. Instone
22	149.3	B	15hp White (steam)	Mr. G.C. Ashton Jonson
23	149.0	B	15hp Darracq	Mr. A. Rawlinson
24	147.8	C	30hp Daimler	Mrs. Herbert Lloyd
25	145.2	C	30hp Daimler	Mr. J.M. Gorham
26	144.4	A	8hp De Dion	Mr. J.W. Stocks
27	143.1	C	24hp Thornycroft	Mr. Guy Baxendale
28	141.0	C	40hp Berliet	Mr. J. Ernest Hutton
29	139.3	A	12-14hp Leader	Mr. Malcolm McCraith
30	139.1	B	12hp Sunbeam	Captain Sir R.K. Arbuthnot, R.N.
31	139.0	B	15hp White (steam)	Mr. Frederick Coleman
32	137.0	A	14hp Minerva	Mr. Herbert Ashby
33	133.5	C	24hp Wolseley	Mr. Chas. J.P. Cave
34	128.6	A	12hp Leader	Colonel C.W. Wilson

1906 – The Second ACGBI Event – Starters in CLASS D

For cars the chassis price of which is over £850.00

No.	Car	Entrant	Driver
1	60hp Napier	Mr. Cecil Edge	Mr. Cecil Edge
2	30-40hp Peugeot	Mr. F. Guy Lewin	Mr. Charles Friswell
3	30hp Westinghouse	Mr. F. Guy Lewin	Mr. C. Martin
4	60hp Napier	Mr. S.H. Pearce	Mr. S.H. Pearce
5	60hp Napier	Mr. Ernest Owers	Mr. Ernest Owers
6	60hp Berliet	Mr. J. Ernest Hutton	Mr. J. Ernest Hutton
12	35-45hp Daimler	Mr. Herbert Musker	Mr. Herbert Musker
14	35-50hp Pipe	Mr. Claude Watney	Mr. Claude Watney
16	35hp Daimler	Mr. E.M.C. Instone	Mr. E.M.C. Instone
17	35hp Daimler	Mr. Allen D. Grigg	Mr. Allen D. Grigg
18	35hp Daimler	Mr. E. Manville	Mr. E. Manville
19	35hp Daimler	Mr. E.M.C. Instone	Mr. G. Davenport Powell
21	60hp De Dietrich	Mr. Chas. Jarrott	Mr. C. Bianchi
22	30-40hp Peugeot	Mr. W. Harold Tribe	Mr. M.F. Mieville

1906 – The Second ACGBI Event – Starters in CLASS C

For cars the chassis price of which is over £500.00 and not more than £850.00

No.	Car	Entrant	Driver
26	22hp Berliet	Mr. J.E. Hutton	Mr. J.E. Hutton
28	30hp Daimler	Mr. G.S. Barwick	Mr. G.S. Barwick
29	50hp Napier	Mr. Fred. W. Baily	Miss Dorothy Levitt
32	25-35hp Fraschini	Mr. H.E. Hall	Mr. H.E. Hall
33	30hp Daimler	Mr. J.M. Gorham	Mr. J.M. Gorham
34	28hp Pipe	Mr. Claude Watney	Mr. G. Dumont
35	30-40hp Daimler	Mr. H. Musker	Mr. Percy Musker
36	40hp Darracq	Mr. A. Rawlinson	Mr. A. Rawlinson
37	24hp Rochet-Schneider	Mr. John M. Courage	Mr. Arthur Haslop
38	30hp Daimler	Mr. Anthony Hordern	Mr. Anthony Hordern
39	35-40hp Iris	Mr. F.R.S. Bircham	Mr. A.C. Earp
40	28hp Daimler	Mr. Philip Wilkins	Mr. Philip Wilkins
41	35hp Rochet-Schneider	Mr. R.St.J. Willans	Mr. R.St.J. Willans
44	24hp Beaufort Princess	Mr. J. Edgar Lound	Mr. Albert E. Oakley
45	30-40hp Daimler	Mr. Paul Brodtmann	Mr Paul Brodtmann
46	30hp Daimler	The Rev. F.A. Potts	Mr. C. Grinham
47	28-36hp Daimler	Mr. G.H. Warne	Mr. G.H. Warne

APPENDIX III TABLES OF ENTRIES AND RESULTS

1906 – The Second ACGBI Event – Starters in CLASS B

For cars the chassis price of which is £300.00 and not more than £500.00

No.	Car	Entrant	Driver
49	22hp Minerva	Mr. J.T.C. Moore-Brabazon	Mr. J.T.C. Moore-Brabazon
50	16-20hp Beeston-Humber	Mr. T.C. Pullinger	Mr. T.C. Pullinger
51	26-30hp Simms-Welbeck	Mr. G. Hubert Woods	Mr. G. Hubert Woods
52	26-30hp Simms-Welbeck	Mr. G. Hubert Woods	Mr. D. McNeill
53	12-16hp Clement-Talbot	Mr. T.H. Woollen	Mr. T.H. Woollen
54	18hp Speedwell	Mr. C.H. Dodd	Mr. R. Chandler
55	14hp Germain	Capt. J.B.T. Masui	Mr. H. Ramoisy
56	20-32hp Darracq	Mr. A. Rawlinson	Mr. S. Girling
57	14-18hp Spyker	Mr. F.F. Wellington	Mr. C. Machin
58	12-16hp Talbot	Mr. Q.O. Grogan	Mr. Q.O. Grogan
59	20-32hp Darracq	Mr. Algernon Lee Guinness	Mr. Algernon Lee Guinness
60	16-20hp Argyll	Mr. A.L. Humphreys	Mr. W.C. Earp
61	20hp Darracq	Mr. Warwick J. Wright	Mr. Warwick .J. Wright
62	20hp Darracq	Mr. Warwick J. Wright	Mr. A.H. Walker
63	20-32hp Darracq	Sir T. Sutherland G.C.M.G.	Mr. G.F. Heath
64	25hp M.M.C.	Mr. C.P. Gosnell	Mr. R.P. Gosnell
65	18-22hp Florentia	Mr. R.St.J. Willans	Mr. Lionel Goldsby
66	14hp Thornycroft	Mr. Tom Thornycroft	Mr J. Sharp
67	18-22hp Whitlock-Aster	Mr. W. Hacker Arnold	Mr. W. Hacker Arnold
70	22hp Minerva	Mr. L. Russell	Mr. L. Russell
71	18hp Star	Mr. L. Russell	Mr. R.A. Cobb
72	10hp Peugeot	Mr. M.F. Mieville	Mr. M.F. Mieville

1906 – The Second ACGBI Event – Starters in CLASS A

For cars the list price of which is £150.00 and not more than £350.00

No.	Car	Entrant	Driver
73	8hp James and Browne	Mr. T.B. Browne	Mr. C.L. Cattell
74	10hp Adams-Hewitt	Mr. F. Leigh-Martineau	Mr. F. Leigh-Martineau
75	10-12hp Coventry-Humber	Mr. Edward Powell	Mr. Louis Coatalen
76	12-16hp Russell	Mr. Percival L.D. Perry	Mr. H.A. Bate
77	10hp Lindsay	Mr. J. Lindsay Scott	Mr. F.H. Arnott
78	8hp Crypto	Mr. John Dring	Mr. W.G. James
79	16hp Reo	Mr. Robert E. Phillips	Mr. F. Graham Sharpe
80	10hp Alldays	Mr. William Alldays	Mr. F.W. Huband
81	10hp Alldays	Mr. William Alldays	Mr. E.J. Blakemore
82	10-12hp Humber	Mr. Herbert Musker	Mrs. Herbert Musker
83	10hp Stanley (steam)	Mr. Arthur H. Bruck	Mr. Arthur H. Bruck
84	6hp Peugeot	Mr. M.F. Mieville	Mr. M.F. Mieville

SOUTH HARTING HILL CLIMB 1905-1924

1906 – The Second ACGBI Event – Results in CLASS D

Time Place	Car	No.	Driver	Points*	Formula Marks	Formula Ranking
1st	35hp Daimler	18	Mr. E. Manville	282.6	151.3	5th
2nd	35hp Daimler	19	Mr. G. Davenport Powell	276.6	150.5	7th
3rd	60hp Napier	1	Mr. Cecil Edge	275.6	160.4	1st
4th	60hp Berliet	6	Mr. J. Ernest Hutton	273.8	144.3	11th
5th	60hp De Dietrich	21	Mr. C. Bianchi	273.2	136.7	13th
6th	35hp Daimler	16	Mr. E.M.C. Instone	272.4	147.7	8th
7th	35-45hp Daimler	12	Mr. Herbert Musker	271.2	147.7	8th
8th	35hp Daimler	17	Mr. Allen D. Grigg	264.8	146.4	9th (sic)
9th	60hp Napier	4	Mr. S.H. Pearce	262.8	151.1	6th
10th	35-50hp Pipe	14	Mr. Claude Watney	248.0	152.2	4th
11th	30-40hp Peugeot	22	Mr. M.F. Mieville	244.0	154.5	2nd
12th	30-40hp Peugeot	2	Mr. Charles Friswell	228.8	154.0	3rd
13th	60hp Napier	5	Mr. Ernest Owers	226.2	139.7	12th
14th	30hp Westinghouse	3	Mr. C. Martin	198.0	145.2	10th

*note: Points are calculated as (400 – actual time in seconds)

1906 – The Second ACGBI Event – Results in CLASS C

Time Place	Car	No.	Driver	Points*	Formula Marks	Formula Ranking
1st	30hp Daimler	28	Mr. G.S. Barwick	278.0	154.4	2nd
2nd	50hp Napier	29	Miss Dorothy Levitt	276.2	136.4	14th
3rd	40hp Darracq	36	Mr. A Rawlinson	273.8	142.4	8th
4th	30-40hp Daimler	35	Mr. Percy Musker	267.6	153.3	4th
5th	30hp Daimler	33	Mr. J.M. Gorham	264.6	152.8	5th
6th	25-35hp Fraschini	32	Mr. H.E. Hall	251.4	140.5	10th
7th	30hp Daimler	46	Mr. C. Grinham	250.4	147.1	6th
8th	30hp Daimler	38	Mr. Anthony Hordern	249.2	145.4	7th
9th	30-40hp Daimler	45	Mr. Paul Brodtmann	236.2	139.4	11th
10th	28hp Pipe	34	Mr. G. Dumont	208.2	171.3	1st
11th	22hp Berliet	26	Mr. J.E. Hutton	186.6	154.3	3rd
12th	24hp Rochet-Schneider	37	Mr. Arthur Haslop	177.4	137.8	13th
13th	28hp Daimler	40	Mr. Philip Wilkins	173.0	139.0	12th
14th	35-40hp Iris	39	Mr. A.C. Earp	169.4	135.5	15th
15th	28-36hp Daimler	47	Mr. G.H. Warne	166.8	140.8	9th
16th	24hp Beaufort Princess	44	Mr. Albert E. Oakley	119.0	130.6	16th
--	35hp Rochet-Schneider	41	Mr. R.St.J. Willans	not placed	137.3	17th

*note: Points are calculated as (400 – actual time in seconds)

APPENDIX III TABLES OF ENTRIES AND RESULTS

1906 – The Second ACGBI Event – Results in CLASS B

Time Place	Car	No.	Driver	Points*	Formula Marks	Formula Ranking
#	20hp Darracq	61	Mr. W.J. Wright	264.0	166.4	5th
#	20hp Darracq	62	Mr. A.H. Walker	254.2	159.5	7th
1st	20-32hp Darracq	56	Mr. S. Girling	231.0	150.0	12th
2nd	20-32hp Darracq	63	Mr. G.F. Heath	229.6	149.4	13th
3rd	20-32hp Darracq	59	Mr. Algernon Lee Guinness	214.4	145.1	17th
4th	12-16hp Talbot	58	Mr. Q.O. Grogan	212.0	179.5	2nd
5th	14hp Germain	55	Mr. H. Ramoisy	200.0	172.2	4th
6th	12-16hp Talbot	53	Mr. T.H. Woollen	197.6	179.7	1st
7th	16-20hp Beeston-Humber	50	Mr. T.C. Pullinger	195.6	147.0	15th
8th	26-30hp Simms-Welbeck	51	Mr. G Hubert Woods	188.2	154.8	10th
9th	22hp Minerva	49	Mr. J.T.C. Moore-Brabazon	187.8	158.7	8th
10th	14hp Thornycroft	66	Mr. J. Sharp	177.6	174.4	3rd
11th	26-30hp Simms-Welbeck	52	Mr. D. Mc Neill	176.0	148.6	14th
12th	16-20hp Argyll	60	Mr. W.C. Earp	167.2	153.5	11th
13th	18hp Speedwell	54	Mr. Mr. R. Chandler	161.6	145.2	16th
14th	18-22hp Florentia	65	Mr. Lionel Goldsby	150.4	141.0	20th
15th	14-18hp Spyker	57	Mr. C. Machin	87.0	157.9	9th
16th	22hp Minerva	70	Mr. L. Russell	84.8	144.8	18th
17th	18hp Star	71	Mr. R.A. Cobb	70.2	142.0	19th
18th	25hp M.M.C.	64	Mr. R. P. Gosnell	41.6	127.6	22nd
19th	18-22hp Whitlock-Aster	67	Mr. W. Hacker Arnold	32.4	137.4	21st
20th	10hp Peugeot	72	Mr. M.F. Mieville	27.6	161.1	6th

#note: Disqualified following protests   *note: Points calculated as (400 – actual time in seconds)

1906 – The Second ACGBI Event – Results in CLASS A

Time Place	Car	No.	Driver	Points*	Formula Marks	Formula Ranking
1st	10hp Stanley (steam)	83	Mr. Arthur H. Bruck	188.4	189.3	1st
2nd	10-12hp Coventry-Humber	75	Mr. Louis Coatalen	172.4	162.7	4th
3rd	10hp Alldays	81	Mr. E.J. Blakemore	171.0	171.1	2nd
4th	10hp Alldays	80	Mr. F.W. Huband	170.4	166.9	3rd
5th	16hp Reo	79	Mr. F. Graham Sharpe	149.4	134.3	12th
6th	8hp James and Browne	73	Mr. C.L. Cattell	107.6	155.7	5th
7th	10-12hp Humber	82	Mrs. Herbert Musker	91.6	155.6	6th
8th	10hp Lindsay	77	Mr. F.H. Arnott	74.0	150.0	9th
9th	12-16hp Russell	76	Mr. H.A. Bate	66.2	148.3	10th
10th	10hp Adams-Hewitt	74	Mr. F. Leigh-Martineau	-21.4	136.3	11th
11th	8hp Crypto	78	Mr. W.G. James	-45.8	151.8	7th
12th	6hp Peugeot	84	Mr. M.F. Mieville	-139.8	151.4	8th

*note: Points are calculated as (400 – actual times in seconds)

APPENDIX III TABLES OF ENTRIES AND RESULTS

1907 – The Yellow Trophy – Starters and Results

Car	Entrant	Driver	$\dfrac{D^2 n}{2}$	Weight Lbs.	Time mins.	Speed mph	Efficiency %
White (steam)	Frederic Coleman	Frederic Coleman	50.08	4,284	1.927	32.4	79.10
Talbot	W. Stokes	W. Stokes	30.93	3,472	2.720	23.0	72.35
Clement-Talbot	R.E. Deacon	R.E. Deacon	22.50	3,063	3.303	18.9	71.60
Clement-Talbot	T.H. Woollen	J. Hedge	25.10	3,360	3.323	18.8	69.50
Deasy	E.W. Lewis	E.W. Lewis	34.00	3,727	2.750	22.8	69.10
Clement-Talbot	Viscount Ingestre	F. Blake	34.20	2,968	2.237	28.0	68.75
Napier	S.F. Edge	F. Newton	48.00	4,256	2.280	27.4	68.75
Clement-Talbot	Earl of Shrewsbury	G. Day	22.50	2,800	3.173	19.8	66.80
Maudslay	Cyril C. Maudslay	R.H. Verney	50.00	4,676	2.500	25.0	65.00*
Berliet	W. Watson	W. Watson	44.50	3,283	2.063	30.4	65.00*
Deasy	Philip Graham	Philip Graham	34.00	3,808	3.063	20.5	63.20
Daimler	John Goddard	John Goddard	55.75	3,892	2.063	30.4	60.60
Berliet	J.E. Hutton	J.E. Hutton	60.75	3,920	1.950	32.1	59.60
Germain	Capt. Theo Masui	H. Ramoisy	26.20	3,052	3.377	18.6	59.60
Berliet	J.E. Hutton	J. Brookes	44.50	3,279	2.220	28.2	59.30
Daimler	Herbert Musker	Herbert Musker	55.55	3,948	2.132	29.4	58.90
Minerva	Warwick J. Wright	Miss D. Levitt	51.25	4,508	2.610	24.0	58.80
Climax	Josef Latzel	Thos. Watson	29.75	3,500	3.660	17.1	55.80
De Dion Bouton	Walter Munn	Walter Munn	25.00	3,416	4.220	14.8	55.40
Ariel-Simplex	Chas. Sangster	A.E. Harrison	72.00	4,712	1.867	33.6	55.30
Mass	A.F. King	A.F. King	37.50	3,696	3.117	20.1	54.75
Iris	F.R.S. Bircham	F.R.S. Bircham	54.20	4,172	2.483	25.2	54.00
Gracile	C.H. Saunders	C.H. Saunders	56.50	4,088	2.423	25.8	52.20
De Dion	J.W. Stocks	J.W. Stocks	33.00	4,116	4.070	15.3	52.10
Iris	F.R.S. Bircham	G.F.W. Knowles	54.20	4,564	2.844	22.0	51.80
Napier	S.F. Edge	Cecil Edge	75.00	3,808	1.860	33.6	49.35
Brooke	Mawdsley Brooke	S.W. Humphrey	54.20	3,727	2.464	25.4	49.20
Iris	F.R.S. Bircham	H. Clifford Earp	50.00	3,724	2.670	23.4	49.10
Thornycroft	Tom Thornycroft	H. Niblett	40.50	3,920	3.190	19.6	48.75*
Buick	H.H. Sternberg	H.H. Sternberg	20.25	2,968	4.110	15.2	48.40*
Daimler	G.S. Barwick	G.S. Barwick	69.70	3,836	2.037	30.8	48.35
Thames	W.T.Clifford-Earp	W.T.Clifford-Earp	75.00	4,844	2.350	25.6	48.00*
Iris	F.R.S. Bircham	A. Perman	50.00	4,004	3.141	19.9	44.30
Scout	J. Percy Dean	J. Percy Dean	24.50	3,052	4.813	13.0	44.10
Clement-Talbot	Harold Measures	F. Martin	31.00	3,612	4.597	13.6	43.35
Humber	Arthur E. Gould	Arthur E. Gould	30.00	3,220	4.397	14.3	41.80
Cadillac	F.S. Bennett	F.S. Bennett	32.00	2,996	3.890	16.0	41.35
Lorraine-Dietrich	W.H. Phillips	W.H. Phillips	66.20	4,508	2.878	21.8	40.70
Climax	Josef Latzel	Cecil H. Lamb	28.00	3,416	5.500	11.4	37.75
Osterfield	Douglas S. Cox	Douglas S. Cox	24.50	2,716	5.153	12.2	36.50
Thornycroft	Tom Thornycroft	Tom Thornycroft	61.00	4,004	3.377	18.6	33.45
Alldays	Claude M. Taylor	Claude M. Taylor	28.15	3,388	6.147	10.2	33.20
Daimler	E.M.C. Instone	Oliver Bush	69.70	3,808	6.513	9.6	14.32

* Results disputed by *Automotor Journal*

1907 – The R.A.C. Closed Event – Starters and Results

For cars with a D²n value not exceeding 65

Car	Entrant	Driver	No. of Cyls.	R.A.C. Rating	Net Time mins. secs.
Germain	Capt. Theo Masui	H. Ramoisy	4	25.75	2 15.4
Berliet	J.E. Hutton	J.E. Hutton	4	24.75	2 42.2
Arrol-Johnston	John S. Napier	Ernest A. Rosenheim	4	25.60	2 45.8
Clement-Talbot	T.H. Woollen	W. Stokes	4	24.80	2 48.8
Minerva	J.T.C. Moore-Brabazon	J.T.C. Moore-Brabazon	4	25.80	3 04.4
Thornycroft	Tom Thornycroft	Tom Thornycroft	4	22.50	3 12.2
Cadillac	J.S. Bennett	J.S. Bennett	4	25.60	3 23.4
Ford	Percival L.D. Perry	Percival L.D. Perry	4	22.50	3 23.8
Beeston-Humber	Thomas Chas. Pullinger	Thomas Chas. Pullinger	4	24.75	3 31.6
Alldays	William Allday	E.J. Blakemore	2	11.25	3 35.2
De Dion Bouton	Walter Munn	Walter Munn	4	20.05	3 50.8
Alldays	Claude M. Taylor	Claude M. Taylor	4	22.50	5 17.6
Alldays	William Allday	E. Armstrong	2	11.25	5 39.0

1907 – The R.A.C. Closed Event – Starters and Results

For cars with a D²n value of less than 40

Car	Entrant	Driver	No. of Cyls.	R.A.C. Rating	Net Time mins. secs.
Lindsay	J. Lindsay Scott	J. Lindsay Scott	4	15.87	3 36.6
Alldays	William Allday	E.J. Blakemore	2	11.25	3 57.4
Singer	H.E. Hall	H.E. Hall	4	15.93	4 18.0
Peugeot	M.F. Mieville	M.F. Mieville	2	13.60	4 52.8
De Dion Bouton	J.W. Stocks	E.J. Underwood	1	6.18	4 53.6
De Dion Bouton	J.W. Stocks	H.J. Stanton	2	12.37	5 00.6
Alldays	William Allday	E. Armstrong	2	11.25	5 34.4
Adams	A.H. Adams	Reginald R. Smith	1	9.02	5 38.4
Renault	E.B. Waggett	E.B. Waggett	2	12.37	5 57.2
Baby Peugeot	M.F. Mieville	W.H. Tribe	1	6.00	7 52.6

APPENDIX III TABLES OF ENTRIES AND RESULTS

1913 – The Cyclecar Club Open Meeting – Starters and Results

Entrant	Machine	No. Cyls.	Capacity c.c.	Machine Wt. lbs.	Passenger Wt. lbs.	Time mins. secs.	Figure of merit	Place Time	Formula
Class 1 – Single seat cyclecars up to 1100cc, (three or four wheels)									
A.W. Lambert	Morgan	2	1082	574	133	1 33.4	0.3206	1	1
G. Holzapfel	Carden					Failed			
W.G. McMinnies	Morgan					n.s.			
Class 3 – Four wheeled cyclecars up to 750cc, (two seated)									
J.F. Buckingham	Chota	1	746	710	304	2 29.4	2.096	1	1
A.E. Parnacott	Cycar	4	499	756	304	4 4.6	0.7836	2	2
K. Kreitmayer	Zebra	1	644	1092	300	5 26.4	0.2817	3	3
H. Welham	Welham					Failed			
R.V. Patterson	Chota					n.s.			
H.R. Godfrey	G.N.					n.s.			
Class 4 – Three wheeled cyclecars up to 1100cc, (two seated)									
W.G. McMinnies	GP Morgan	2	986	616	340	1 43.0	0.4647	1	1
A.W. Lambert	Morgan	2	1082	560	301	2 6.2	0.2310	2	3
S.W. Spencer	Morgan	2	1082	672	298	2 7.2	0.2584	3	2
Class 5 – Four wheeled cyclecars up to 1100cc, (two seated)									
A.G.F. Nash	G.N.	2	1085	679	284	1 50.8	0.3247	1	3
L. Martin	Singer	4	1097	1260	295	2 14.0	0.3596	2	1
J.T. Wood	G.W.K.	2	1069	1071	295	2 14.8	0.3407	3	2
C.M. Whitehead	G.N.	2	1085	714	307	2 41.0	0.1792	4	8
G.N. Higgs	G.N.	2	1085	896	299	2 56.4	0.1786	5	9
E.H. Armstrong	Armstrong	2	965	728	280	2 56.6	0.2014	6	6
H. Naylor	G.N.	2	985	707	316	2 58.8	0.1917	7	7
J. Chater Lea	Chater Lea	2	965	966	296	3 00.0	0.2436	8	4
A.P. Bradley	Duo	2	965	1092	317	3 19.2	0.2255	9	5
Lt. L. Hook	G.W.K.	2	1069	1148	304	3 39.0	*		
F.W. Vallat	V.C.					Failed			
G.A. Turner	Turner					Failed			
M. Furneaux	Swift					Failed			
Lord Exmouth	G.N.					Failed			
M. Barrett	Crouch					Failed			
C. Hallsall	Wilton					Not weighed			
V. Wilberforce	G.W.K.					n.s.			

* Time recorded by *Motor Cycle*, but listed as Failed by *Cyclecar*.

Note: Abbreviations used for 1913 and later events:
n.s. = Non-starter.
n.r. = Not reported.

– 191 –

1914 – The Inter Club Meeting – Results

Driver   *Car*   *Position*

Class I – Cars up to 10hp (3 starters)
H.R. White   10-12hp Bifort   1st
R. Van Namen   10hp Bugatti   2nd
N.S. Hind   10hp Bugatti   3rd

Class II – Cars up to 16hp (6 starters)
Capt. H. Heath   12-20hp Benz   1st
C.B. Stainer   15-20hp Talbot   2nd
A.T. Duka   16-18hp Austro-Daimler   3rd

Class III – Cars up to 26hp (9 starters)
D. Jones   25hp Prince Henry Vauxhall   1st
R.W. Radclyffe   20hp Vauxhall   2nd
J. Guthlac-Birch   16hp Clegg-Darracq   3rd
H.F.W. Farquharson   15hp Mass   5th

Class IV – Cars over 26hp (6 starters)
N.S. Hind   25hp Berliet   1st
C.E.S. Gillett   25-50hp Talbot   2nd
Baldwin S. Millard   38hp Lanchester   3rd
Hugh Garnett   38.8hp Metallurgique   n.r.
W. Nash Vinson   25hp Talbot   crashed

Class V – Inter club team competition (4 teams)
Hampshire A.C.   1st 3.805 points
Capt. H. Heath   12-20hp Benz
J. Guthlac-Birch   16hp Clegg-Darracq
C.E.S. Gillett   25-50hp Talbot
Dorset A.C.   2nd 3.723 points
R. Van Namen   10hp Bugatti
N.S. Hind   25hp Berliet
H.F.W. Farquharson   15hp Mass

Class VI – Cars of any capacity made before 31st December 1909 (5 starters)
R.W. Radclyffe   1908 20hp Vauxhall   1st
Hugh Garnett   1909 38.3hp Metallurgique   2nd

APPENDIX III TABLES OF ENTRIES AND RESULTS

1914 – The Cyclecar Club Meeting – Entries & results on time

Driver	Car	Time mins. secs.	Position on time
Class I – Touring cyclecars under 750cc			
J.F. Buckingham	6hp Buckingham	scratched	
Class II – Standard touring cyclecars and light cars under 1100cc			
A.G.F. Nash	10hp G.N.	1 51.0	1st
H.R. Godfrey	10hp G.N.	1 59.8	2nd
F. Thomas	10hp G.N.	2 4.4	3rd
G.H. Thurlow	8hp Thurlow	2 14.8	4th
H.D. Leno	9hp Charronette	n.r.	
A.L. Greenhill	10hp Singer	n.r.	
E.G.M. Sturt	12hp Buckingham	n.r.	
H.F. Burford	10hp de P	n.r.	
F.R. Samson	8hp G.W.K.	n.r.	
Dr. Colver-Glauert	10hp G.N.	n.r.	
J.A. Tickell	10hp Calthorpe Minor	n.r.	
W. Chater-Lea	8hp Chater-Lea	n.r.	
H.C. Taylor	8hp Crouch Carette	n.r.	
A.E. Walter	8hp Crouch Carette`	n.r.	
L. Davies	10hp Morris Oxford	n.r.	
G. Brooking	8hp G.W.K.	n.r.	
S. de Beers	9-11hp Nova	failed	
A. Noble	10hp A.C.	scratched	
C.L. Scott	10hp A.C.	n.r.	
W.J. Slee	10hp A.C.	n.r.	
J.T. Wood	8hp G.W.K.	n.r.	
F.E. Moccatta	10hp G.N.	n.r.	
Barton Adamson	9hp Adamson	n.r.	
G. Griffiths	8hp Morgan	failed	
W.D. Hawkes	10hp Victor	n.r.	
A. Warren-Lambert	9.8hp Warren-Lambert	n.r.	

1914 – The Cyclecar Club Meeting – Entries & results on time

Driver	Car	Time mins. secs.	Position on time
Class III – Standard touring light cars exceeding 1100cc but under 1500cc			
D. Cohen	8hp Bugatti	2 55.2	1st
E.A. Lippold	10.5hp Calcott	2 57.2	2nd
P. Boult	10.5hp Calcott	3 3.6	3rd
J. Coop	10.5hp Calcott	3 8.8	4th
R.F. Langdon	10.5hp Calcott	n.r.	
N.S. Hind	Bugatti	failed	
Class IV – Lady drivers of standard machines			
Mrs. Warren Lambert	9.8hp Warren-Lambert	2 52.4	1st
Miss Portwine	10hp A.C.	3 9.6	2nd
Miss Henry	8hp G.W.K.	3 18.4	3rd
Miss Kent	8hp Humberette	n.s.	
Miss Adyce Price	8.3hp Mathis	n.r.	
Miss Douglas	8hp de P	failed	

APPENDIX III TABLES OF ENTRIES AND RESULTS

1914 – The Cyclecar Club Meeting – Entries and results on time

Driver	Car	Time mins. secs.	Position on time
Class V – Standard touring monocars			
W.E. Humphries	5hp Carden	1 29.4	1st
J.V. Carden	5hp Carden	1 50.4	2nd
H. Hurlin	5-6hp Aviette	n.r.	
A.M.N. Holzapfel	5hp Carden	failed	
L.W. Spencer	8hp Morgan	reclassified	
A.P. Bradley	8hp Morgan	reclassified	
Class VI – Racing machines			
J.V. Carden	8hp Carden	1 25.0	1st
A.G.F. Nash	10hp G.N.	1 30.8	2nd
W.E. Humphries	5hp Carden	1 31.0	3rd
L. Brooking	8hp Morgan	1 35.8	4th
J.W. Leno	6hp Baby Peugeot	n.r.	
W.G. McMinnies	"The Jabberwock"	n.r.	
K. Crawford	9hp Crawford	n.r.	
J.F. Buckingham	12hp Buckingham	failed	
A.G.F. Nash	10hp G.N.	n.r.	
G.L. Holzapfel	8hp Carden	n.r.	
L.W. Spencer	8hp Morgan	n.r.	
J.T. Wood	8hp G.W.K.	n.r.	
T.B. Andre	8-10hp Marlborough	n.r.	
A.P. Bradley	8hp Morgan	n.r.	
R..A. Whatton	8.3hp Mathis	n.r.	
H.D. Leno	9hp Charronette	n.r.	
A.M.N. Holzapfel	5hp Carden	scratched	
G. Griffith	8hp Morgan	n.r.	
W.D. Hawkes	10hp Victor	failed	
Percy Newbold	9.8hp Warren-Lambert	n.r.	

Team Prize

G.N. Team - Winners	Carden Team	A.C. Team
A.G.F. Nash	A.M.N. Holzapfel	A. Noble
H.R. Godfrey	G.L. Holzapfel	C.L. Scott
Dr. Colver-Glauert	J.V. Carden	W.J. Slee

1914 – The Cyclecar Club Meeting – Results on formula

Driver | *Car* | *Fig. Of Merit* | *Position* | *Award*

Class II – Standard touring cyclecars and light cars under 1100cc
Driver	Car	Fig. Of Merit	Position	Award
W.R. Morris	10hp Morris Oxford	.001140	1st	Gold Medal
L. Davies	10hp Morris Oxford	.001070	2nd	Silver Plaque
A.G.F. Nash	10hp G.N.	.001040	3rd	Bronze Plaque

Class III – Standard touring light cars exceeding 1100cc but under 1500cc
Driver	Car	Fig. Of Merit	Position	Award
D. Cohen	8hp Bugatti	.001390	1st	Torkington Trophy
E.A. Lippold	10.5hp Calcott	.000771	2nd	Silver Plaque
P. Boult	10.5hp Calcott	.000655	3rd	Bronze Plaque

Class IV - Lady drivers of standard machines
Driver	Car	Fig. Of Merit	Position	Award
Miss Henry	8hp G.W.K.	.000695	1st	Gold Medal
Mrs. Warren Lambert	9.8hp Warren-Lambert	.000655	2nd	Gold Medal

Class V – Standard touring monocars
Driver	Car	Fig. Of Merit	Position	Award
W.E. Humphries	5hp Carden	.001120	1st	Gold Medal
J.V. Carden	5hp Carden	.000840	2nd	

LIEUT. D.S. MACASKIE DRIVING HIS 8hp A.V. IN CLASS 7. (1919)

APPENDIX III TABLES OF ENTRIES AND RESULTS

1919 – The Junior Car Club Meeting – Results on time and formula

Driver	Car	Time in mins.	Position on Formula
Class 1 – Standard three-wheeled cyclecars up to 1100cc			
F.J. Findon	8hp Morgan	2.050	only starter
Class 2 – Standard two-seated light cars and cyclecars up to 1100cc			
Capt. A.G. Frazer-Nash	10hp G.N.	2.420	3rd
C. Finch	10hp G.N.	2.590	6th
W.H. Ogilvie	10hp G.N.	2.803	7th
W. Wadham	9.5hp Standard	2.993	1st
H.D. Leno	8hp Charronette	3.043	2nd
S.C. Westall	10hp A.C.	3.150	5th
J.H. Wadham	7.5hp Baby Peugeot	3.463	4th
A.P. Bradley	8hp Horstmann	4.257	8th
Class 3 – Standard two-seated light cars and cyclecars up to 1500cc			
G.C. Stead	10hp A.C.	2.310	1st
J.T. Wood	10.8hp G.W.K.	2.436	2nd
H.R. White	10hp Bifort	2.737	3rd
A. Noble	10hp A.C.	2.850	4th
A.P. Bradley	10hp A.C.	3.220	5th
Lieut. Burroughes	10hp A.C.	3.240	6th
W.G. Brownsort	10hp A.C.	4.827	7th
Class 4 – Standard four-seated light cars up to 1500cc			
J.T. Wood	10.8hp G.W.K.	n.r.	only starter
Class 5 – Lady drivers in standard cars and cyclecars up to 1500cc			
Miss J.A. Hill	10hp A.C.	n.r.	walkover
Mrs. A.G. Frazer-Nash	10hp G.N.	failed	
Class 6 – Non standard three wheeled cyclecars up to 1100cc			
Major A.C. Hardy	8hp G.P. Morgan	1.951	2nd
F.G. Layzell	8hp G.P. Morgan	2.433	1st
Class 7 – Non standard light cars and cyclecars up to 1100cc			
Capt. A.G. Frazer-Nash	10hp G.N.	1.346 (ftd)	2nd
H.R. Godfrey	10hp G.N. Vitesse	1.666	3rd
R.O. Lowe	8hp A.V.	1.700	4th
Capt. J.S. Coats	10hp Singer	1.833	1st
Lieut. D.S. Macaskie	8hp A.V.	1.853	5th

1919 – The Junior Car Club Meeting – Results on time and formula

Driver	Car	Time in mins.	Position on formula

Class 8 – Non standard light cars and cyclecars up to 1500cc

Driver	Car	Time in mins.	Position on formula
H.R. Godfrey	10hp G.N. Vitesse	1.584	3rd
G. Bedford	11.9hp Hillman	1.720	1st
Capt. J.S. Coats	10hp Singer	1.733	2nd
H.G. Severn	6hp A.V.	1.827	6th
C.A.S. Peto	10hp Eric-Campbell	1.976	7th
G. Caithness	10hp A.C.	2.160	4th
B. Marshall	11.9hp Chiribiri	2.353	5th
Capt. A.G. Frazer-Nash	10hp G.N.	failed	
McCulloch	10hp A.C.	disqualified	

Team Prize

Second A.C. Team – Winners　　　　　　　　**First A.C. Team – Second**
S.C. Westall　　　　　　　　　　　　　　　　　A. Noble
Lieut. B.H. Burroughs　　　　　　　　　　　　W.G. Brownsort
Lieut. G.C. Stead　　　　　　　　　　　　　　 Miss J.A. Hills

G.N. Team – Third

APPENDIX III TABLES OF ENTRIES AND RESULTS

1919 – The Junior Car Club Meeting – Weights of competing cars

Car	Net weight empty			Gross weight with passengers		
	cwt.	qr.	lb.	cwt.	qr.	lb.
8hp Morgan	5	2	25	7	3	6
10hp G.N.	8	0	2	10	2	12
8hp Horstmann	9	3	6	12	1	12
10hp G.N.	7	0	2	9	3	2
10hp G.N.	6	3	26	9	1	14
10hp A.C.	10	0	22	12	2	26
8.5hp Charronette	11	3	18	14	2	0
9.5hp Standard	12	1	16	14	3	22
7.5hp Baby Peugeot	8	3	4	11	1	22
10hp G.W.K.	12	1	10	15	1	6
10hp A.C.	12	2	14	15	2	14
10hp A.C.	12	2	10	15	1	0
10hp A.C.	11	3	10	14	1	3
10hp Bifort	14	3	20	16	3	10
10hp A.C.	13	0	7	15	2	24
10hp A.C.	12	0	13	14	3	10
10hp G.W.K.	12	1	4	17	1	24
10hp A.C.	13	0	7	15	2	24
8hp Morgan	6	1	2	8	3	20
8hp Morgan	5	3	6	7	0	13
10hp Singer	9	3	10	11	0	14
5hp A.V.	2	1	26	3	3	6
10hp G.N.	6	0	2	7	1	3
10hp G.N.	5	3	7	7	1	11
8hp A.V.	3	3	19	5	1	0
8hp A.V.	3	2	4	5	0	0
10hp Hillman	12	3	4	15	1	26
10hp Eric-Campbell	7	2	4	8	2	11
10hp A.C.	10	0	6	11	3	3
10hp A.C.	10	0	26	12	2	5
11.9hp Chiribiri	9	3	6	13	1	18

Note: Data as published, individual cars not identified.

1920 – The Junior Car Club Meeting – Entries

No.	Driver	Car	Capacity cc
Class 1 – Three-wheeled cyclecars up to 1100cc			
1	W.D. Hawkes	Morgan	1098
2	H.J. Fisher	6hp Reindeer	688
Class 2 – Touring two-seated cars up to 1100cc			
3	G.L. Hawkins	10hp G.N.	1086
4	S. Watson	10hp Deemster	1086
5	C. Finch	10hp G.N.	1086
6	W. Phillips	10hp Deemster	1086
7	A.G.F. Frazer-Nash	10hp G.N.	1086
8	Major R.C. Empson	8hp Lawrence-Jackson	998
9	W.S. Marchant	8hp Bleriot-Whippet	998
10	E.A. Tamplin	8hp Tamplin	998
52	A.E. Barrett	10hp G.N.	1086
11	E.R.R. Starr	10hp Deemster	1086
	(entrant: Major Baskerville Cosway)		
Class 3 – Touring two-seated cars up to 1500cc			
12	J.A. Evans	10.5hp Ashton	1498
14	Hon. Victor Bruce	10hp A.C.	1495
15	A. Noble (sub. Mrs. Hatton)	10hp A.C.	1495
16	G.M. Giles	10hp Bugatti	1327
17	B.S. Marshall	8-10hp Mathis	1130
5	C. Finch	10hp G.N.	1086
18	J.T. Wood	10.8hp G.W.K.	1368
19	E.A. Falconer	10.8hp G.W.K.	1368
20	G.C. Stead	10hp A.C.	1495
4	S. Watson	10hp Deemster	1086
21	Major A. Warren-Lambert	10hp Warren-Lambert	1330
22	H. Leno	10hp Charron-Laycock	1460
23	H.L. Field	10hp Warren-Lambert	1330
24	S.C. Westall	11hp McKenzie	1330
25	G.W. Waterlow	10hp Warren-Lambert	1330
9	W.S. Marchant	8hp Bleriot-Whippet	998
26	W.D. Hawkes	Horstmann	1460
27	R.E.H. Allen	10hp Bugatti	1368
10	E.A. Tamplin	8hp Tamplin	998
28	Miss V. Meeking	10hp A.C.	1495
6	W. Phillips	10hp Deemster	1086
50	W.F. Taylor	10hp A.C.	1495
51	E. Herrington	9.5hp Hurtu	1328

APPENDIX III TABLES OF ENTRIES AND RESULTS

1920 – The Junior Car Club Meeting – Entries

No.	Driver	Car	Capacity cc
Class 4 – Touring four-seaters up to 1500cc			
29	C.M. Keiller	10.8hp G.W.K.	1368
30	D.H. Owen Edmunds	10.8hp G.W.K.	1368
31	H.G. Pope	10.8hp G.W.K.	1368
32	R.A. Pope	10.8hp G.W.K.	1368
33	F.M. Harding	10.8hp G.W.K.	1368
34	D. Stevenson	10.8hp G.W.K.	1368
Class 5 – Touring cars up to 1500cc – Lady drivers			
51	Mrs. Hatton	10hp A.C.	1495
21	Mrs. A. Warren-Lambert	10hp Warren-Lambert	1330
26	Mrs. W.D. Hawkes	Horstmann	1327
7	Mrs. Nash	10hp G.N.	1085
28	Miss V. Meeking	10hp A.C.	1495
11	Miss Adyce Price	10hp Deemster	1086
36	Miss Violet Cordery	10hp Silver Hawk	1498
Class 6 – Monocars sold and used as single seaters up to 1100cc			
37	E.W. Scofield	5-6hp A.V.	654
38	Major R.C. Empson	8hp A.V.	998
39	K. Don	8hp Tamplin	998
40	W.F. Davenport	8hp A.V.	998
Class 7 – Racing cars up to 1100cc			
41	H.R. Godfrey	10hp G.N. Vitesse	1086
42	A.G.F. Frazer-Nash	10hp G.N. (Kim I)	1086
38	Major R.C. Empson	8hp A.V.	998
1	W.D. Hawkes	Morgan	1098
Class 8 – Racing cars up to 1500cc			
43	C.H. de Lapalud	J.L.	1496
44	B.S. Marshall	8-10hp Mathis	1327
41	H.R. Godfrey	10hp G.N. Vitesse	1086
42	A.G.F. Frazer-Nash	10hp G.N.	1086
45	Capt. N. Macklin	10hp Silver Hawk	1498
1	W.D. Hawkes	Morgan	1098

1920 – The Junior Car Club Meeting – Entries

No.	Driver	Car	Capacity cc
Class 9 – Sporting cars up to 1500cc			
46	T. Gilmore Ellis	8.7hp G.N. (Green Bug)	1086
41	H.R. Godfrey	10hp G.N. Vitesse	1086
45	Capt. N. Macklin	10hp Silver Hawk	1498
21	Major A. Warren-Lambert	10hp Warren-Lambert	1330
47	A.P. Bradley	10hp Silver Hawk	1498
48	W.D. Hawkes	10hp G.N.	1086
44	B.S. Marshall	10hp Mathis	1327
49	H.L. Field	10hp Silver Hawk	1498
36	A. Bray	10hp Silver Hawk	1498

APPENDIX III TABLES OF ENTRIES AND RESULTS

1920 – The Junior Car Club Meeting – Results

No.	Driver	Car	Time mins. secs.	Position on time	Position on formula
Class 1 – Three-wheeled cyclecars up to 1100cc					
1	W.D. Hawkes	Morgan	1 15.2	1	
2	H.J. Fisher	6hp Reindeer	n.s.		
Class 2 – Touring two-seated cars up to 1100cc					
10	E.A. Tamplin	8hp Tamplin	1 40.2	1	
4	S. Watson	10hp Deemster	1 41.4	2	1
5	C. Finch	10hp G.N.	1 42.8	3	3
6	W. Phillips	10hp Deemster	1 45.0	4	2
7	A.G.F. Nash	10hp G.N.	2 03.0	5	
52	A.E. Barrett	10hp G.N.	2 07.8	6	
11	E.R.R. Starr	10hp Deemster	2 09.0	7	
8	Major R.C. Empson	8hp Lawrence-Jackson	2 47.2	8	
3	G.L. Hawkins	10hp G.N.	n.s.		
9	W.S. Marchant	8hp Bleriot-Whippet	failed		
Class 3 – Touring two-seated cars up to 1500cc					
6	W. Phillips	10hp Deemster	1 38.0	1	1
21	Major A. Warren-Lambert	10hp Warren-Lambert	1 40.0	2	
4	S. Watson	10hp Deemster	1 42.2	3	2
5	C. Finch	10hp G.N.	1 43.6	4	3
9	W.S. Marchant	8hp Bleriot-Whippet	1 44.4	5	
10	E.A. Tamplin	8hp Tamplin	1 45.6	6	
18	J.T. Wood	10.8hp G.W.K.	1 46.6	7	
25	G.W. Waterlow	10hp Warren-Lambert	1 52.4	8	
20	G.C. Stead	10hp A.C.	1 55.0	9	
22	H. Leno (J. Sedcole in results)	10hp Charron-Laycock	2 00.6	10	
16	G.M. Giles	10hp Bugatti	2 01.2	11	
50	W.F. Taylor	10hp A.C.	2 13.6	12	
23	H.L. Field	10hp Warren-Lambert	2 15.6	13	
17	B.S. Marshall	8-10hp Mathis	2 19.0	14	
24	S.C. Westall	11hp McKenzie	2 20.2	15	
28	Miss V. Meeking	10hp A.C.	2 25.8	16	
51	E. Herrington	9.5hp Hurtu	2 32.6	17	
12	J.A. Evans	10.5hp Ashton	2 34.2	18	
15	Mrs. Hatton	10hp A.C.	2 36.8	19	
27	R.E.H. Allen	10hp Bugatti	2 39.0	20	
14	Hon. Victor Bruce	10.8hp G.W.K.	n.s.		
19	E.A. Falconer	10hp A.C.	n.s.		
26	W.D. Hawkes	Horstmann	n.s.		

1920 – The Junior Car Club Meeting – Results

No.	Driver	Car	Time mins. secs.	Position on time	Position on formula
Class 4 – Touring four-seaters up to 1500cc					
30	D.H. Owen Edmunds	10.8hp G.W.K.	2 11.8	1	1
32	R.A. Pope	10.8hp G.W.K.	2 18.0	2	2
34	D. Stevenson	10.8hp G.W.K.	2 30.4	3	3
31	H.G. Pope	10.8hp G.W.K.	2 34.8	4	
33	F.M. Harding	10.8hp G.W.K.	2 42.6	5	
29	C.M. Keiller	10.8hp G.W.K.	3 04.0	6	
Class 5 – Touring cars up to 1500cc – Lady drivers					
21	Mrs. A. Warren-Lambert	10hp Warren-Lambert	1 49.2	1	1
7	Mrs. Frazer-Nash	10hp G.N.	2 04.4	2	2
28	Miss V. Meeking	10hp A.C.	2 17.8	3	3
51	Mrs. Hatton	10hp A.C.	2 33.8	4	
26	Mrs W.D. Hawkes	Horstmann	n.s.		
11	Miss Adyce Price	10hp Deemster	n.s.		
36	Miss Violet Cordery	10hp Silver Hawk	1 37.0	(disqualified)	
Class 6 – Monocars sold and used as single seaters up to 1100cc					
39	K. Don	8hp Tamplin	1 27.0	1	
40	W.F. Davenport	8hp A.V.	1 34.0	2	
37	E.W. Scofield	5-6hp A.V.	1 55.2	3	
38	Major R.C. Empson	8hp A.V.	n.s.		
Class 7 – Racing cars up to 1100cc					
42	A.G.F. Frazer-Nash	10hp G.N. (Kim I)	1 04.6 (ftd)	1	
41	H.R. Godfrey	10hp G.N. Vitesse	1 12.6	2	
1	W.D. Hawkes	Morgan	failed		
38	Major R.C. Empson	8hp A.V.	n.s.		
Class 8 – Racing cars up to 1500cc					
42	A.G.F. Frazer-Nash	10hp G.N. (Kim I)	1 05.6	1	
41	H.R. Godfrey	10hp G.N. Vitesse	1 14.4	2	
45	Capt. N. Macklin	10hp Silver Hawk	1 20.2	3	
47	A.P. Bradley (from Class 9)	10hp Silver Hawk	1 22.8	4	
44	B.S. Marshall	8-10hp Mathis	1 24.8	5	
49	H.L. Field	10hp Silver Hawk	1 19.2		
36	A. Bray	10hp Silver Hawk	n.r.*		

* *The Autocar* and *Motor* credited Bray with 3rd place. *Light Car and Cyclecar* did not record the run.

APPENDIX III TABLES OF ENTRIES AND RESULTS

1920 – The Junior Car Club Meeting – Results

No.	Driver	Car	Time mins. secs.	Position on time
	Class 9 – Sporting cars up to 1500cc			
46	T. Gilmore Ellis	8.7hp G.N. (Green Bug)	1 15.8	1
41	H.R. Godfrey	10hp G.N. Vitesse	1 18.6	2
21	Major A. Warren Lambert	10hp Warren-Lambert	n.s.	
48	W.D. Hawkes	10hp G.N.	n.s.	
44	B.S. Marshall	10hp Mathis	n.s.	

Team Entries	Drivers	Position
1 – A.C.	W.F. Taylor, G.C. Stead, Hon. Victor Bruce	
2 – A.C.	Miss V. Meeking, Mrs. Hatton, A. Noble	
3 – G.W.K.	C.M. Keiller, D. Stevenson, D.H. Owen Edmunds	3
4 – G.W.K.	E.A. Falconer, R.G. Pope, H. Pope	
5 – Silver Hawk	Capt. N. Macklin, A.P. Bradley, A. Bray	
6 – Deemster	Stanley Watson, W. Phillips, Major Baskerville Cosway (E.R.R. Starr)	2
7 – Warren-Lambert	A. Warren-Lambert, H.L. Field, G.W. Waterlow	
8 – G.N.	A.G.F. Frazer-Nash, H.R. Godfrey, T.G. Ellis	1

SOUTH HARTING HILL CLIMB 1905-1924

1921 – The Junior Car Club Meeting – Entries and Results

Driver	Car	Time secs.	Position on time	Position on formula
Class 1 – Touring three-wheelers up to 1100cc				
Single entry merged with Class 2.				
Class 2 – Touring two-seaters up to 1100cc				
E.A. Tamplin	8hp Tamplin	90.2	1	
Capt. A. Frazer-Nash	8.7hp G.N.	94.2	2	1
A.E. Moss	8.7hp G.N.	96.2	3	2
V.G. Lloyd	7hp Carden	123.4		
H. Debnam	9.5hp Deemster	n.s.		
W.J.H. Phillips	10hp Deemster	n.s.		
A.E. Barrett	9.5hp Little Greg	102.2		
T.H. Short	10hp Deemster	n.s.		
H.A.J. Wilson	8.7hp G.N.	160.6		
G.C. Formilli	7hp Carden	135.0		
Capt. J.V. Carden	7hp Carden	106.0		3
A.E. Hartfall	10hp Morgan	110.2 (moved from Class 1)		

APPENDIX III TABLES OF ENTRIES AND RESULTS

1921 – The Junior car Club Meeting – Entries and Results

Driver	Car	Time secs.	Position on time	Position on formula
Class 3 – Touring two-seaters from 1100cc to 1500cc				
W.G. Hedges	10/30 Alvis	94.8	1	1
G.C. Stead	11.8hp A.C.	95.6	2	3
S. Watson	10hp Warren-Lambert	99.6	3	
L. Geach	10/30hp Alvis	101.2		2
R.W. Pradier	10hp Charron-Laycock	109.4		
C.E. Maney	11.8hp A.C.	166.4		
C.J. Sleep	10.4hp Calthorpe	147.8		
A.A. Pollard	11.9hp A.C.	n.s.		
H.E. Phillips	10hp Eric-Campbell	163.6		
W.D. Hawkes	10hp Horstmann	150.4		
A.H. Cranmor	11.9hp Lagonda	117.2		
A.R. Simmins	11.8hp A.C.	135.6		
J.T. Wood	10.8hp G.W.K.	n.s.		
M. Keddie	10hp Alvis	failed		
Hon. V.A. Bruce	11hp A.C.	n.s.		
C. Caithness	11.9hp A.C.	123.4		
G.W. Cosens	10hp Warren-Lambert	08.8		
R.E.H. Allen	11.3hp Bugatti	n.s.		
Class 4 – Touring four-seaters up to 1500cc				
D.L. Underwood	11.8hp A.C.	124.8	1	1
G.F. Reeve	11.8hp A.C.	132.4	2	
F.M. Harding	10.8hp G.W.K.	133.4	3	
F. Harris	10.8hp G.W.K.	163.4		2
R.A. Pope	10.8hp G.W.K.	135.2		3
H.R. Tollemache	11hp Lagonda	153.4		
A.W. Lambert	10hp Warren-Lambert	failed		
D.A. Parsons	11.8hp A.C.	163.2		
Class 5 – Lady Drivers in standard cars up to 1500cc				
Mrs. A. Frazer-Nash	8.7hp G.N.	102.0	1	1
Mrs. W. Lambert	10hp Warren-Lambert	109.4	2	
Miss V. Meeking	11.8hp A.C.	173.8	3	
Miss G.M.F. Keddie	10/30hp Alvis	n.s.		
Class 6 – Special Class for Tamplin, A.V., and Carden machines				
E.A. Tamplin	8hp Tamplin	87.2	1	
W.F. Davenport	8hp A.V.	99.4	2	
V.G. Loyd	7hp Carden	101.2	3	
G.C. Formilli	7hp Carden	106.4		
Capt. J.V. Carden	7hp Carden	115.0		

1921 – The Junior Car Club Meeting – Entries and Results

Driver	Car	Time secs.	Position on time	Position on formula
Class 7 – Racing cars up to 1100cc				
Capt. A. Frazer-Nash	8.7hp G.N.(Kim II)	70.0	1	
G.L. Hawkins	8.7hp G.N.	73.2	2	
H.R. Godfrey	8.7hp G.N.	74.8	3	
W.D. Hawkes	10hp Morgan	n.s.		
H.R. Wilding	9.5hp Little Greg	76.6	(moved from Class 9)	
J.V. Carden	7hp Carden	111.2		
Class 8 – Racing cars up to 1500cc				
Capt. A. Frazer-Nash	8.7hp G.N. (Kim II)	69.8 (ftd)	1	
W.M.W. Thomas	11hp Aston-Martin	75.0	2	
H.J.C. Smith	10hp Eric Campbell	84.0		
R.W. Pradier	10hp Charron-Laycock	81.2		
L. Martin	11hp Aston-Martin	n.s.		
E.G. Lefrere	11.3hp Bugatti	77.6	3	
W.D. Hawkes	10hp Morgan	n.s.		
T.G. Ellis	10hp Silver Hawk	84.6		
H.R. Godfrey	8.7hp G.N.	n.s.		
W.H. Oates	11.9hp Lagonda	82.8		
R. Mays	9.8hp Hillman	83.2	(moved from Class 9)	
W. Harris	8.9hp Marlborough	90.6	(moved from Class 9)	
E.L. Mather	10.5hp Douglas	87.0	(moved from Class 9)	
Class 9 – Sporting cars up to 1500cc				
G.L. Hawkins	8.7hp G.N.	81.2	1	1
W.M. Thomas	11hp Aston-Martin	84.8	2	2
J. Addis	11hp Aston-Martin	94.2	3	3
R.W. Pradier	10hp Charron-Laycock	106.0		
E.G. Lefrere	11.3hp Bugatti	disqualified		
L. Humphries	8.7hp G.N.	97.0	(moved from Class 2)	
W.G. Brownsort	11.8hp A.C.	106.8		
H.R. Godfrey	8.7hp G.N.	failed		
A. Hester	10hp Deemster	n.s.		
G.C. Formilli	7hp Carden	136.0		
V.G. Loyd	7hp Carden	127.8		
L. Geach	10hp Alvis	108.6		
E. de W.S. Colver	8.7hp G.N.	failed	(moved from Class 2)	
W.R. Steele	8.7hp G.N.	98.8	(moved from Class 2)	
A.W. Lambert	10hp Warren-Lambert	113.2	(moved from Class 3)	
C.M. Harvey	10hp Alvis	113.6	(moved from Class 3)	
H. Hagens	11.9hp A.C.	failed	(moved from Class 3)	

APPENDIX III TABLES OF ENTRIES AND RESULTS

1921 – The Junior Car Club Meeting – Entries and Results

Team Entries	Drivers	Position
G.N. No. 1	- Capt. A. F. Nash, H.R. Godfrey, G.L. Hawkins	1
G.N. No. 2	- E. de W.S. Colver, W.R. Steele, A.E. Moss	
G.N. No. 3	- A.F. Nash, H.A.J. Wilson, L. Humphries	
A.C. No. 1	- W.G. Brownsort, G.F. Reeve, G.C. Stead	
A.C. No. 2	- A.A. Pollard, H. Hagens, D.A. Parsons	
A.C. No. 3	- V. Bruce, C.E. Maney, G. Caithness	
A.C. No. 4	- Miss V. Meeking, D.L. Underwood, A.R. Simmins	2
Aston-Martin	- J. Addis, W.M.W. Thomas	3
Warren-Lambert	- A.W. Lambert, S. Watson, G.W. Cosens	
Deemster	- W.J.H. Phillips, T.H. Short, H. Debnam	
Alvis	- M. Keddie, C.M. Harvey, L. Geach	
Carden	- V.G. Loyd, J.V. Carden, G.C. Formilli	
G.W.K.	- J.T. Wood, F.M. Harding, R.A. Pope	

R.W. PRADIER DRIVING THE 10hp CHARRON-LAYCOCK ON ITS FIRST COMPETITION OUTING. HE FINISHED FOURTH IN CLASS 9. (1921)

1922 – The Junior Car Club Meeting – Entries and Results

Driver	Car	Time secs.	Position on time	Formula marks	Position on formula
Class 1 – Standard two-seater cars up to 1100cc					
W.H. Holmes	8hp Morgan	88.8	1	136.9	7
J. Parsley	8hp Morgan	92.0	2	144.5	5
J.F. Slaughter	8hp Talbot	95.8	3	235.4	1
R.W.B. Billinghurst	8hp G.N.	102.6	4	150.0	4
F.M. Avey	8hp A.V.	103.2	5	139.0	6
W.D. Hawkes	8hp Talbot	104.8	6	216.4	2
A.E. Bull	8hp Amilcar	110.8	7	176.3	3
A.J. Graham-Wigan	8hp Lewis	140.6	8	103.1	8
Class 2 – Standard two-seater cars up to 1500cc					
W.G.H. Hedges	10/30 Alvis	82.8	1	224.2	1
E.G. Lefrere*	11.5hp Bugatti	84.6	2	190.2	3
A.R. Linsley	11.5hp Bugatti	87.0	3	189.2	4
J. Parsley	8hp Morgan	90.0	4	148.8	8
W.H. Oates	11.9hp Lagonda	92.6	5	161.8	7
R.W.B. Billinghurst	8hp G.N.	96.2	6	162.5	6
D.M.K. Marendaz	Marseal	101.4	7	146.8	9
W.D. Hawkes	8hp Talbot	102.6	8	222.4	2
A.E. Bull	8hp Amilcar	107.6	9	183.1	5
Class 3 – Standard four-seater cars up to 1500cc					
W.G.H. Hedges	10/30 Alvis	106.4	1	193.0	1
D. Chinery	11.9hp Albert	145.0	2	132.6	2
Miss Viola Meeking	11.8hp A.C.	147.0	3	113.2	3
C.E. Maney	10/20 Enfield-Allday	156.0	4	111.7	4
S.C. Westall	11.9hp Albert	178.2	5	111.3	5
Class 4 – Private owners cars up to 1500cc					
A.R. Linsley	11.5hp Bugatti	85.4	1	193.8	3
A.A. Pollard	10/30 Alvis	93.6	2	213.1	1
P. Bennett	10/30 Alvis	95.0	3	205.5	2
L.H. White	12hp A.B.C. Sports	113.2	4	169.7	4
W.H. Shepherd	12/20 Calthorpe	137.6	5	124.4	5
R. D'Oyley Hughes	8.7hp G.N.	failed			
C.E. Maney	10/20 Enfield-Allday	145.8	6	122.3	6

* The *J.C.C. Gazette* and *Light Car and Cyclecar* list Lefrere as driver, *Motor*, and *Autocar* list Cushman.

APPENDIX III TABLES OF ENTRIES AND RESULTS

1922 – The Junior Car Club Meeting – Entries and Results

Driver	Car	Time secs.	Position on time	Formula marks	Position on formula
Class 5 – Lady Drivers					
(sporting cars subdivision) *					
Miss Viola Meeking	11.8hp A.C.	77.0	1	155.2	1
(touring cars subdivision) *					
Mrs. W.D. Hawkes	8hp Talbot	101.8	1	224.8	1
Mrs. A.G. Frazer-Nash	8.7hp G.N.	106.8	2	143.1	2
Mrs. F.N. Picket	8.7hp G.N.	126.0	3	119.2	3
Class 6 – Disabled Drivers					
N. Fielden	8.7hp G.N.	124.0	1	121.6	1
F. Harris	10.8hp G.W.K.	127.0	2	118.1	2
Class 7 – Sporting cars up to 1500cc					
R. Mays	Brescia Bugatti	64.2	1	215.2	3
G.L. Hawkins	10hp G.N. Vitesse	75.6	2	231.6	2
W.G.H. Hedges	10/30 Alvis	80.4	3	232.8	1
W.F. Knight	10.8hp McKenzie	96.4	5	149.3	5
Hon. V.A. Bruce	11.8hp A.C.	82.0	4	188.7	4
P.A. Denney	12/20 Calthorpe	failed			
S.H. Newsome	10/30 Alvis	failed			
Class 8 – Racing cars up to 1100cc					
A.G. Frazer-Nash	8.7hp G.N. (Kim II)	62.2	1		
W.D. Hawkes	10hp Morgan (Land Crab)	62.4	2		
F.N. Picket	8.7hp G.N.	77.6	3		

* The *J.C.C. Gazette* shows this subdivision of Class 5; it also allocates Formula marks not reported by other sources.

1922 – The Junior Car Club Meeting – Entries and Results

Driver	Car	Time secs.	Position on time
Class 9 – Racing cars from 1100cc to 1500cc			
R. Mays	Brescia Bugatti (Cordon Rouge)	59.8 (ftd)	1
L. Cushman *	Brescia Bugatti	65.0	2
H.J.C. Smith	10hp Eric Campbell	69.2	3
A.G. Frazer-Nash	1219cc G.N.	failed	
N. Hort-Player	10hp Marlborough	75.4	6
F.M. Luther	Austro-Daimler	71.2	5
S.H. Newsome	10/30 Alvis	81.6	7
H.K. Moir **	11hp Aston-Martin	70.2	4
A. McCulloch	12hp A.B.C. Sports	91.0	=8
G.L. Hawkins	10hp G.N. Vitesse	failed	
L. Little	J.V.C.	91.0	=8

* *J.C.C. Gazette* lists Lefrere as driver, every other source names Cushman.
** *J.C.C. Gazette* lists Lionel Martin as driver, every other source lists Moir.

Note: *J.C.C. Gazette* alone also lists Team Prize Silver Medals
    1st Bugatti – E.G.A. Lefrere, R. Mays, and A.R. Linsley

APPENDIX III TABLES OF ENTRIES AND RESULTS

1923 – The Junior Car Club Meeting – Entries and Results

Driver	Car	Time secs.	Position on time	Position on formula
Class 1 – Standard two-seat touring cars up to 1100cc				
F.A. Houghton	8hp Tamplin	28.4	1	4
D. Chinery	8hp Gwynne	35.6	2	1
A.J. Dixon	Singer	39.2	3	3
L. Horn	Gwynne	41.2	4	2
J.F. Deverill	Gwynne	n.s.		
B.E. Lewis	Frazer Nash	n.s.		
A.R. Simmins	Talbot-Darracq	n.s.		
J.F. Crundall	Humber	n.s.		
V. Balls	Amilcar	n.s.		
H.W. Holmes	Morgan	failed		
Class 2 – Standard two-seat touring cars up to 1500cc				
L. Cushman	Bugatti	21.0	1	5
A. Noble	Deemster	24.0	2	7
Miss W.M. Pink	Aston-Martin	26.4	3	3
H.W. Holmes	Morgan	26.6	4	13
W.G.H. Hedges	Alvis	29.4	5	5
F.A. Houghton	Tamplin	31.6	6	14
A.R. Simmins	Talbot-Darracq	33.0	7	1
S.H. Newsome	Cooper	34.6	8	8
A.R. Linsley	Bugatti	39.0	9	10
L. Horn	Gwynne	39.2	10	2
W.H. Oates	Lagonda	39.6	11	11
D. Chinery	Gwynne	40.6	12	4
F. King	Lagonda	41.0	13	12
L. White	A.B.C.	54.4	14	9
H.J.C. Smith	Eric Campbell	92.8	15	15
L. Goossens	Eric Campbell	95.4	16	16
A. Frazer-Nash	Frazer Nash	n.s.		
P.N. Hills	Bugatti	n.s.		
J.F. Crundall	Humber	n.s.		

1923 – The Junior Car Club Meeting – Entries and Results

Driver	Car	Time secs.	Position on time	Position on formula
Class 4 – Private owners touring cars up to 1500cc				
A.A. Pollard	Alvis	34.0	1	1
A.R. Linsley	Bugatti	34.8	2	2
L. White	A.B.C.	53.6	3	3
E. Hancock	Talbot-Darracq	71.2	4	4
L. Goossens	Eric Campbell	97.4	5	5
R.E.H. Allen	Bugatti	n.s.		
Class 5 – Lady members driving cars up to 1500cc				
Miss W.M. Pink	Aston-Martin	20.0	1	1
The Lady Belper	A.C.	25.8	2	2
Miss I. Cummings	Frazer Nash	n.s.		
Mrs. A. Frazer-Nash	Frazer Nash	n.s.		
Class 6 – Disabled drivers in cars up to 1500cc				
R.A. Pope	G.W.K.	42.6	1	1
N. Fielden	G.N.	67.2	2	2
Class 7 – Standard sporting cars up to 1500cc				
C.M. Harvey	Alvis	16.6	1	3
J.A. Hall	Frazer Nash	16.8	2	5
L. Cushman	Bugatti	18.2	3	4
Miss W.M. Pink	Aston-Martin	19.6	4	1
W.G.H. Hedges	Alvis	24.6	5	6
N.J. Norwood	Frazer Nash	26.4	6	7
B.E. Lewis	Frazer Nash	36.6	7	8
A.R. Simmins	Talbot-Darracq	32.4	8	2
A.R. Linsley	Bugatti	34.6	9	11
C.A.H. Mason	A.B.C.	39.0	10	10
A.R. Simmins	Wolseley	44.2	11	9
O. Wilson Jones	Salmson	58.4	12	12
I. Bradley	G.N.	n.s.		
B.H. Austin	Bugatti	n.s.		
I. Buchanan	Horstman	n.s.		
A. Frazer-Nash	Frazer Nash	n.s.		
L. Bradley	Riley	n.s.		
E.R. Hall	Bugatti	n.s.		

APPENDIX III TABLES OF ENTRIES AND RESULTS

1923 – The Junior Car Club Meeting – Entries and Results

Driver	Car	Time secs.	Position on time	Position on formula
Class 8 – Racing cars up to 1100cc				
J.A. Hall	8.7hp Frazer Nash	6.4	1	
H.S. Eaton	G.N.	9.6	2	
O. Wilson Jones	Salmson	11.8	3	
J.G. Lindsay	Amilcar	17.6	4	
F.H.B. Samuelson	F.S.	22.6	5	
Capt. E. Gribben	Ariel Nine	30.4	6	
G.C. Formilli	New Carden	39.4	7	
E.C. Gordon England	Austin Seven	44.8	8	
N. Black	G.N.	n.s.		
Miss I. Cummings	Frazer Nash	n.s.		
A. Frazer-Nash	8.7hp Frazer Nash	n.s.		
G.L. Hawkins	G.N.	n.s.		
V. Balls	Amilcar	n.s.		
Class 9 – Racing cars from 1100cc to 1500cc				
E.R. Hall	11.9hp Bugatti	0.0 (ftd)	1	
A. Frazer-Nash	G.N.	0.4	2	
C.M. Harvey	Alvis	1.0	3	
G.E.T. Eyston	Aston-Martin (alcohol fuelled)	1.8	4	
L. Cushman	Bugatti	3.8	5	
J.A. Joyce	A.C.	4.8	6	
B.H. Austin	11.4hp Bugatti	7.0	7	
H.J.C. Smith	Eric Campbell	9.0	8	
I. Buchanan	Horstman	9.6	9	
A.J. Graham Wigan	A.B.C.	n.s.		
N. Black	G.N.	n.s.		
L. Martin	Aston-Martin	n.s.		
H.S. Eaton	G.N.	n.s.		
R. Mays	Bugatti	n.s.		

1924 – The Surbiton Motor Club Meeting – Entries and Results

Driver	Car	Time secs.

Class 19 – 1100cc Racing Cars
Driver	Car	Time
Ivy Cummings	1086cc Frazer Nash	31.4
Wilson Jones	1086cc Salmson	33.8
J.P. Dingle	747.5cc Austin	34.8

Class 20 – 1500cc Touring and Sports Cars
Driver	Car	Time
L. Cushman	1452cc Bugatti	36.6
Kaye Don	1497cc Darracq	38.6
J.W. Ewen	1496cc Palladium	49.6
Stuart	1496cc Palladium	n.r.
V.W. Derrington	Salmson	n.r.
J.A. Joyce	A.C.	n.r.
B.S. Marshall	1496cc Bugatti	n.r.

Class 21 – 1500cc Racing Cars
Driver	Car	Time
Ivy Cummings	1086cc Frazer Nash	29.8
J.A. Joyce	1496cc A.C.	32.0
L. Cushman	496cc Bugatti	32.8

APPENDIX III TABLES OF ENTRIES AND RESULTS

1924 – The Surbiton Motor Club Meeting – Entries and Results

Driver	*Car*	*Time*
		secs.

Class 22 – 2000cc Touring and Sports Cars
L. Cushman	1452cc Bugatti	35.8
Kaye Don	1497cc Darracq	38.2
J.W. Ewen	1496cc Palladium	49.2
B.S. Marshall	1496cc Bugatti	n.r.

Class 23 – 2000cc Racing Cars
D. Resta	1988cc Sunbeam	26.6
R.G. Oats	1987cc Ansaldo	31.0
L. Cushman	1496cc Bugatti	30.2

Class 24 – 3000cc Touring and Sports Cars
R.G. Oats	1987cc Ansaldo	31.0
L. Cushman	1452cc Bugatti	34.6
B.S. Marshall	1496cc Bugatti	35.8

Class 25 – 3000cc Racing Cars
D. Resta	1988cc Sunbeam	26.4
H. Cook	2996cc Vauxhall	29.2
L. Cushman	1496cc Bugatti	30.2
Cyril Paul	1996cc Beardmore	30.2

Class 26 – Unlimited cc Touring and Sports Cars
B.S. Marshall	1496cc Bugatti	34.8
Ivy Cummings	5000cc Bugatti	n.r.

Class 27 – Unlimited cc Racing Cars
D. Resta	1988cc Sunbeam	25.8
H. Cook	2996cc Vauxhall	30.0
J.A. Joyce	1496cc A.C.	32.2

Note: The results quoted for this event are those published in *The Motor*. The results published in *The Autocar* were significantly different for Classes 20, 22, and 24.

1924 – The Sixth Junior Car Club Meeting – Entries and Results

Driver	Car	Time rel. secs.	Position on time	Position on formula
Class 1 – Standard two-seat touring cars up to 1500cc				
Miss W.M. Pink	Aston-Martin	0.0	1	1
D.E. Calder	Horstmann	5.6	2	5
A.A. Pollard	Aston-Martin	10.4	3	2
H.S. Eaton	Aston-Martin	12.8	4	3
J.C. Douglas	Aston-Martin	15.4	5	4
R.H. McBean	Aston-Martin	18.8	6	6
A.R. Linsley	Bugatti	failed		
T.A.N. Leadbetter	Alvis	n.r.		
Class 2 – Touring cars up to 1500cc				
Miss W.M. Pink	Aston-Martin	0.0	1	1
H.S. Eaton	Aston-Martin	7.4	2	4
A.A. Pollard	Aston-Martin	9.8	3	3
A.H. Ely	Talbot Eight	16.8	4	2
R.H. McBean	Aston-Martin	18.8	5	5
L.H. White	Crouch	29.2	6	7
E. Hancock	8hp Talbot-Darracq	40.2	7	6
J.C. Douglas	Aston-Martin	43.2	8	8
A.R. Linsley	Bugatti	103.0	9	9
D.E. Calder	Horstmann	n.r.		
Class 3 – Sports cars up to 1500cc				
B.H. Austin	11.9hp Bugatti	0.0	1	5
Miss W.M. Pink	Aston-Martin	3.2	=2*	3
A.Y. Jackson	12hp Alvis	3.2	=2	2
A.R. Linsley	Bugatti	4.2	4	4
H.C. Hordern	Alvis	7.2	5	1
Mrs. R.U. Dykes	Alvis	21.6	6	7
L.H. White	Crouch	30.8	7	9
P.A. Denney	Calthorpe	31.6	8	8
C.J. Randall	10hp Talbot	38.0	9	6
Strachan	Alvis	n.r.		
D.E. Calder	Horstmann	n.r.		
E.R.H. Hill	Riley	n.r.		

* Note: Results as reported in *Junior Car Club Gazette*. Other reports had Miss Pink 2nd on her own with 3rd variously reported as Jackson or Linsley.

APPENDIX III TABLES OF ENTRIES AND RESULTS

1924 – The Sixth Junior Car Club Meeting – Entries and Results

Driver	Car	Time rel. secs.	Position on time	Position on formula
Class 4 – Standard sports cars up to 1500cc				
H. Heath	12hp Darracq	0.0	1	1
B.H. Austin	11.9hp Bugatti	0.6	2	10
Miss D. Heath	12hp Darracq	2.6	3	5
Miss W.M. Pink	Aston-Martin	3.4	4	6
A.Y. Jackson	Alvis	4.4	5	4
A.R. Linsley	Bugatti	5.2	6	7
T.A.N. Leadbetter	Alvis	7.4	7	2
H.C. Hordern	Alvis	9.2	8	3
D.E. Calder	Horstmann	11.4	9	11
Mrs. R.U. Dykes	Alvis	20.2	10	9
E.R.H. Hill	Riley	20.4	11	12
C.J. Randall	10hp Talbot	35.2	12	8
Strachan	Alvis	n.r.		
C.M. Harvey	Alvis	n.r.		
A.D. Makins	Darracq	n.r.		
Class 5 – Racing cars up to 1100cc				
J.A. Hall	Frazer Nash (Kim II)	0.0	1	
B.E. Lewis	Frazer Nash (Rodeo Special)	1.0	2	
B.H. Davenport	Frazer Nash	4.0	3	
Ian Bradley	G.N.	5.0	4	
H.S. Eaton	Gwynne	6.4	5	
A.A. Hordern	Austin Seven	11.0	6	
G. Hendy	Austin Seven	11.2	7	
J.P. Dingle	Austin Seven	11.4	8	
A.R. Simmins	Talbot-Simmins	12.0	9	
B. Tebbutt	Morgan	27.2	10	
Class 6 – Racing cars 1100cc to 1500cc				
R. Mays	Bugatti (Cordon Bleu)	57.2 (ftd)	1	
E.R. Hall	Aston-Martin (Bunny)	59.4	2	
J.A. Joyce	A.C.	59.8	3	
A. Frazer-Nash	Frazer Nash	60.4	4	
Major C.M. Harvey	Alvis	61.2	5	
R. Mays	Bugatti (Cordon Rouge)	62.0	6	
H. Heath	Darracq	68.0	7	
D.E. Calder	Horstman	68.6	8	
Miss D. Heath	Darracq	71.2	9	
J.A. Hall	Frazer Nash (Kim II)	n.r.		

THE PORTRAIT OF EARL RUSSELL
PUBLISHED IN *THE AUTOCAR* WITH HIS
OBITUARY IN MARCH 1931.

South Harting Hill Climb

APPENDIX IV

Earl Russell
The Father of the South Harting Hill Climb

John Francis Stanley, 2nd Earl Russell (1865-1931), was one of that small group of pioneers who fought public hostility and official short-sightedness to get the motor car accepted in Britain. He and John Montagu (Lord Montagu from November 1905) were perhaps the two most influential advocates in Parliament, although from very different political perspectives, who separately piloted through Westminster two of the most important Acts of Parliament concerning the motor car, The Motor Car Act of 1903 and the Road Traffic Act of 1930. Contrary to what the separation in time between these two Acts might indicate, Earl Russell and John Montagu were in fact the same age and had almost identical life spans, give or take a year or so.

An early life member of The (Royal) Automobile Club, he was also an active Committee member. To get the flavour of the man, and to place him firmly in the context of South Harting, a letter he wrote to the Editor of *Automotor Journal* on 13th June 1907 is here reproduced in full:

"Sir,
At the last (Automobile) Club Committee I called attention to the fact that the regulations for the South Harting Hill Climb appeared to be framed in such a manner as to exclude steam cars. Several members spoke on behalf of the Competitions Committee, but not one was ingenuous enough to tell me that this fact was clearly recognised, and that the rules themselves stated that only vehicles "fitted with internal combustion engines" were eligible. One speaker went so far as to say that steam cars would be allowed to compete if they could come within the rules. It was largely due to the Committee not being dealt with straightforwardly in this matter that my motion to the effect that all touring cars should be eligible to compete received very little support. I note with great

regret, and I think the fact worth emphasising , that the Committee of the Royal Automobile Club, which ought to be independent, continues to allow itself to be dominated by the interests of the petrol car manufacturers, and is closing one event after another to steam cars. From the point of view of the buyer of a motor car (and it is the class of buyers that the Royal Automobile Club professes to represent) the Tourist Trophy has already been deprived of half its usefulness by the exclusion of steam cars.

This principle has now been extended to the South Harting Hill Climb. I started this hill climb three years ago in the hope that it might be a friendly closed event , but the Committee have steadily altered the rules year by year until it has degenerated into an ordinary trade competition of the worst type.

The buyer of a motor car does not care one iota for the Club's formula or for handicapping, or for any other ingenious device which makes one car turn out better than another. All he cares about is what his car costs him, and at what speed it can climb the hill, and possibly what it weighs. The South Harting Hill Climb has been run for two years on a price basis with perfect satisfaction to the buyer, and I regard the Club as neglecting the interests of the larger number of its members, who are private gentlemen, and owners of motor cars, in running competitions entirely in the interests of the trade, and basing them upon formulae which afford absolutely no information to the private buyer, and to which he is indifferent.

I am, Sir,
Your obedient servant
Russell"

The Russell family dynasty can be traced with certainty back to Stephen Russell of Dorchester and Weymouth who died in 1438. Four generations later, John Russell was created 1st Earl of Bedford in 1550 by King Edward VI. William, the 5th Earl, was created 1st Duke of Bedford in 1694 by King William III. Lord John Russell, born in 1792, was the youngest son of John Russell, the 6th Duke of Bedford.

The title Earl Russell, of Kingston Russell in the county of Dorset, was created in 1861 for Lord John Russell, who was at that time Foreign Secretary but had previously been Prime Minister on two occasions, the first from 1846 to 1852, and the second from 1865 to 1866. The Earldom held the subsidiary title of Viscount Amberley, of Amberley in the county of Gloucester, and of Ardsalla in the county of Meath.

The 3rd Earl Russell (younger brother of the 2nd) was Bertrand Russell, who achieved fame as a mathematician and philosopher, but never used the title professionally. His second son, Professor Conrad Sebastian Robert Russell, the 5th Earl Russell, Professor of British History at King's College, London, and outspoken Liberal Democrat peer, died in October 2004. The present Earl Russell is his son Nicholas Lyulph Russell born in 1968.

John Francis Stanley Russell, known as Frank, was born on 12th August 1865 at Rodborough Manor, the family home in the Stroud valley. He was the first son of Viscount Amberley M.P., and his wife Katherine Louisa, the daughter of the 2nd Lord Stanley of Alderley in the county of Cheshire. Viscount Amberley was the eldest son of the 1st Earl Russell, who was still alive at this time.

EARL RUSSELL – THE FATHER OF THE SOUTH HARTING HILL CLIMB

A PORTRAIT OF THE YOUNG EARL RUSSELL, AGED 20, TAKEN IN SALT LAKE CITY DURING HIS AMERICAN TOUR IN 1885.

As he later reminisced:

"I am a Stanley in appearance and largely in temperament, although I have inherited from the Russells bad eyes, some sense of art, a certain capacity for speech and writing coupled with a certain ineffectiveness and hesitation which prevent my being good at games, taking any interests in competition, and blustering my way through life with the superb assurance and self-satisfaction of the true Stanley".

The young Frank Russell had a far from settled childhood. His parents went from deep piety to agnosticism and espoused such radical ideas for the time as birth control, religious freedom, votes for women and, according to one report, free love. Viscount Amberley had lost his seat in Parliament largely as a result of his views on birth control. In 1874, when Frank was only nine, his mother, and six year old sister Rachel, contracted diphtheria and died within days. His mother was only 32 years old. Two years later his father died "from heartbreak and strain" at the age of 34. A fairly traumatic first eleven years.

Viscount Amberley had appointed Frank Russell's tutor, one D.A. Spalding, who was both scientist and atheist, and another atheist friend as guardians for Frank and Bertrand "to protect them from the evils of a religious upbringing". This, along with certain unconventional sleeping arrangements involving Mr. Spalding and Lady Amberley, persuaded their grandparents, Lord and Lady Russell, to have the boys made wards in Chancery and delivered to Pembroke Lodge, their home in Richmond Park.

Lady Russell, her brother George Elliott and her son Rollo were appointed guardians. Life at Pembroke Lodge was to be very different to anything the young Frank Russell had experienced before. Pembroke Lodge had been granted to Lord Russell and his wife by Queen Victoria for their life-time occupation as a reward for his services to the nation. There was clearly more than a simple monarch/subject relationship between Queen Victoria and Lord and Lady Russell however, as Frank Russell in his autobiography later recounted some fascinating details of the etiquette and protocol involved when Queen Victoria occasionally visited Pembroke Lodge to take tea.

Lady Frances Anna Maria Elliot Russell was the second wife of Lord John Russell and only half his age when they married in 1841. The four children they had were all either mentally ill or incapacitated in adult life. Possibly as a result of all this trauma, Lady Frances was an austere, highly religious, shy, but very widely read and cultured woman. She was a founding figure in the Unitarian Church. Bertrand Russell, in his autobiography, recalled that Lord and Lady Russell never understood the unruly Frank and "regarded him from the first to be a limb of Satan".

When Lord Russell's health deteriorated the whole household was moved temporarily to Broadstairs. A new tutor was appointed to whom Frank took an intense dislike. Things generally became so intolerable that Frank decided to run away and, at 3am one morning, he made his way to Broadstairs Station to catch a train to London. There were however no trains till morning and he was spotted by a policeman and returned to the house. He was left in the pantry while the butler roused the household, but promptly ran away again, slept in a haystack, and made his way to Margate the following day where he thought the train service might be better. He was again recognised by a policeman and returned to the house just in time for morning prayers.

After breakfast Lady Russell gave him a long and serious lecture, and asked to him to promise never to do anything similar again. He absolutely refused, and later recalled that ......
"I regard this as one of the wisest and happiest actions of my life. It was their intention to

save me from the awful contamination of public schools and to endeavour to turn me out a perfect replica of the Uncle Rollo. Bertie, whom they caught younger and who was more amenable, did enjoy the full benefits of a home education in the atmosphere of love with the result that until he went to Cambridge he was an unendurable little prig."

Soon after the family returned to Pembroke Lodge, Frank, now beginning to be called Viscount Amberley, was sent to the private school run by the Rev. R.S. Tabor at Cheam. He later recalled… "Old Tabor the headmaster was an unctuous and pious person but very soothing to parents."

In May 1878 a carriage was sent to the school to fetch Frank and take him back to Pembroke Lodge. His grandfather, Lord John Russell, was dead. A gloomy week later Frank and Rollo were chief mourners during a two day procession back to the Russell family mausoleum at Chenies in Buckinghamshire.

"It will be readily imagined how odious the whole proceedings were to me but I observed them with propriety and decorum. I was no longer Viscount Amberley, I was Earl Russell – wretched child of twelve."

The young Earl Russell came more under the influence of his uncle and guardian Rollo. The Hon. Francis Albert Rollo Russell was an academic and scientist, specialising in meteorology. He also shared his mothers passion for the Unitarian Church and "wrote Unitarian hymns with a scientific flavour".

Rollo set the young Earl off on an engineering path, particularly the study of "electricity of the frictional variety". The teaching was based on the writings of Professor Tyndall. Frank was fascinated and soon progressed onto "voltaic electricity…in which my uncle was not well up." He became obsessed by wireless telegraphy and, self taught at the age of thirteen, became a sufficiently proficient operator to be allowed to use real post office equipment at rural locations in Scotland while on holiday there. He continued his experiments back at Pembroke Lodge.

Frank's other grandmother, Lady Stanley, lived at 40 Dover Street, in London. His guardians at Pembroke Lodge restricted his visits there, as they tried to restrict all contact with the outside world, but Frank loved going there because of the completely different atmosphere of freedom and open mindedness. "Throughout the whole of my adolescence the one relief, the one escape, the one freedom from the oppression of Pembroke Lodge, was represented by 40 Dover Street." Nearby was the Royal Institution, where Tyndall was the resident Professor. As now, they ran a series of Christmas lectures for children and Frank became a regular attendee. On the advice of Lady Stanley, Frank became a Life Member as soon as he was old enough. A pattern of interest in things scientific and mechanical was emerging.

In October 1879, at the age of fourteen, Frank was sent to Winchester School. This was to be a turning point in his life, and a period that, in later life, he would look back on as one of the happiest in his life. Frank found the freedoms, intellectual as well as physical and social, quite intoxicating after the constraints of Pembroke Lodge. He had pocket money to spend, a bicycle to roam the countryside and also made many life long friendships. "The greatest individual influence of my life at Winchester was my friendship with Lionel Johnson, and it is to this stimulus that I owe my intellectual and to some extent my emotional development." Lionel Johnson was of Irish descent and later became a respected poet, literary critic and passionate advocate for all things Irish. It has been his misfortune to be mainly remembered for introducing Oscar Wilde to Lord Alfred Douglas in 1891.

Frank continued his experiments with electricity and even developed a talent and liking for mathematics. (There must have been at least one gene in common with his brother Bertrand.) He deeply resented being taken away a term early in 1883 to prepare himself for entry to Oxford. "If I was doing well at school, and if I actually had the audacity to be happy there, that showed that the public school system had finally corrupted me, and the sooner I was removed from its baneful influence the better."

In October 1883 Frank took up residence at Balliol College, Oxford under the Master Benjamin Jowett, to read classics. His justification for this seemingly unlikely choice was that "I think the classical training is far wider from a human point of view." He developed an active social life but took his work very seriously. His private reading was mainly philosophy and theology, and he even records that he began teaching his younger brother Bertie some philosophy.

He also had an active fitness regime and began to take up cycling more seriously on a "56inch Rudge with solid tyres"… "I was completely at home on the machine….my record was Arundel to Chichester, 10½ miles in 45 minutes…I could detach both hands from the handle bar for long periods, sufficiently long to wind up and set my watch and make notes about times with a pencil on a piece of paper. I have never ridden on these modern and dangerous machines which for some reason are called Safetys." The first stirrings of interest in personal transport.

This happy state of affairs was rudely shattered late in his second year. His relationship with Jowett had always been slightly ambiguous; outwardly friendly but lacking the respect and closeness of his relationship with some masters at Winchester. Jowett suddenly announced that he had been informed of Frank's "disgusting conduct in writing some scandalous letter" and suggested he should stand down for one month as punishment. Totally baffled by the accusation Frank demanded to see the letter, but Jowett refused.

Jowett declined to discuss the matter any further, he also refused Frank's request for an independent inquiry. Frank completely lost his temper, Jowett increased the penalty to one year, but Frank upstaged him by removing his name from the college records and leaving Oxford completely. That was in May 1885. The issue has never been fully resolved, but was still presented in evidence against him at later unrelated court proceedings. Years afterwards Jowett virtually admitted that he had never actually seen any letter, but he still declined to name the complainant.

The last thing Frank could contemplate was a return to the claustrophobia of Pembroke Lodge, but as he was still eighteen months away from his coming of age, and with only his £400 a year allowance to live on, that presented him with a problem. He found a small house near the river at Hampton and signed a lease on it. Uncle Rollo pointed out that, as a minor, he could sign any form of contract. To which Frank replied that the lease was signed and what was Pembroke Lodge going to do about it. The answer was a summons to the House of Lords to see the Lord Chancellor, Lord Selborne. They do things differently in aristocratic circles.

Lord Selborne was very friendly and insisted that Frank kneel with him and pray for divine guidance. The compromise found was that Frank should have a tutor live with him. The tutor chosen was Graham Balfour, a cousin of Robert Louis Stevenson, with whom Frank got on extremely well. They named the house Ferishtah, after "Ferishtah Fancies", a new book of poetry by Browning, and settled into a comfortable routine helped by a resident "general servant".

The two year stay at Ferishtah included a six month "grand tour" of America. In October

1885 Frank and Graham Balfour arrived in New York aboard the brand new ship Etruria. Frank was not impressed with 1880's New York, a "disgustingly untidy and unfinished city", although the people were "kind and hospitable". They travelled widely and did the sort of things touring aristocrats do, like being invited to the White House by President Cleveland and debating polygamy with the leaders of the Mormon Church.

Prophetically, in those pre-motoring days, they climbed Pikes Peak on horseback. In his autobiography (written in 1923) Frank also said some quite unrepeatable things about black Americans. Frank and his tutor returned to England on the Umbria in May 1886.

In August 1886 the 2nd Earl Russell came of age and inherited whatever monies were held in trust for him. His first action was to buy Broom Hall at Teddington, an old house, one of the main attractions of which was extensive grounds which ran down to the river and had a long private frontage just above Teddington Weir. There was a boat house, and a steam launch called Isobel, on which Frank made long expeditions up river, sleeping on board. He soon got to know the river Thames from Westminster up to Lechlade in detail and hankered after something more adventurous; something sea going.

He acquired the 50 foot steam yacht Royal, a sea going vessel built by White of Cowes. With a crew of two, she was commissioned on the Thames but then taken down river to Margate, cross channel to Ostend, through the Belgian canals, and back across the Channel to the Thames. Frank had taught himself navigation because he could not afford a qualified skipper but, for the more ambitious journey Frank had in mind, he had already realised that the Royal was underpowered and not fast enough.

After a summer cruising the east coast and Norfolk Broads, the Royal was taken to Plenty & Sons of Newbury to have new engines fitted. Throughout the winter of 1886/7 Frank spent many days in the workshops, staying at a local hotel, watching and learning the engineering procedures and skills involved in making, building up and fitting the new steam engines and boiler from scratch.

In April 1887 the work was completed and the Royal was taken for sea trials on runs between Dover and Southampton. The speed was up from 4 to 8 knots. She was then based at Shoreham and provisioned for the year long trip Frank planned.

With a crew of six, and two passengers, the Royal set off on 23rd August 1887 on an initial course for Cherbourg. They were held up for two weeks by bad weather in Jersey before setting off for the Bay of Biscay via Ushant. They spent a week in Bordeaux before making for Marseilles through the Canal du Midi. There they stayed a month, having a new propeller fitted, before cruising via Nice and Monte Carlo into Italian waters and round the coast to Elba. It was by then November and they were fighting their way against storms and heavy weather. They finally reached their destination, Naples, on 14th December. There they stayed until mid May. They returned via Corsica to Bordeaux, and back to the English Channel through the French canal system. The Royal finally moored back at Broom Hall, Teddington on the 3rd July 1888

They had travelled a total of over 3000 nautical miles, in a period of a year less a few days, and without major incident. There had been a few changes of crew, a surprising number being caused by dismissal for drunkenness. A quite extraordinary journey for a 22 year old, self taught navigator in only his second season of deep water sailing. He was justifiably very pleased with himself.

One of the first things Frank had done when he bought Broom Hall was to install electric lighting, putting to good use his years of experimentation and study of electrical engineering.

Soon after his return from Naples, in October 1889, he helped set up Swinburne & Company, operating initially from a small shed in the grounds of Broom Hall. The senior partner was James Swinburne, who had been employed by Crompton the electrical pioneers, but who now wanted to promote an invention of his called the "Hedgehog Transformer". The company subsequently moved to larger premises near Teddington Station and were involved in the manufacture of transformers, alternators and later voltmeters and ammeters. Frank was elected a member of the Institution of Electrical Engineers in 1890.

They took a stand at an electrical exhibition at Crystal Palace, generating four foot long mock lightning to get attention, and with the girls dressed in green and chocolate, the company colours. However the business never made money and in October 1892 the partnership was dissolved. Frank immediately set up a new company, Russell & Company, with offices in Queen Victoria Street, near Blackfriars in London, as general electrical contractors. This company also failed to make any money and only lasted three years.

As a backdrop to this business activity, Frank's private life degenerated into a horror story. In 1889, while living the bachelor life in some comfort at Broom Hall, he had two unexpected visitors one day. They turned out to be Lady Scott and her twenty year old daughter, Mabel Edith. Lady Scott made all sorts of excuses about mistaking the address, thinking somebody else lived there, and asking his pardon for the mistake. What Frank did not find out until much later was that the visit was in fact the carefully planned first step in a process of entrapment to find a suitable husband for Mabel Edith. They had recently failed in a similar plan with Lord Craven as the target, and had now picked the young Lord Russell as the next target.

"My unsuspecting and simple mind swallowed these protestations whole, and the pride of the proprietor was flattered when she (Lady Scott) expressed a wish to look over the grounds. Moreover the daughter was beautiful and very attractive, and we had common interests in the river, so that it was not very surprising that by the time the ladies left I had promised to run up in my launch and look them up in Walton."

Friends soon began to warn Frank of Lady Scott's history and reputation, but Lady Scott sensed what was going on and cleverly contracted the new Russell & Company to install lighting and a Parsons turbine, with Plenty boiler, in their house at Walton. Parsons turbines were state of the art in 1889 and Frank could not resist. Thus began a much closer relationship between Frank and Lady Scott and her daughter.

After a while Mabel told Frank that people were beginning to talk, and perhaps they should stop seeing each other. Frank swallowed the bait and proposed. After a few ominous delays, until Mabel came of age and inherited some money her mother needed badly, they were married on 1st February 1890.

Frank had by now fallen hopelessly in love with Mabel Edith. Only slowly did it sink in that Lady Scott had huge debts, and that even Mabel had considerable debts of her own. Sir Claude Scott had left his wife after she had had several notorious affairs, after which she had become "an adventuress".

The newly-weds had taken a furnished house in Eaton Square, London, because Mabel hated Broom Hall, but Frank was taken aback to find that Lady Scott became a virtually permanent resident. Society would accept the new Lord and Lady Russell, but not Lady Scott. Relationships became increasingly strained. He was very "tidy and faddy", she lived "like a butterfly". A mere three months after the wedding Mabel left Eaton Square to live with her mother at Walton. They then began a twelve year campaign of persecution to extract money from Lord Russell.

EARL RUSSELL – THE FATHER OF THE SOUTH HARTING HILL CLIMB

Before Mabel actually went back to her mother, Frank and Mabel had chosen a new riverside residence in Maidenhead. This was later called Amberley Cottage. Broom Hall had been sold, at a huge loss, and the lease on the Eaton Square house given up. From June 1890 Frank was therefore based at Amberley Cottage.

Mabel, encouraged by Lady Scott, sought an allowance of £1000 per year from Frank. His response was that, since they were still married, and Mabel was welcome to come and live at Amberley Cottage, any talk of "allowances" was completely inappropriate. An unfortunate error by their bankers in changing the previous joint account into separate accounts resulted in some of Mabel's cheques being returned. This was construed as a deliberate insult and Mabel then wrote to the Dowager Lady Russell at Pembroke Lodge saying that she was seeking a judicial separation on the grounds of cruelty. The trial began on 1st December 1891.

Threatened additional "gross" charges were dropped on the opening day of the trial. These apparently related to night time visits by Frank to the room of a Mr. "X" while he was staying at Eaton Square. The evidence for this seems to have been based on an unseen letter to Mabel from Lady Cardigan. There were even oblique references to the mystery letter which had caused Frank to walk out of Oxford University.

The trial was a complete fiasco for Mabel and Lady Scott as all the cruelty charges were exposed for the fabrications they were. The trial lasted four days, but the jury took less than one hour to acquit Frank completely of all charges. This was not, however, to be the end of the matter. Indeed, the very next day Mabel repeated all the dropped charges to The Hawk, a contemporary society gossip magazine.

Meanwhile Frank had reverted to the bachelor life at Amberley Cottage. He had constructed a large engine house in the grounds to generate electricity for electric lighting, he still had the launch Isobel, and commuted up to London from Taplow Station, a 10 minute drive by horse and carriage.

In 1894, when the new Parish Councils Act was passed, friends persuaded Frank to stand for the new Cookham Parish Council, which he did and won the seat. He greatly enjoyed it and soon progressed to a seat on the larger District Council, where among other duties he was responsible for administering the Maidenhead Workhouse. He abhorred the conditions he found there, and the attitudes of many of the local "established" politicians. He ruffled many feathers. After a few years of local politics in rural Buckinghamshire he was appointed a Justice of the Peace and ruffled a few more feathers. His political career was well and truly launched.

Mabel had not gone away, in fact she and her mother were living only a few miles up river from Frank at Bray. She had refused to withdraw the charges against Frank but still repeatedly requested meetings to discuss things; her finances were getting desperate. Frank refused to talk at all until all the charges were formally withdrawn. Stalemate. In March 1894 Frank received a petition for restitution; he cross petitioned for a judicial separation on the grounds of cruelty! By this ploy, Mabel could be cross examined on all the charges she had made. In April 1895, five years after the original trial, a new hearing began. Again Mabel and Lady Scott were publicly discredited and the jury took only 20 minutes to find against them.

Even then Lady Scott and Mabel would not accept the verdict. An appeal court reversed the conviction for cruelty but decided that Mabel's conduct had been so infamous that no Court would ever grant a decree of restitution. Lady Scott was still not satisfied and persuaded Mabel to appeal to the House of Lords.

To support their case in the House of Lords, Lady Scott then made a fatal mistake. She bribed past employees of Lord Russell, from his electrical contracting company and the crew of the Royal, to concoct a series of highly libellous statements. She even sent copies of these statements to the Law Lords involved in the appeal. Frank sued for criminal libel and all the conspirators, including Lady Scott, were sent to prison. In July 1897 The House of Lords dismissed the appeal.

Since 1892, when he was running Russell & Company from offices in Queen Victoria Street, Frank had rented a pied-a-terre in Temple Gardens. In the evenings he was an active member of the nearby National Liberal Club. He was a Committee member and also belonged to a very influential group of people who used to meet regularly to discuss the topics of the day. Knowing of his background in local politics in Maidenhead, they persuaded him, in 1894, to run for West Newington on behalf of the Progressive Party in the London County Council elections. He did and he won. He was squeezed out of the nomination at the next election, but fought the Hammersmith constituency instead. He was not successful, but was rewarded by the Progressive Party for all his hard work by being nominated as an Alderman which carried a six year term of office. During this period Frank was very active on several LCC committees. Because of his experiences in Maidenhead he was on the Asylums Committee, he was also on the Parliamentary Committee, and was Chairman of the Highways Committee when the Motor Car Act was passed in 1903.

When he was fighting the 1898 LCC election in the Hammersmith constituency, one of his leading supporters was a Mrs. Somerville, who was prominent in the womens suffrage movement. They became good friends and she visited Amberley Cottage on several occasions. It soon became clear that they were more than just good friends but Mollie, as she was called, made it clear that marriage was the only basis on which the relationship could proceed. Any prospect of a divorce between Lord Russell and Mabel Edith in England seemed impossible. Mollie, however, said she would settle for an American wedding if Frank could first get an American divorce.

Mrs. Marion (Mollie) Somerville was born Marion Cooke in Ireland in 1857. The family moved to Scotland and she first married one James Watson in Glasgow in 1881. He left her and their son Stanley, and went to join a spiritualist community in New Mexico. She filed for divorce in 1888, and in 1889 married George John Somerville and had two further sons. By coincidence it seems George Somerville was also an electrical engineer. The circumstances of the divorce between Mollie and George, or the reason she was living in London in 1898, are not recorded.

A source not directly related to the Russells described Mollie in 1895 as "a fat florid coarse Irishwomen of forty, with black curls, friendly manners and emotional opinions; a political agitator and reformer." Younger brother Bertrand also wrote some less than flattering things about Mollie's appearance.

To avoid unwanted attention, Frank and Mollie sailed on La Bretagne from Le Havre to New York in July 1899 and made their way slowly by train and stage coach to Nevada. They stayed initially at the Lake Shore Hotel at Glenbrook on Lake Tahoe, but later rented a house, took on two Chinese servants, brought Mollie's son Stanley over, and settled in for the winter in order to secure the six months residency necessary to acquire domicile in Nevada and file a petition for divorce. Judge Mack of Ormsby County heard the petition and granted the divorce. Three days later on a Sunday, in the Riverside Hotel in Reno, they were married by Judge Curler.

In May 1900, pausing only for a few days in Chicago, where Frank went to Kokomo to buy a Haynes-Apperson motor car, they headed for New York where they boarded the Ivernia for the return crossing to England.

Back in England they set up home in rented accommodation in Grays Inn in London. Frank had become tired of Amberley Cottage, which had been completely rebuilt after it was destroyed by fire just before the House of Lords Appeal hearing. He knew every inch of the river, he was no longer involved in the local politics, and he had developed a "passion" for the open spaces and long vistas of the South Downs.

Some years previously Frank had bought, for £450, a small cottage, standing in one acre of land, near the summit of Beacon Hill in West Sussex. It stood 625 feet above sea level and commanded magnificent views across Portsmouth and the Solent to the Isle of Wight. It was called Telegraph House because, until 1849 when the electric telegraph came in, it had been part of a chain of Admiralty Semaphore Stations enabling Portsmouth Dockyard to communicate directly with the Admiralty in London. The adjacent stations were at Fernhurst and Compton. When Frank bought it, the four room cottage, with a kitchen annexe, was being used by the wife of Sir Rennell Rodd, the British Ambassador in Italy, as a summer home for London children. The housekeeper had told Frank that the children hated the isolation and yearned for "pavements and shops". Frank had put a nominee in possession as he wanted to buy more adjacent land without driving up prices.

Frank bought a few more acres, from neighbouring landowner Willie James, and built a modest extension. Frank and Mollie moved in in 1901. They had sold Amberley Cottage, including the launch and steam engine, but Frank "removed to Telegraph House all my furniture, my radiators, my dynamo, my faithful Moyse (his second engineer from the Royal), my gardener and his family, my plants, and my horses and my carriages". Further extensions were soon built to properly house the servants and stable the horses, as well as greenhouses and potting sheds.

The only access to Telegraph House at that time was by an unmade road with steep gradients, which must have made moving day interesting. A new road was needed. "After long surveying I chose the easiest route and constructed a road entirely of local flints embedded on the chalk rock. I had from five to seventeen men at work and in less than a year had completed an excellent road 1580 yards long and 13 feet wide at a cost of £700....I also acquired a quarter of an acre opening off it on which I built a motor stable." It would have been this road that competitors and officials from The South Harting Hill Climb took when invited back to tea at Telegraph House after the events in 1905 and 1906.

Frank had always coveted a much larger piece of land which lay between Telegraph House and the existing metalled road (now the B2141), which belonged to Captain Hornby, son of Admiral Hornby. Every year he had made an offer but had always been refused; it was ten years before an offer was accepted. The acquisition of this extra 220 acres transformed the original cottage into an estate.

What was now needed was an appropriate mansion house. Before that however Frank built another road, through his new land, which led from Telegraph House to the edge of Kill Devil Copse, which was part of the Up Park Estate and fronted onto the existing metalled road. One and a quarter miles long, it took three years to construct, between 1909 and 1911, and cost £540.

To build his mansion, Frank decided to demolish the original cottage, which was "being held up by the wallpaper", and build a new two storey house incorporating a tower. The tower was important, since he had originally bought Telegraph House largely for the views. The stables were converted into a motor house. The house was innovative for the time incorporating double glazing, steam radiators, and an electricity generator. The first architect appointed would have nothing to do with double glazing and was sacked.

One Monday morning in the spring of 1901, having been home a year, Frank and Mollie had travelled up by train from Telegraph House to London when, at Waterloo Station, they were accosted by a man who asked if he was Lord Russell. When Frank said yes, the man said he had a warrant for his arrest on a charge of bigamy. Frank thought the matter must be a trivial technicality, but later found himself in Bow Street Magistrates Court being remanded on bail of £2000.

Frank had not realised that the six month domicile requirement in Nevada for obtaining a divorce was not recognised in English law. Nor was he aware that bigamy was one of the three exceptions for which a British citizen could be tried in England even if the crime were committed abroad. The other two exceptions were duelling and bomb making. In the passion of the moment Frank had not bothered to seek advice from an English lawyer before embarking on his American trip. Because he was a peer of the realm, the trial was removed to the House of Lords.

The hearing was on 10th July 1901, and the whole affair seemed more of a social occasion than a formal trial, with the galleries filled with ladies in all their finery. Frank pleaded guilty but made a long plea in mitigation. Lord Halsbury, summing up, said he recognised all the mitigating circumstances, but still felt that some token punishment was called for. He proposed that three months in Holloway would be appropriate. This was put to their Lordships, none dissented, so that was the sentence passed.

As a "first class misdemeanant" Frank had certain privileges in Holloway. He wore his own clothes, had his own furniture, excellent food was supplied by an outside caterer, he was allowed visitors three times a week, he exercised only with other first class misdemeanants, and a debtor prisoner was assigned to him to clean his cell as a paid servant. Even Frank admitted that, once his sense of injustice had subsided, for the second half of his sentence "I really had a fairly happy time….and more or less ran the prison as St. Paul did after they had got used to him."

Mabel Edith had filed for dissolution of the marriage on the grounds of bigamy and adultery as soon as she learned of events in America. This was not defended and a Decree Nisi was granted. Soon after the House of Lords hearing she was granted a Decree Absolute. "Two or three years later Mabel Edith died of consumption, the normal end to a life of that kind."

Frank soon settled back into normal life again after his release from Holloway. He resumed work at the LCC "with not much more interruption than if I had been away on a three month journey." The National Liberal Club "had taken the sensible view that the prosecution and the conviction were both farcical, and had resolved unanimously that, although a convicted felon, there was no reason why I should lose my membership."

The "convicted felon" tag still rankled though. Eventually, in 1911, he went to talk to Mr. Asquith about it, "and found him very kind and sympathetic." Soon afterwards he was granted a free pardon under the Great Seal.

Ironically, at the time Frank was convicted of bigamy he was half way through his studies to become a barrister. By nature, and by circumstance, Frank had always been interested in the law. In 1899 he was admitted as a student at Grays Inn to read for the Bar. After passing the initial exams, he placed himself under the tutelage of Ernest Cockle. His studies were interrupted by his visits to America and Holloway, but he was finally called to the Bar on 17th May 1905. He set up chambers with Ernest Cockle in New Court.

Because of his interests in motoring, Frank attracted many briefs to defend motorists. But, in deference to Mollie, he declined a prosecution brief for a hearing in the House of Lords because the plaintiffs were suffragettes. He practised for five years in all, getting involved in a wide variety of cases, and became a member of the South East Circuit.

In the wider field of business Frank became involved in many ventures over the years which met with varying degrees of success. After his own electrical contracting business failed, however, none could be considered truly entrepreneurial. He was usually invited onto the board of companies because of his name.

One which was successful before he joined, and remained so, was Plenty and Son, who had fitted the new engines to his steam yacht Royal before his voyage to Naples. They had an excellent reputation and did work for the Admiralty supplying steam launch engines. When one of the partners left, the business was turned into a limited company in 1890 and Frank was appointed Chairman. He stayed with the company for over thirty years.

Another more exotic involvement was with Companhia do Nyassa, a Portuguese company with a charter from the Portuguese Government to administer territories in Mozambique. The company was largely financed through London and therefore had a second London based board. Frank was Chairman of this London board.

Costs were exceeding revenue so Frank was sent to Lisbon to negotiate with the Portuguese Government. Some form of settlement was reached and the London board was disbanded. In the process however Frank managed upset a local nobleman and was challenged to a duel. Despite the challenge being more symbolic than real, Frank declined to get involved.

Following two insurance company ventures, both of which failed and cost Frank considerable sums of money, he was offered a seat on the board of the Globe & Phoenix Gold Mining Company in Rhodesia. The directors were paid very handsomely, £2-3000 a year each, and shareholders were beginning to express their displeasure at general meetings. Eventually the company was restructured and Frank was offered the Chairmanship at a fee of £700 per annum. He accepted and spent three weeks in Rhodesia in 1915.

However he resigned after a year or so following prolonged litigation when a property company sued Globe & Phoenix. The case lasted 144 days, but Globe won and were awarded a record £50,000 in costs.

His last known business venture was a company exploiting patents in electrical metal smelting. A company called Thermo Electric was set up to produce tungsten, which was a vital component of tool steels and strategically important during the first world war. However the company expanded too quickly on borrowed money and when the price of tungsten dropped after the war they became insolvent. The bank intervened and called in the receiver.

Yet another parallel strand in Franks complex life was the House of Lords. He first took his seat in 1887, when he was twenty two years old.

This was about the time he bought Broom Hall, and had just returned from his trip to Naples in his steam yacht Royal. He would have much preferred to be involved in the House of Commons, but over the years he became involved in the work of various Joint Select Committees.

On one he became heavily involved in developing the standards for electric traction (tramcars) which was just beginning to be commercially developed in Britain. On another he became involved in the water supply for London; he personally had favoured nationalising the water companies, building a huge reservoir in the Welsh hills and piping the water to London. This was rejected in favour of using the Thames as a source and building the series of reservoirs near Staines.

After ten years or so he became an occasional speaker in the House and focussed his attention on reforming the divorce laws. His Divorce Reform Bill in 1902 was flatly rejected, but he persisted in his crusade by running the Divorce Reform Society outside the House.

His own marital problems were far from over. In 1916 Mollie sued Frank for divorce, and the agreed settlement was £400 a year for life. This was to be paid through the "Marion Countess Russell Fund", which had been set up in 1914. This led to some accusations of collusion in setting up the divorce. Mollie outlived Frank by some ten years.

At some time before his divorce from Mollie, Frank had become friendly with Elizabeth von Arnim. She had been born Mary Annette Beauchamp in Sydney, Australia in 1866, was raised in England, but in 1891 married Count Henning von Arnim, the great-great-great grandson of King Friedrich Wilhelm I of Prussia. She became a prolific and successful novelist. Count von Arnim died in 1910.

Elizabeth flirted with Frank, "because he was safely married" and therefore quite suitable as a lover. Frank became infatuated, but when he announced he was getting divorced from Mollie, Elizabeth was horrified. Among the reasons she gave to Bertie for not wanting to marry his brother Frank was that "he slept with seven dogs on the bed". Frank was very fond of animals and bred Maltese terriers at Telegraph House. Elizabeth, nevertheless, allowed things to drift and they were married in 1916. It was a disaster and they were divorced in 1919.

After all his failed business ventures and marriages, Frank's finances were becoming perilous. As early as January 1921, in a letter to brother Bertie, he said that his creditors were threatening to bankrupt him.

In 1927 his financial pressures were eased slightly when brother Bertie and his wife Dora rented Telegraph House, at a rent of £400 a year, to open a progressive school which they named Beacon Hill School. In Bertie's opinion the "house was ugly and absurd, but the situation was superb."

Meanwhile, back on the political scene, Frank was still active in the House of Lords. For a peer of the realm, Frank's politics had always been rather left wing, and when the Labour Party developed from the Labour Representation Committee, just before the first World War, Frank became the first peer to officially join. He was not included in the first Labour minority government in 1924, but was appointed Parliamentary Secretary to the Department of Transport in the second Labour government in 1929. He was valued by Ramsey MacDonald for his lawyers mind and debating skills, which were fairly rare among trade unionists. An observant country clergyman discovered that the number of Under-Secretaries in the House of Commons exceeded the statutory limit by one. The remedy for this involved Frank being transferred to the office of Under Secretary for India.

He was still in this post when he died in the Hotel de Noailles in Marseilles on the 3rd March 1931 at the age of 65. He had been recuperating from a severe bout of influenza, aggravated by worsening heart problems. In 1923 he had written….. "with the exception of a week of influenza in 1899, when it was first invented, (I have only once) had to stay in bed since the age of seventeen."

EARL RUSSELL – THE FATHER OF THE SOUTH HARTING HILL CLIMB

As Frank was childless, his younger brother Bertrand became the 3rd Earl Russell on Frank's death;

"I inherited a title but not one penny of money, as he was bankrupt. A title is a great nuisance to me and I am at a loss what to do."

Bertie had also had a stormy married life and had, at this juncture, been married and divorced twice, with more to come. His now divorced second wife, Dora, had continued to run Beacon Hill School at Telegraph House on her own until Bertie returned from a period abroad in 1934 and told her to move out because he wanted to live there. Dora continued to run the school elsewhere up until the second World War. In 1937 Bertie sold Telegraph House, in part to fund the Marion Countess Russell Fund, which still had to provide Mollie with £400 a year income, but also to save on running costs and fund his own growing alimony bills. Bertie himself did not pass on the Earldom to his own eldest son, John Conrad Russell, until 1970.

SOUTH HARTING HILL CLIMB 1905-1924

EARL RUSSELL ON THE HAYNES-APPERSON CAR HE BROUGHT
BACK FROM AMERICA AFTER HIS STAY IN NEVADA TO
SECURE A DIVORCE FROM HIS FIRST WIFE MABEL.
HE PRAISED THE GENERAL RELIABILITY OF THE CAR BUT
CRITICISED THE QUALITY OF ENGINEERING.
(1900)

South Harting Hill Climb

APPENDIX V

Earl Russell and the Motor Car

John Francis Stanley, 2nd Earl Russell, led a very complex life, as outlined in Appendix IV. Our primary interest here is his motoring activities, but to weave those into an overall account of his life would be to make them fragmentary. In his autobiography, *My Life and Adventures* written in 1923, "Motors and Motoring" is only one chapter in a 36 Chapter book. To create an illusion of continuity, the motoring aspects of his life have been separated out and are here presented as a single narrative.

With his early love of all things scientific and mechanical, and his equally strong love of travel, it was almost inevitable that the young Frank would be fascinated by the development of the motor car. He had even served the cycling apprenticeship common to so many motoring pioneers.

He bought his first car in 1898, it was a 2½hp, single cylinder, belt drive, Benz; "a queer contraption with two seats back to back mounted on four bicycle wheels…no motorist who has graduated on a Benz has any reason to be afraid of tackling any other kind of car."

In 1898 Frank was living at Amberley Cottage in Maidenhead, a flat, forgiving landscape for a low powered car that would not climb anything more than a 1:20 hill without the risk breaking a belt. In a strong headwind, or in more than two inches of mud, it would not hold high gear. Despite this, Frank frequently used the car to commute between Amberley Cottage and Hanwell Asylum, where he was Chairman.

His next car was the 8hp Haynes-Apperson that Frank brought back from America in 1900. "This was an enormous improvement, it was larger, it had pneumatics, it had two cylinders and could go about twenty miles an hour. Its principle disadvantage was the method of engaging the gears; the sliding fingers had tiny friction bands; these were perpetually going wrong." He was also fairly scathing about the quality of American castings which "let water into my cylinder, (despite which) it ran home fairly well with a leak into the cylinder so large that as soon as it became stationary the whole of the cooling water drained off."

The following year Frank acquired a rather more sporting vehicle from S.F. Edge, "which had an international reputation having run second in some continental race." Although, writing twenty years later, Frank did not positively identify the car, we know from other sources that it was originally "Number 8", the Panhard-Levassor which had come second in the 1896 Paris-Marseilles-Paris race, and which Edge had bought from Harry Lawson. The winning Panhard, Number 6, had been sold by Lawson to Charles Rolls.

"When I first drove this car I was terrified by its appalling speed and feeling of power. Even at second speed one felt as if it was running away with one, so ferociously fast did it appear in those days...It had one appalling and incredible fitment, a large shoe brake operating directly upon the outside of the pneumatic tyre. It stopped the car, but generally destroyed the tyre."

Around this time Edge was in discussion with Montague Napier, who he had known from Bath Road (cycling) Club days, about building a British car to take on the French cars, such as the Panhards. "Number 8" had, in fact, been used as a development car by Edge and Napier and, by the time Frank acquired it, had been extensively modified with wheel steering, pneumatic tyres, external radiator and a prototype 2-cylinder Napier engine. The brake operating directly on the rear tyre was presumably a left-over from its pre-pneumatic days.

As a result of his contacts with Edge and Napier, Frank "placed an order at enormous expense for a 12hp (Napier) which was at last delivered to me, but I never got any satisfaction out of it, and never found it anything but a dud car." One of the reported problems was again losing all its cooling water. The precise timing of this purchase is not clear; however he still had a Napier at the end of 1903, since it was a Napier which he adorned with registration number "A1" when he was Chairman of the LCC Highways Committee. It is not known if it was the same car. At later times in his motoring career he had several White Steam Cars, many Humbers and at least one 30hp Daimler.

In March 1899, when he was still running the Benz, Frank had bought, for the princely sum of £20, one of the first life memberships of the Automobile Club of Great Britain and Ireland, which had been formed by Frederick Simms in August 1897. When it received its Royal Charter in March 1907 it became the Royal Automobile Club.

Frank became a very active member and served on all the committees. He was a steward at the Irish Gordon-Bennett Race in 1903, but that did not stop him from complaining that the Main Committee was "manned by wealthy racing car owners". One committee which gave him enormous influence was the small editorial committee for the Journal and the Year Book. Later, in 1910 when the Club moved from Whitehall Court into palatial new purpose built premises in Pall Mall, Frank used his lawyers brain to re-draft the Club Rules.

The seeds for internal strife in the club, however, were sown from the beginning. The one word which sums it up is perhaps "elitism". When the club was formed motoring was an expensive, elite activity, and the club had the appropriate social and political aspirations. As motoring descended the social ladder, motorists rapidly became more numerous. Trade interests began to dominate the Main Committee, and the "establishment" club was very reluctant to criticise increasing police persecution of motorists. Who would speak for the ordinary, amateur motorist.

In an effort to counter this potential loss of influence, the ex Legal Secretary of the Automobile Club, Rees Jefferies, created the Motor Union in 1901. This allowed the ever increasing number of provincial motor clubs, and other individual motorists, to become "affiliated members" of the Automobile Club for half a guinea a year per member. It also ensured that the Club had control of all competitions organised by the "Branch Clubs". Frank

THE THIRD CAR THAT EARL RUSSELL OWNED
WAS THIS PANHARD-LEVASSOR WHICH HE BOUGHT FROM
S.F. EDGE IN 1901. IT HAD ORIGINALLY FINISHED SECOND IN
THE 1896 PARIS-MARSEILLE-PARIS RACE BEFORE
BEING USED AS A DEVELOPMENT CAR BY EDGE AND NAPIER.
(1901)

immediately became involved in the MU, becoming Chairman of the Touring Committee, with responsibility for appointing hotels.

The MU inevitably grew rapidly and was soon much bigger than the parent Club; it began to demand more and more privileges, which the parent Club were not prepared to grant. There followed a very public and acrimonious row, aggravated when the MU began to copy the anti-police tactics of the newly formed Automobile Association, with the end result that, in November 1907, the Automobile Club severed all links with the Motor Union. Frank sided with the MU and stood down from the Automobile Club Main Committee. The MU went into decline and in 1910 was integrated with the AA. The resulting organisation dwarfed the Automobile Club.

Just to confuse the issue even further, Frank had been involved with the AA since its inception. Formed initially by a group of dissident Automobile Club activists, including Edge and Jarrott, who wanted more active support for motorists against police harassment, the AA was formed in June 1905. In July the provisional committee invited Frank to join a sub-committee to formulate the Rules. These were accepted at a meeting in August and Frank was confirmed as a member of the 20-man committee.

At this point Frank was a main committee member of all three motoring organisations, the Automobile Club, the Motor Union and the Automobile Association, despite their conflicting interests.

Frank gained valuable publicity for the AA by fighting, and winning, a high profile case at Guildford Assizes involving an AA patrolman. The patrolman had given evidence in defence of an AA member summonsed for speeding on The Fairmile, Cobham. The driver was found guilty and fined anyway, but the patrolman was then accused of perjury and sent to Brixton prison pending trial. The AA decided to defend their employee with all the resources they could muster; Earl Russell K.C. led the defence and, against the judges summing up, the jury acquitted the patrolman.

Frank remained a committee member of the AA until the end of 1907, when he resigned. This was about the same time he stood down from the Automobile Club Main Committee. Even Frank's lawyer's mind must have found it difficult to reconcile the conflicting interests of the three main motoring organisations.

Another spin-off from the Automobile Club which Frank became involved in was the Motor Volunteer Corps. To promote the motor car, the pioneers realised that they must convince the people in power of the merits of mechanised transport, and that included the military. In 1903 the War Office sanctioned the formation of the Motor Volunteer Corps, although their vision of its function did not stretch much beyond that of chauffeurs and baggage carriers. The Commandant was Mark Mayhew, who was a member of the Automobile Club, a founder member of the AA, and a member of the LCC, as well as being a lieutenant in the Imperial Yeomanry. One of the first recruits was Private the Earl Russell, who went on manoeuvres in his chauffeur driven White Steam Car. Rudyard Kipling was another early recruit.

After a couple of years the Corps became accepted by the military and its members were given commissions to distinguish them from ordinary army drivers. A little later the Corps was formally made a branch of the army with the title Army Motor Reserve. As Frank later commented:

> "It thus happened that I twice had the honour of receiving His Majesty's commission as an officer whilst still technically a convicted felon."

As would be expected, Frank also had some direct involvement with the motor industry. The first recorded contact was as early as 1895, when he was still only thirty years old and had yet to own a motor car. Frank was approached by a young city type, on behalf of Harry John Lawson, and offered the Chairmanship of the Great Horseless Carriage Company, a new company being set up to top the pyramid of companies Lawson was building with the intention of controlling the nascent British motor industry by buying all the key patents. Frank was flattered and interested, but when he enquired how a promised payment of "£500 for joining the board" would be made, he was told it would be paid "in a bag of gold so there would be no trace of it." The young city type was shown the door.

Lord Winchelsea became Chairman of the Great Horseless Carriage Company with some very distinguished directors on the board. On paper at least these included Gottlieb Daimler,

EARL RUSSELL AND THE MOTOR CAR

EARL RUSSELL ON HIS "A1" CAR, WHICH IS PROBABLY THE
12hp NAPIER WHICH HE BOUGHT NEW DIRECT FROM S.F. EDGE
SOME TIME IN 1903. *CAR ILLUSTRATED* WERE
"SURPRISED TO NOTE" THAT "SO ASTUTE A PERSON AS EARL RUSSELL"
WOULD USE A NUMBER PLATE NOT MEETING THE REGULATIONS,
WHICH APPARENTLY REQUIRED A DASH BETWEEN
THE LETTER AND FIGURE.
(1903)

Comte de Dion and H.H. Mulliner. Edward Pennington was also a director, and Frederick Simms was consulting engineer. The company took up residence in the "Motor Mills", which Lawson had converted from the old Coventry Cotton Mills, with all Lawson's other pyramid of companies. One of these companies, who were on the ground floor, was Humber & Company, and a fire which started in their premises destroyed the whole building. After much rebuilding, and company restructuring, the remnants of the Great Horseless Carriage Company, by then called the Motor Manufacturing Company, eventually went bust in 1904.

Perhaps not entirely a coincidence, the only manufacturer who Frank subsequently became directly involved with was the Humber Company. After an inauspicious start operating under the Lawson umbrella, the company reformed as Humber Ltd. in 1900 with a share issue of £500,000. Frank became a stockholder. In 1901 the company recruited Louis Coatalen as chief engineer; the company prospered developing a reputation for quality and some success in competition.

The success of the company led to some over confidence and over investment, which all came to a head in 1907. The situation was not helped by Louis Coatalen moving to Hillman. A new share issue in 1907 was only 40% subscribed and in 1908 the company recorded a £23,000 loss. At a difficult shareholders meeting Frank proposed that a committee be appointed to investigate the whole affair. When that committee reported to an extraordinary general meeting in February 1909 it presented a damning indictment of the management. The committee's recommendation was that the company go into voluntary liquidation and that a new company be formed with the same name. All but one of the directors resigned and Frank was appointed as Chairman of the new board.

The Beeston plant had been closed in 1908 and the spare capacity at Folly Lane was used initially for a foray into aviation, initially putting Humber engines under Bleriot wings, but later building complete aircraft. This was not a success however and ceased in 1911. Nevertheless the company made a slow recovery and by 1913 turned in a £50,000 profit. W.G. Tuck, the works driver, was breaking all sorts of class records at Brooklands, competing in hill climbs, and setting a benchmark for W.O. Bentley who was developing the French D.F.P. car before embarking on his own design. Frank remained a director of Humber from 1909 until 1924; he was either Chairman or Deputy Chairman for all of those years except 1911 and 1912. Outside of Humber Frank does not seem to have been directly involved in the motor industry, with the exception of such appointments as President of the Motor and Cycle Trades Benevolent Fund in 1909.

If there was a common thread running through the 2nd Earl Russell's complex life it was perhaps politics in it's widest sense. It seems he could not be involved in anything without wanting to run it. His involvement with motoring politics could be said to have started when he became Chairman of the Highways Committee of the LCC, but it did not become high profile until 1903 when what eventually became the Motor Car Act of 1903 was being drafted.

The prime mover was John Montagu, later to become Lord Montagu. He had been an elected Conservative member of the House of Commons since 1892, and was Chairman of the Parliamentary Automobile Committee. However the main interaction between John Montagu and Frank, who sat in the House of Lords, was in the committees of the Automobile Club.

The Automobile Club were becoming increasingly concerned that the 1896 Light Locomotives on Highways Act, which first legitimised private motoring on public roads in Britain, needed replacing with a new Act giving motorists greater freedoms, particularly from the 12mph speed limit. At the same time, however, they were concerned that the general prejudice against the motor car, still widespread in the country and in Parliament, might actually lead to yet more punitive legislation.

Local Authorities were arguing strongly for all motor cars to carry a ready means of identification, the more easily to prosecute people caught speeding. The Automobile Club were against vehicle registration and numbering as long as speed limits were in force. They recognised however the possibility of compromise, trading one off against the other. John Montagu had already, in June 1902, secured a first reading in the House of Commons of a Private Members Bill accepting vehicle registration but abolishing speed limits. In place of speeding offences the Bill relied on prosecutions for "furious" driving under an 1835 Act aimed at horse riders. The Bill did not get a second reading.

The Legislative Committee of the Automobile Club asked John Montagu to draft a new Bill, accepting vehicle numbering, but abolishing speed limits and introducing new offences of dangerous or reckless driving. In order to get members support, a special meeting was called in March 1903 to debate the new draft Bill. The turnout was disappointing in that only 81 out of 2263 members attended.

At the meeting there was strong opposition to any system of vehicle numbering, and that opposition was led by Earl Russell. He asked the meeting:

> "Who…believes that any number three inches in height can be identified on the back of a car travelling at 40mph…the only thing you will see is a cloud of dust…Vaseline smeared over the number will cause the dust to stick…and the number will be illegible."

John Montagu made a passionate speech in defence of his draft Bill stressing that only by accepting numbering would any concessions on speed limits be gained. The meeting concluded that the issue should be put to a ballot of all members of the Automobile Club and it's affiliated clubs in the Motor Union. Two papers were sent to all members, one in favour of the draft Bill written by John Montagu and one opposing it written by Earl Russell.

A total of 1,671 votes were cast, and in a ratio of 2:1 they were in favour of vehicle numbering in return for the abolition of speed limits. Thus was the Automobile Club able to present a united front in favour of John Montagu's draft Bill. Unfortunately the carnage in the Paris-Madrid race in May 1903 did nothing to ease public hostility to the motor car, led by a lurid press campaign.

In early July 1903 the Government introduced its own Bill, which was much like John Montagu's draft. John Montagu therefore dropped his Private Members Bill and supported the Government. Their Bill got it's second reading with some amendments, but the basic principles remained intact. In late July it went before a House of Lords Committee and had some further amendments added, including driver licences, but no driving test. A proposal for a 20mph speed limit was voted down.

On 4th August the Bill came back to the House of Commons but, with pressure for the House to finish its business before the summer recess, it was clear that the Bill could only be carried by giving a promise to the Local Government Board to reconsider the abolition of speed limits. At this point the Automobile Club asked John Montagu to block the Bill but he refused. In the final debate in the Commons on 6th August a 20mph speed limit was agreed and that became law on 1st January 1904.

Earl Russell's response to this very disappointing outcome was both predictable and pragmatic. His immediate response, in lawyer mode, was to write a lengthy article under the title "An Analysis of the New Act" which was published in *The Autocar* on 12th September 1903. The first half of the article spelt out in detail the sixteen new penalties imposed on motorists by the Act. The second half of the article were his "observations", beginning:

> "The Act is now in a very incoherent form, and bears the obvious evidence of hasty legislation at the fag end of a session, and the acceptance of amendments without due consideration…The only satisfactory Clause is the last, providing that this blot on the Statute Book shall not endure for more than three years."

It remained on the Statute Book for twenty six years, until the Road Traffic Bill of 1930 which Earl Russell himself piloted through the House of Lords as the current Parliamentary Secretary to the Ministry of Transport.

In January 1904 Earl Russell expanded on his "observations" at great length in a paper he read to the Automobile Club. The dissertation was also published in *The Car Illustrated*, which was very magnanimous of the proprietor and editor, John Montagu, since not only had Frank opposed him over the drafting of the Bill, but the *Automobile Club Journal*, which Frank influenced by being on the editing committee, had been very critical of John Montagu. This extended to Frank's paper:

> "There has been a disposition on the part of some people – notably Mr. Scott Montagu, who is always optimistic – to assume that the Act does not matter much, and that we shall all get on all right if it is reasonably interpreted. If it were reasonably interpreted I should be inclined to agree, but our experience of magistrates in the past has not been such as to give us any confidence in their commonsense."

Frank's pragmatic response to the new Act was to be first in the queue for the registration number "A 1". When the new Act became law Frank was Chairman of the Highways Committee of the LCC, who were responsible for the registration and licensing of cars in London, in this role he "obtained the number A 1". However this number "became too well known in Surrey", and the police branded him "a hooligan driver". A series of reports of prosecutions, mainly for speeding, appeared in the motoring press in 1904. Frank relinquished the number and proposed it should be assigned to the Chairman of the LCC.

He retained a proprietary interest in "Cherished Numbers" however, since when the Roads Act of 1920 laid down that registration numbers should always remain with the car they were first allocated to, Frank led the public outcry which culminated in a circular from the Minister of Transport in July 1921 to all local authorities saying that the Minister would "raise no objection to Councils acceding to a request for the transfer of an identification mark and registration number on payment of a fee of £5." This extra-statutory provision remained at the discretion of local authorities until 1985, when it was eventually enshrined in law. It was of course pure coincidence that the DVLA had recently expressed an interest in selling "Cherished Numbers."

"A 1" was certainly the first registration number to be issued in London, but not in Britain as a whole. The Act required vehicles to be registered from 1st January 1904. Although the

London records have been destroyed, the evidence suggests that A 1 was issued in December 1903; Somerset, Buckinghamshire and Hastings had all commenced issuing numbers in November.

It was fairly common practice for issuing authorities to retain the local number "1" for mayoral or council use. The apocryphal stories of Earl Russell "queuing on the pavement all night" to obtain the number A 1, for which no direct evidence has been found, seems highly improbable. If you are Chairman of the Highways Committee for the issuing authority why would you queue all night outside your own office ? Frank's autobiography is very detailed; if the story were true he would surely have mentioned it. Perhaps it was politically unacceptable for Frank to "reserve" the number for his personal use; if so, it is just possible that he got some minion to queue all night on his behalf, which he chose not to discuss afterwards.

The next time we hear the name Earl Russell in connection with motor car politics is not until 1926, when he introduced a Private Members Bill into the House of Lords for compulsory car insurance. Insurance for motor cars had been available since the Brighton Emancipation Run in 1896, and the first specialist company was the Car and General formed in 1903. There was however, to modern ears, a surprisingly strong opposition to the very concept of "compulsory insurance" of any form. Concerns ranged from civil liberties to those of the insurance industry that the government would want to control premiums.

The main pressure however came from Local Authorities who, in the mid twenties, were finding it increasingly difficult to actually recover damages awarded by the courts against convicted car drivers, who were in turn becoming less affluent as motoring penetrated the lower middle classes. Opposition slowly crumbled however; some estimates put the number of motorists who already had car insurance as high as 90%, and the increasing number of cars bought on Hire Purchase had to have it anyway. The matter eventually got swept up in the drafting of the 1930 Road Traffic Act. The Government were adamant that insurance was needed for public service vehicles, and therefore argued that it should be applied to all vehicles.

The Ministry of Transport was not established until 1919. The first Minister was Sir Eric Geddes, and his first action was to set in train a review of road traffic law. His Ministry of Transport Committee drafted a new Road Traffic Bill in February 1922. This still had speed limits but introduced the offence of "dangerous driving" for those who exceeded them. Nothing was done however and the old 1903 Motor Car Act continued to be renewed annually.

When the second Labour government, under Ramsey MacDonald, was elected in June 1929, Frank was appointed to be Parliamentary Secretary to the Ministry of Transport, his first public office in government. The Minister at the time was Herbert Morrison. In July 1929 the Royal Commission on Transport, appointed by the previous government, reported. They concluded that the 20mph speed limit had become an anachronism, but beyond that they could find no sustainable argument for any specific higher limit. They therefore proposed that it be abolished but that new penalties be introduced for "dangerous driving". The definition of a lesser offence of "careless driving" was thought to be legally too difficult. The Commission favoured compulsory insurance, but rejected driving tests as too expensive and difficult to devise. They proposed a Highway Code (later to become central to driving tests) to soothe disputes between motorists and a still partly hostile public. Although not a legal document, evidence in court that the Code had not been followed would be admissible for the prosecution. The Commission could see no reason for the Ministry of Transport not to prepare a new Bill for cabinet discussion, based largely on the original 1922 draft. The task dropped straight into Earl Russell's in-tray.

The main outside pressure for new legislation had been road safety and vehicle insurance, in the face of over 6,000 road deaths a year and a rapidly escalating vehicle population. Herbert Morrison and the Labour cabinet, however, saw the tidying up of the vehicle licensing system and public transport as the main priorities. A new section had therefore to be written in a hurry as the Commission had not addressed these issues. The Motor Car Act of 1903 had been specifically drafted to address the issue of motor cars, this Act was more to do with regulating road transport in general. The new Bill was introduced into the House of Commons in December 1929. There was much disagreement about speed limits but unanimity against driving tests. The Bill got its first reading without major amendment.

It went straight to the House of Lords, introduced by Earl Russell.

He clearly saw echoes of the 1903 arguments and commented;

"I wish my noble friend Lord Montagu of Beaulieu , who chafed as I did at the delay of this long overdue legislation were still among us today, though I have little doubt if he were that he would give me plenty of trouble in committee."

Lord Montagu had died in March 1929, after a prostate operation, at the age of 62. After an unexciting debate the Bill went back to the Commons virtually unaltered.

The final debate in the Commons during the committee stages was much more heated. An effort to reintroduce speed limits was easily defeated. A proposal from the Lords to allow magistrates to confiscate cars from convicted motorists was supported by the Ministry of Transport and Earl Russell, but opposed by the Home Office on practical grounds; what would happen if the car had been lent to a friend. Frank seriously proposed that "borrowing" cars should be an offence in itself, but he was overruled by the Home Office.

The Road Traffic Act became law in January 1930. It defined seven motor vehicle classifications, raised the age limit to ride a motor cycle from 14 to 16, required a declaration of fitness when applying for a driving licence but imposed no driving test, abolished the speed limit for cars but retained them for commercial vehicles, imposed heavy penalties for dangerous driving and introduced the offence of "careless driving", to include driving when drunk, imposed compulsory insurance, brought in the Highway Code, and allowed Local Authorities to restrict vehicle use on particular roads, but also obliged them to put up sign and direction posts of authorised types and remove unauthorised signs.

This was to be Earl Russell's last act as Parliamentary Secretary to the Ministry of Transport. His last public office was to be Under-Secretary for India, and it was this title that most of the obituaries used as headline in March 1931.

South Harting Hill Climb

APPENDIX VI

A Brief History of Speed Limits

The first occasion on which the speed of mechanically propelled vehicles on British roads was restricted by law was the Locomotives on Highways Act of 1865; the infamous "Red Flag Act". This sought to regulate the use of heavy steam driven traction engines pulling loads. The Act required three persons to be in attendance, with one walking 60 yards ahead with a red flag to warn oncoming traffic. The maximum speeds allowed were 4mph in open country and 2mph in towns.

The Locomotives on Highways Amendment Act of 1878 relaxed these restrictions slightly in that the man walking in front need only be twenty yards ahead and did not have to carry a red flag. Many however chose to continue carrying the flag as a means of recognition for the public. The very first motor cars took to the roads of Britain under this legislation.

It was not until the Locomotives on Highways Act of 1896 that a new class of vehicle, defined as a "light locomotive" (less than 3 tons), was recognised. The need for three persons in attendance was removed, and the speed limit raised to 14mph. The Local Government Board however promptly reduced it to 12mph. The Act also introduced the concept of Construction & Use Regulations, but only horns and lights were specified. This was the famous "Emancipation Act" that triggered the first "Motor Car Tour to Brighton", organised by Harry Lawson and his Motor Car Club. Nothing to do with red flags.

The 1896 legislation governed the use of motor cars in Britain until the Motor Car Act of 1903. The expectation was that this Act would abolish speed limits in return for vehicle registration and numbering; in fact it retained the general limit but increased it to 20mph. This Act, amazingly, remained in force until the 1930 Road Traffic Act abolished speed limits in Britain for motor cars.

This means that the entire sequence of fourteen events held at South Harting over the period from 1904 to 1924 almost certainly involved breaking the law. In the era of the Speed Six Bentley, Mercedes SSK, Vauxhall 30/98, and Lea Francis Hyper the 20mph speed limit still technically applied throughout Britain. The expression "still technically applied" is appropriate since the law was, from the very beginning, widely resented and eventually became completely discredited.

The early arguments soon became polarised very much as a town versus country issue. There was in 1904 no central funding for road maintenance, and rural roads had to be maintained out of local taxes. The local rural population saw increasing numbers of cars, mainly owned by townies, wreaking havoc on their roads. One remedy was seen to be police "speed traps", actively supported by local magistrates, raising revenue through fines on "speeding" motorists.

The declared purpose of the Automobile Association when it was founded in 1905 was to patrol the roads, spot the speed traps, and warn their members. The Royal Automobile Club with its establishment ethos, had problems with being seen to challenge the police. Their "ordinary motorist" offshoot however, the Motor Union, began to follow the example of the AA, which contributed to a souring of relations between parent and offshoot and the eventual merging of the Motor Union with the AA in 1910.

It had just about become accepted that there was a case for law reform when the First World War intervened and different priorities prevailed. The world slowly recovered after the war and as normality returned the same basic contradictions in motor car legislation resurfaced.

In 1919 the AA patrols began to be motorised and the numbers were increased. With an elaborate "stop and ask why if I don't salute" routine to avoid prosecution for police obstruction, there was soon a stand off between police and motorist and the 20mph speed limit was effectively discredited. Even the Home Secretary recommended that prosecutions should only proceed if the public safety was threatened.

The extent of the farce was illustrated at the 1926 AA Annual Dinner when the then Home Secretary, Sir William Joynson-Hicks, who also happened to be a Vice President of the AA, was guest of honour. You therefore had the man responsible for the police being entertained by an organisation who employed an army of patrols whose express purpose was to thwart the police. The AA at this stage had 300,000 members.

The 1930 Road Traffic Bill went to the other extreme and abolished speed limits for motor cars. It substituted new offences of "dangerous driving" and "careless driving", and also brought in compulsory insurance. The AA patrols were joined on the road by the new mobile police; this "necessitated some reorganisation of the patrol service".

The new regime of no speed limits and prosecutions for dangerous or careless driving did nothing to bring down the escalating death toll on the roads. Supposedly road safety had been the prime motivation behind the 1930 legislation. In 1935 the 30mph speed limit in built up areas, which is still with us, was introduced. Eventually, in 1967, limits were imposed on all roads, the highest being 70mph on the motorways. These are also still with us.

The main effect of this bizarre situation on the running of the South Harting Hill Climb was in the reporting of the results. Only once in the twenty years that events were run were actual speeds officially published. This was for the Yellow Trophy in 1907, where the rules for the event, and the Trophy, were supplied by a magazine, *Automotor Journal*. The highest (average) speed recorded was 33.6mph. For some events times were published, but mostly results were based on formulae of varying complexity (See Chapter 3) and "relative times". However some journals vented their frustration in print. *Motoring Illustrated* as early as 1905 expressed "much dissatisfaction" over the rule of "strict secrecy as to times and speeds". They did private timings and published speeds up to 27.5mph. Raymond Mays record of

57.2secs., set in his Bugatti at the last meeting in 1924, represented an **average speed** of some 63mph.

There was in the early days a seeming ambivalence in the police attitude to motor sport on the public road. In 1905 they were quoted at South Harting as "welcoming such meetings" and helped the organisers control the spectators. Speed limits apart, however, there did not seem to be any real recognition or concern on either side of the potential dangers of motor sport on public roads. It was not until the first reported accident in 1925 at Kop Hill in Buckinghamshire that the R.A.C. eventually proscribed speed events on public roads.

South Harting Hill Climb

APPENDIX VII

The Organising Clubs

The Automobile Club of Great Britain & Ireland (ACGBI)

The origins of the ACGBI go right back to the very beginnings of motoring in Britain. It was founded by Frederick Simms in 1897, just one year after the Emancipation Run to Brighton. Frederick Simms has been called "the father of the British motor industry".

Arguably the two most significant figures involved in the birth of the British motor industry were Harry Lawson and Frederick Simms. Two men inextricably linked and yet very different in character. Harry Lawson, the avaricious entrepreneur who intended nothing less than complete control of the industry by buying up all the key patents, and Frederick Simms, the engineer, prolific inventor, and friend of Gottlieb Daimler, who granted to him the British and Empire rights to the crucial Daimler engine patents.

Another key motoring pioneer was Sir David Salomons, a keen and wealthy amateur engineer who staged the very first Motor Show in Britain at Tunbridge Wells in 1895. In that same year he announced that he was going to set up a club to promote motoring, and duly formed the Self Propelled Traffic Association. Harry Lawson joined but Frederick Simms did not, since he claimed that he had suggested the idea first and that Salomons had simply upstaged him. Subsequent published correspondence indicates that Simms was right. Lawson immediately tried to make the SPTA into a promotional vehicle for his companies but Salomons blocked him.

Frederick Simms then set up the Motor Car Club with Lawson as Chairman. The stated purpose was non commercial but Lawson soon began to use it as a business platform. John Scott Montagu and Selwyn Francis Edge, two other prominent motoring pioneers, publicly accused Lawson of perverting the purpose of the Motor Car Club.

The first major act of the Motor Car Club was to organise the Emancipation Run to Brighton in November 1896. Pictures of the start show Lawson, all 5ft. of him, in the ludicrous militaristic uniform he designed for members of the Motor Car Club.

This run was seen by Lawson as promoting his business interests, but it back fired partly because the press reaction was very mixed, not helped by the confusion over the results and actual list of finishers.

Lawson, however, was unperturbed and a week later floated the British Motor Syndicate and associated it with the Motor Car Club. Even Simms now accepted that the Motor Car Club was being exploited by Lawson for commercial purposes, although his loyalties must have been divided since he was also consultant engineer to the British Motor Syndicate.

However, by the middle of 1897 it was clear that the whole motoring movement had failed to take off. Public hostility was if anything increasing, not helped by Queen Victoria letting it be known that she was "not amused" by the motor car. A largely hostile press suggested that only a really independent body, like the influential Automobile Club de France, stood any chance of building public confidence.

Frederick Simms blamed both the Self Propelled Traffic Association and the Motor Car Club for being institutions under the control of single individuals. The former had not been a success, partly because Sir David Salomons had turned out to be another self publicist, but also because he had publicly backed the steam car against the petrol engine.

Frederick Simms enlisted the support of Harrington Moore, secretary of the Motor Car Club, and announced in July 1897 that he was going to form a new club to be called the Automobile Club of Great Britain. In August 1897 he persuaded The Hon. Evelyn Ellis, another prominent motoring pioneer, to chair a successful exploratory meeting.

The inaugural meeting of The Automobile Club of Great Britain & Ireland (ACGBI), as it had by then become, was held in December 1897. The constitution was based on a translation of that of the Automobile Club de France, done by Harrington Moore, and the first elected Chairman was Roger Wallace Q.C. One hundred and twenty members attended including the Hon. C.S. Rolls. This rose to 380 within the year.

Sir David Salomons had been suspicious of Simms motives and had even tried to register the name "Automobile Club of Great Britain" to thwart him. Under threat of legal action however he caved in, became a founder member, and in 1898 the SPTA was incorporated into the ACGBI.

The club quickly became rather exclusive with members including not only the Hon C.S. Rolls, but Lord Carnavon, Earl Russell, Montague Graham-White, the Hon. Rupert Guinness, and Alfred Harmsworth the newspaper proprietor. Cars were, after all, still very expensive toys at this time. Progressively however more industrialists, military men and other professional people joined, women though were still barred.

The initial years were difficult. Public antipathy was slow to subside, unlike France and Germany for instance where acceptance of the motor car was much more widespread. One contributing factor was that developing technology meant that cars were rapidly becoming more powerful and therefore faster. The potential for "frightening the horses" was increasing.

The real driving force behind the ACGBI was the secretary Claude Johnson, later to become "the hyphen in Rolls-Royce". Even he nearly fell victim to public apathy when the Richmond Show that he organised in June 1899 was a commercial flop. His resignation was wisely not accepted. The ACGBI remained stubbornly elitist with membership only by nomination and election, thus avoiding the issue of how to remain influential but yet become a mass movement. Political clout, which it also sought, sat uncomfortably between these two positions. The membership at the turn of the century was no more than 540.

One significant move the ACGBI made at this time, almost by chance in the absence of any other contenders, was to become the self appointed regulator of motor sport. The first real fruits of this came in the year 1900 with the One Thousand Mile Trial, organised by Claude Johnson and financially backed by Alfred Harmsworth. This colossal event, in which 84 cars visited virtually every major city in Britain from London to Edinburgh over a period of nearly three weeks was a huge success and finally got a favourable press for the motor car. It was the turning point for public acceptance of the motor car in Britain.

In 1902 the ACGBI organised the first recognisable motor race meeting in Britain. This was held on Whitsun weekend at Bexhill, along the private sea front road on the estate of the Earl De La Warr, attracted a crowd of some 30,000 people, and was won by Leon Serpollet in his steam car at a speed of 54mph.

Another major event in 1902 was that S.F. Edge won the important Gordon Bennett race in France on a Napier, the first time a British car & driver had won a race abroad. One consequence of this was that Britain had to organise the race in 1903. Since racing on public roads was illegal in Britain, and dedicated race tracks were still a few years away, the ACGBI, as motor sport controller, organised the race in Ireland. It was won by Camille Jenatzy in a Mercedes.

By the end of 1904 ACGBI membership had reached 2500, but still the public perception was gaining ground that the club was for wealthy racers only. Secretary Claude Johnson had left in 1903 which caused something of an organisational vacuum. The ACGBI response, under the guidance of the new secretary Julian Orde, was to organise the first Tourist Trophy race for standard cars in the Isle of Man, which allowed racing on public roads.

King Edward VII had been an early motoring enthusiast and became patron of the ACGBI in 1903. In March 1907 he granted the club his Royal Seal of Approval and it became the Royal Automobile Club.

The Cyclecar Club

The ACGBI had set up the Auto-Cycle Club, (later called the Auto-Cycle Union), to look after the interests of motor cyclists in 1903. There was at that time already a perception in England and France that a market existed for a hybrid vehicle; more sociable than a motor cycle but lighter and cheaper than a car. Tri-cars, typified by the French Leon Bollee, with tandem seats and steered (from the rear) by a pair of front wheels either side of the front passenger, were an early attempt to meet this need.

By 1909 several rather more practical prototype machines were running, with people such as H.F.S. Morgan, Archie Frazer-Nash, and H.R. Godfrey involved in England. Simple, light, lively vehicles with some weather protection. Some were four wheeled, some three.

The editor of *Motor Cycling*, W.G. McMinnies, was intrigued by the idea of a very light car powered by a motor cycle engine. In the autumn of 1910, in Paris for the Motor Show, he was completely captivated by the ingenious but crude prototype Bedelia that he saw one day in the street.

This "unpainted wooden coffin", with four motor cycle wire wheels, two passengers seated in tandem with the rear one steering, had a V-twin 1056cc engine at the front driving through twin belts without clutch or gearbox to duplicate twin pulleys on the back axle. Gear changing was effected with two sticks heaving the drive belts onto the other pulleys. Neutral was achieved by moving the rear axle forward to slacken the belts. There was no reverse.

McMinnies recognised that a new, but as yet un-named, form of motoring had been born.

Nor had it yet been claimed by either the motoring or motor cycling press. Surely, he thought, it needed its own dedicated journal, and on November 27th 1912 *The Cyclecar* appeared on the bookshelves. The name had been invented by Col. Lindsay Lloyd, the Clerk of the Course at Brooklands, at a meeting convened by the Auto-Cycle Union who had decided to take the new machines under their wing before the already wealthy R.A.C. grabbed the potential membership subscriptions. What was then needed, if for no other reason than to allow competitions to be organised, was a proper definition of a cyclecar to distinguish it from a light car. At the same ACU meeting therefore two classes were defined:

Small Class   660lb. max. weight, (min. 330lb.) 750cc max. engine capacity

Large Class   772lb. max. weight, 1100cc max. engine capacity

This proposal was put to the Federation Internationale des Clubs Motorcyclistes in Paris and was adopted as an international category. All that was now needed was a dedicated club to organise the competitions.

At the offices of Temple Press, the publishers of *The Cyclecar*, and while the first issue was still in preparation, an exploratory meeting was held to discuss the formation of a club. The outcome was that an open meeting was called to be held at the Holborn Restaurant in London on the 30th October 1912.

Some sixty people attended and C.S. Burney (of Burney & Blackburn) formally proposed the formation of a club. This was unanimously accepted and by the end of the meeting The Cyclecar Club had been formed, draft rules accepted, and officers nominated to be elected at the inaugural meeting to be held at the Motor Cycle Show at Olympia on the 29th November 1912.

At that meeting the officers were confirmed as Glyn Rowden; Chairman, W.G. McMinnies; Captain, Frank Thomas; Secretary, and Arthur Armstrong; Treasurer. The subscription was fixed at one guinea for full members and half a guinea for country members and ladies. Some sixty people joined on the spot. It was also agreed that the first organised event would be a social run from London to Wisley Hut, on the Portsmouth Road near Esher, on Saturday 7th December 1912. Some thirty vehicles attended.

The Cyclecar magazine, in early 1913, identified some seventy different makes of vehicle, albeit some only prototypes. These included now familiar names such as A.C., Riley, Humber, Lagonda, Singer, Frazer-Nash and Morgan. Nine were three wheelers, five were French and four German. Most had V-twin air cooled engines and prices were mainly in the £80-£120 range.

During 1913 The Cyclecar Club organised its first full year of events including a hill climb at South Harting. It also participated in the first Cyclecar Grand Prix at Amiens in France contributing 10 entries out of a total of 29; McMinnies in a Morgan won but was denied his prize because the French would not recognise the Morgan as a cyclecar. In hindsight however the summer of 1913 could already be seen as the high point for the cyclecar movement; the first Morris Oxford light car had been launched in 1912 at a price of £175. In October 1913 *Cyclecar* magazine, still less than one year old, was renamed *Light Car and Cyclecar*.

By 1914 the distinction between light cars and cyclecars had become blurred. Cyclecar manufacturers upgraded their vehicles to compete with the ever increasing number of light cars from the traditional motor manufacturers. True cyclecars virtually disappeared. Then in August the country went onto a war footing and most normal activity ceased.

The Cyclecar Club however continued to meet and plan for 1915, it also began to discuss a change of name. The name Junior Automobile Club was suggested, partly because any move to include light cars would mean raising the engine limit to at least 1500cc; it seemed probable therefore that affiliation would have to change from the ACU to what was now the R.A.C., with the attendant increase in subscriptions. Nobody, including the R.A.C., was happy with this prospect. However in April 1915 all activities were suspended and the club funds put into War Loan.

Junior Car Club

At the eleventh hour of the eleventh day of the eleventh month in 1918 the church bells rang as the Armistice was signed. Surviving members of the Cyclecar Club trickled home and started thinking of peacetime pursuits. A reunion committee meeting was called in February 1919 and, after the pleasantries, the main subject for discussion was how to get rid of the name "cyclecar", which had almost become a derogatory term and now only represented a minority interest in the club. Arthur Armstrong proposed the name Junior Car Club, which was well received. It was further suggested that four wheeled members affiliate with the R.A.C. and three wheeled members with the ACU.

These proposals were all put to the first post war general meeting of the Cyclecar Club in March 1919, held at the palatial R.A.C. premises in London, at which many more pre war faces appeared. The R.A.C. were happy with the new name and promised to form a new light car sub-committee to liaise with the reformed club. By the end of the meeting Hugh McConnell had been elected club Captain, Percy Bradley was the new Secretary, along with four Vice Presidents and a full committee of twelve. An events calendar was a high priority, including a revival of the South Harting hill climb and the associated Lobster Weekend at Selsey afterwards.

The renamed club attracted new members, including some distinguished and influential names. The Hon. Victor Bruce, later the first British driver to win the Monte Carlo Rally, General Sir John Nixon, S.C.H. Davis, Leslie Callingham, The Earl of Macclesfield, Capt. N. Macklin and Miles Thomas. The one factor linking most of the new members was a passion for motor sport. The JCC was becoming increasingly identified with motor racing.

After much discussion the club defined the classes of car which would be eligible for their events:

1. Light cars up to 1500cc with four seats weighing at least 15cwt.
2. Light cars up to 1100cc with two seats weighing at least 13cwt.
3. Cyclecars up to 1100cc with a minimum catalogue weight for an open two-seater of 9cwt.

A politically significant move at the Annual General Meeting in January 1920 was the invitation to Sir Arthur Stanley, Chairman of the R.A.C., to become the first President.

Another significant move in 1920 was that the JCC asked the Brooklands Automobile

Racing Club to included events for 1100cc and 1500cc machines in their programmes. In May 1920 they held their first Members Meeting at Brooklands and at other times members were busy establishing Brooklands records for their new classes. In BARC meetings JCC members were soon successfully mixing it with the big boys in handicap racing. In March 1921 the JCC staged the 200 Mile Race, the first big International race to be held at Brooklands, and the first in a long series held at various circuits.

Assisted by the funds raised from the successful 200 Mile Race the JCC advanced rapidly, forming regional centres in the north and south west of England. The very professionally produced *Junior Car Club Gazette* was launched in 1922. The focus was increasingly on racing, but long distance road trials, hill climbs and social events were still organised. The traditional first meeting of the year at the Burford Bridge Hotel near Dorking was always well supported. By 1924 the South Harting Hill Climb was only one of some 16 events organised by the JCC.

By 1926 the JCC had 880 members, but the social events and road trials were losing popularity. Even in racing the JCC had to innovate to attract spectators. The 200 Mile Race was replaced by the Double Twelve, an attempt at Le Mans style 24 hour racing. However night-time racing was prevented by noise regulations around Brooklands so that two twelve hour daytime sessions were substituted. This race was significant in JCC history in that they removed the 1500cc limit and allowed lady drivers.

The JCC continued to innovate throughout the thirties with such novelties as the 1000 Mile Race, and the International Trophy, a split track method of running handicap races with scratch starts. In 1935 the Donnington track opened to provide competition for Brooklands, who responded by laying out the Campbell Circuit to mimic road racing. JCC membership was now pushing 2000 and a new Midland centre was opened.

About this time the whole debate about the club name was reopened. Since they now ran races for cars over 1500cc the name "Junior" seemed inappropriate. Nothing better was agreed however and the matter was shelved. The 200 Mile Race was revived at Donnington in 1936 but for unlimited capacity single seaters. In 1938 The 200 Mile Race was run at Brooklands again on the Campbell Circuit, but by now dark clouds were gathering over Europe again.

At a 1939 committee meeting the name issue came up yet again and the clumsy name "The British Motor Club" was eventually agreed and then put to the next AGM. Only 50 members attended; they agreed that a name change was needed but did not accept the one suggested. On September 3rd war was declared and all JCC business put on hold.

The next General Meeting was not held until January 1944. The gloomy gathering was told that both Brooklands and Donnington were in ruins and unlikely to be available for racing for years to come if ever.

At the first post war AGM in 1946 it was confirmed that Brooklands had been sold to the aircraft manufacturer Vickers Ltd., who already operated from the site. The meeting was also told that the Brooklands Automobile Racing Club had accordingly been wound up. Efforts were immediately made to take over the BARC, which still had 1275 members, since it provided a golden opportunity to acquire a new name while still honouring an old one. By changing the meaning of "B" from "Brooklands" to "British" both ends would be served. The concept of the British Automobile Racing Club had been born.

At the same 1946 meeting the Duke of Richmond & Gordon (aka Freddie March the racing driver) was elected President. On his Goodwood estate was RAF Westhampnett airfield which was no longer required as an active airbase. Wing Commander Tony Gaze, who had flown from the airfield, first had the idea of developing the perimeter road into a race track; via Tommy Wisdom, the Duke needed little persuasion and the first race meeting was held in September 1948. Better still the Duke offered it to the JCC, soon to become the BARC, as their home circuit.

At the 1949 Annual General Meeting of the Junior Car Club the membership voted to change the name to The British Automobile Racing Club and a new, long and successful chapter began.

South Harting Hill Climb

APPENDIX VIII

Source Documents, Picture Credits & Acknowledgments

The majority of the information in the text has been drawn from the contemporary reports in the motoring press, as listed in Appendix II. However much supplementary information has been gleaned from a wide range of sources, including the following books;

Uphill Racers, Chris Mason, Bookmarque Publishing, 1990
Sprint, T.R. Nicholson, David & Charles, 1969
The Beaulieu Encyclopaedia of the Automobile,
edited by Nick Georgano, The Stationary Office, 2000
The Motor Car & Politics, William Plowden, Bodley Head, 1971
Brooklands, The Complete Motor Racing History, William Boddy, MRP, 2001
Brooklands to Goodwood, Rodney Walkerley, Foulis, 1961
Split Seconds, Raymond Mays, Foulis, 1951
The Shelsley Walsh Story, Simon Taylor, Haynes, 2005
The Motoring Century, Piers Brandon, Bloomsbury, 1997
Romance Among Cars, St. John C. Nixon, Foulis, 1937
Golden Milestones, David Kier & Bryon Morgan, AA, 1955
The AA, Hugh Barty-King, AA, 1980
The Singer Story, Kevin Atkinson, Veloce, 1996
Aston Martin, Inman Hunter, Osprey, 1992
The Vintage Alvis, Peter Hull & Norman Johnson, McDonald, 1967
AC, Martyn Walkins, Haynes, 1976
The Humber Story, 1868-1932, A.B.Demaus & J.C.Tarring, Alan Sutton, 1989
Humber, An Illustrated History, 1868-1976, Tony Freeman, Academy Books, 1991
A History of Motor Vehicle Registration in the United Kingdom, L.H. Newman, 1999
My Life & Adventures, Earl Russell, Cassell, 1923
Bertrand Russell Autobiography, Routledge, 1971
The Russells, Christopher Trent, Frederick Muller, 1966

Picture Credits and Acknowledgments

The source of each picture used in the book is identified in the individual captions. Very few previously unpublished pictures were found, so that the vast majority of the images used originated in the contemporary journal reports. Of these, the only ones where original artwork could be found were the pictures from *The Autocar*; the original negatives for most of which are held in the LAT Photographic Archive. I am indebted to LAT for their efforts in identifying, cataloguing and copying these high quality, evocative images.

Some pictures from other contemporary journals were scanned from original copies of those journals. In these cases the source given is just the journal title concerned. All these images are beyond the seventy year statutory limit for copyright, but nevertheless every reasonable effort has been made to establish any current proprietary interests. Most of the journal titles in question are, in fact, now either defunct, or have become completely lost in a succession of name changes, mergers and take-overs.

Specific acknowledgment and thanks are due to The Royal Automobile Club for permission to reproduce complete front covers, and other images, from contemporary issues of *The Royal Automobile Club Journal*.

Individual acknowledgments and thanks for pictures, and other assistance, are gratefully extended to the BARC Archive, the West Sussex Record Office, Jeremy Bacon, John Wheeley, A.B. Demaus, Malcolm Green, Jeremy Wood, and Humphrey Sladden, parish councillor and local historian in South Harting.

South Harting Hill Climb

APPENDIX IX

Index of Motoring Personalities

Page numbers in **bold** type refer to illustrations.

Adamson, Barton **95**
Addis, Jack 124, 126, 132
Allchin, T.R. 174
Allday, William 64
Allen, R.E.H. 119
Arbuthnot, Capt. Sir R.K. 20
Armstrong, Arthur 253, 254
Arnold, W.H. 31, **35**
Amott, Ernest 52
Austin, B.H. 151, 166

Bale, Major 117
Baillie, G.H. 52
Barrett, A.E. **114**
Barwick, George S. 31, **76**
Beaumont, W. Worby 20, 30
Bedford, G 103, 104, **109**
Belper, Lady 145, 148
Bennett, F.S. **76**
Bennett, P. 142
Bennett-Stanford, Mrs. E. 22
Bentley, W.O. 242
Billinghurst, R.W.B. 138, 140
Bircham, F.R.S. **66**, **76**
Blake, F. **63**, **73**
Blakemore, E.J. 69
Bradley, A. Percy 82, 122, 170, 254
Bray, A. 122
Brewer, Robert 52
Brooks, A.J. **74**
Brownsort, W.G 103.
Bruce, Hon. Victor 115, 119, 122, 142, 147, 254
Bruck, A.H. 31

Buckingham, J.F. 86, 87, 99
Bull, A.E. **135**, 140
Burney, C.S. 253
Burns, Mr. 78
Bush, Oliver 68, **76**
Byrd, H. Linley 52

Calder, D.E **164**, 165
Callingham, Leslie 254
Carden, J.V. 99, 131
Carnavon, Lord 251
Chinery, D. 141, 142, 170
Churchill, Frank 21
Citroen, D. **74**
Clifford-Earp, W.T. 67, 73
Coatalen, Louis 19, 22, 31, 242
Coats, Capt. J.S. 104, 111
Cohen, D 98, 101
Coleman, Frederick 31, **38**, **67**, **73**
Colver, E.de W.S. 132
Colvert-Glauert, Dr. 97
Cooke, Humphrey 153, 157, **159**
Coop, J. 98
Cooper, C.H. **10**
Cordery, Miss Violet 115, **118**, 121, 122
Cosway, Major Baskerville 119
Courage, John **41**
Cox, Douglas S. **76**
Cummings, Ivy 145, 148, 154, **155**, **156**, 157
Curzon, Viscount 174
Cushman, Leon **124**, 132, **139**, 144, 148, 151, 153, 154, 157

Cutler, Mr. 21

Daimler, Gottlieb 240, 250
Davenport, B.H. 166, 168
Davenport, W.F. 121, 131
Davies, L. 97
Davis, S.C.H. 115, 117, 254
Day, G. **73**
Dean, Percy **72**
De Dion, Comte 242
De Lapalud, C.H. 121
De La Warr, Earl 252
De Peyrecave, L.F. 99
Deacon, R.E. 67
Demaus, A.B. 147
Derrington, V.W. 154
Dingle, J.P. 154, **163**, 166
Dixon, A.J. 148
Don, Kaye **120**, 121, 157
Douglas, Miss 98
D'Oyley Hughes, R. 142
Dumont, G. 31
Dykes, Mrs. 163, 166
Dykes, Professor 16

Earp, A.C. 28, **69**, **75**
Eaton, H.S. 150, 166, 168
Ebblewhite, A.V. 31
Edge, Cecil 30, 31, 42, 64, 68, **74**, 87, 94
Edge, S.F. 30, **35**, 42, 43, 51, 53, 64, 67, 147, 150, 151, 237, 238, 250, 252
Edmunds, D.H. Owen 121

– 259 –

SOUTH HARTING HILL CLIMB 1905-1924

Ellis, Hon. Evelyn 251
Ely, A.H. 166, **171**
Empson, Major 119, 121
England, E.C. Gordon 147, 148
Ewen, J.W. 154
Exmouth, Lord **84**, 87
Eyston, G.E.T. 145, **146**, 151

Falconer, E.A. 122
Farquharson, H.F.W. **90**, 94
Fetherstonhaugh, Col. Hon. Turnour 15
Field, H.L. 122
Fielden, N. 142, 148
Findon, F.J. 103
Finch, C.I 19, 120
Fisher, H.J. 119
Formilli, G.C. 148
Frazer-Nash, Capt. A.G. 103, 104, 119, 121, 122, **123**, 131, 132, **140**, 144, **149**, 151, 168, 252
Frazer-Nash, Mrs. 104, 121, 131, 142, 148

Gallop, Clive 147
Garrard, C.R. 52
Gamett, Hugh 94
Gaze, Wing Commander Tony 256
Geddes, Sir Eric 245
Gillett, C.E.S. 94
Gilmore-Ellis, T. 122
Girling, Sydney 31
Giveen, F.W. 174
Goddard, John **74**
Godfrey, H.R. 85, 97, 103, 104, 121, 122, 131, 252
Goossens, L. 148
Gorham, J.M. **32**
Gould, Arthur E. **76**
Graham, Philip **74**
Grahame-White, Montague 251
Graham-Wigan, A.J. 138
Green, Fred M. 51
Griffith, G. **95**, 97
Guinness, Algernon Lee 30
Guinness, Hon. Rupert 251
Guthlac-Birch, J. 94

Hall, H.E. 69
Hall, J.A. 148, 150,166, **167**, 168
Hall, E.R. **150**, 151, 168

Harding, F.M. 131
Hardy, Major. A.C. 104
Harmsworth, Alfred 251, 252
Harris, F. **129**, 131, 142
Harris, W. **130**
Harrison, A.E. 67
Hartfell, A.E. 126
Harvey, Major Cyril Maurice **146**, 147, 148, 151
Hatton, Mrs. **116**
Hawkes, Mrs. 121, 142
Hawkes, W.D. 99, **112**, 119, 121, 122, 131, 140
Hawkins, G.L. 131, 132, 142, 144
Heath, Capt. H. **93**, 94
Heath, Doris **161**, 166
Heath, Harold 163, 166, **167**
Hedge, J. **73**, **77**
Hedges, W.G. 131, 140, 141, 142, **143**, 144, 148
Henry, Miss Nan **98**
Herrington, E. 120
Hester, A. 132
Hill, J.A. 104
Hind, N.S. **92**, 94, 98
Holmes, H.W. 140, 148
Holzapfel, A.M.N. 99
Holzapfel, G.L. **84**, 87, 99
Houghton, F.A. 148
Humphrey, S.W. **73**
Humphries, W.E. 99
Hutton, J.E. 68, 69

Instone, E.M.C. **23**

Jackson, A.Y. 163, 166
Jarrott, Charles 30, 53, 54, 132
Jefferies, Rees 238
Jenatzy, Camille 252
Johnson, Claude 20, 46, 47, 251, 252
Jones, S. **89**, 93
Jones, Wilson 150,154
Joyce, J.A. 147, **149**. 150, 154, 157, 168
Joynson-Hicks, Sir William 248

Keddie, Maitland 130, 131
Keddie, Miss 131
Kent, Miss 98

Kenilworth, Lord (see Siddeley)
King, A.F. **75**, 148
Kipling, Rudyard 240
Knight, Vaughan 141
Knowles, G.F.J. **76**
Kreitmayer, K. 87

Lamb, Cecil H. **75**
Lambert, A.W. **86**, 87, 94
Lawson, Harry 240, 242, 247, 250, 251
Layzell, F.G. 104
Lefrere, E.G. 132, 140
Leno, H.D. 97, **109**
Leno, J.W. 99
Levitt, Dorothy **3**, 20, 21, **23**, 30, 31, 38, 63, 64, 67, 71, **76**, 87, 115
Lewis, B.E. 148, 166, 168
Lewis, E.W. **73**
Linsley, A.R. 141, 142, 148, 165, 166
Lloyd, Col. Lindsay 253
Low, Dr. A.M. 97, 103, 119, 126
Lowe, Godfrey 53
Loyd, V.G. 131
Lucas, G.W. 132
Luther, F.M. **138**

Macaskie, D.S. **196**
Macclesfield, Earl of 254
Macklin, Capt. N. 115, 122, 254
Makins, A.D. 166
Maney,C.E. 130, 142
Manville, E. 31, 63
March, Freddie (Duke of Richmond and Gordon) 255
Marchant, W.S. 119
Marendaz, Capt. D.M.K. 135
Marshall, B.S. 122, 153, 154, 157
Martin, F.S. **76**
Martin, Lionel **85**, 87, 117, 124, 126, 135, 145, 151, 157, 165
Martin, Mrs. L. **129**, 132
Mayhew, Mark 240
Mays, Raymond 125, 131, 132, 135, **141**, 142, 144, 151, 153, 163, 165, 168, **169**, 174
McConnell, Hugh 117, 122, 125, 132, 136, 254
McCulloch, A. 104, 144

– 260 –

INDEX OF MOTORING PERSONALITIES

McMinnies, W.G. 8, 86, 87, 99, 252, 253
Meeking, Miss Viola 115, 121, **127**, 131, **136**, 141, 142
Mieville, M.F. 31
Moir, H.K. 135, 144, 145
Morgan, Bobby 147, **156**, 157, **158**
Morgan, H.F.S. 252
Moore, Harrington 251
Moore-Brabazon, J.T.C. 30, 64
Montagu, Lord 64, 221, 242, 243, 246, 250
Morris, W.R. 97
Morrison, Herbert 245,246
Moss, A.E. **128**
Mulliner, H.H. 242
Munn, Walter **75**
Musker, Herbert **76**

Napier, J.S. 53
Napier, Montague **35**, 238
Nash, A.G.F. (see Frazer-Nash) 85, 87, 97, 99
Newsome, S.H. 142
Newton, F. 68
Niblett, H. **75**
Nixon, General Sir John 254
Noble, A 97,117,122,148
North, O.D. 52

Oates, R.G. **152**,154
Oates, W.H. 140, 148
Orde, Julian W. 21, 30, 66,252
Owers, Ernest **41**

Parnacott, A.E. 87
Parsley, J. 140
Parsons, D.A. 131
Paul, Cyril 157
Pennington, Edward 242
Pennington, H. **75**
Perman, A. **75**
Peto, C.A.S. **105**
Picket, F.N. 144
Picket, Mrs. F.N. 142
Pink, Winifred M. 145,148, 151, **162**, 163, 166
Phillips. W. 119,120

Phillips, W.H. 67
Pollard, A.A. 142, 148, 165
Pope, R.A. 121,148
Portwine, John 117, 147
Portwine, Miss 98
Powell, Davenport 31
Pradier, R.W. **209**
Price, Miss Adyce 98, 119

Radclyffe, R.W. 94
Radley, James 99
Ramoisy, H. 68, **75**
Rawlinson, A. **13**
Reeve, G.F. 131
Resta, Dario 153, 157, **158**
Roebuck, J.W. 45, 46, 48, 53
Rolls, Hon. C.S 20, 46, 238, 251
Rosenheim, Ernest A. 68
Royce, Henry 20, 46, 47, 48, 51
Rowden, Glyn 253
Russell, Countess 22, 31, 87
Russell, Earl 19, 21, 22, 30, 41, 63, **71**, 87, 126, **220**, 221-235, **236**, 237-246, 251

Salomons, Sir David 250, 251
Sampson, Lyons 27, 28
Sangster, Chas. 53
Saunders, C.H. 66, **74**
Scofield, E.W. 121
Scott, C.L. 97
Scott, J. Lindsay **69**
Seelhaft, Mr. 135
Segrave, Henry 174
Serpollet, Leon 252
Siddeley, J.D. 14,15
Simms, Frederick 250, 251, 238
Simmins, A.R. 148, 163, 170
Slaughter, J.F. 140
Smith, H.J.C. **137**, 144
Smith-Clarke, G.T. 147
Stanley, Sir Arthur 254
Starr, E.R.R. 119
Stead, G.C. 103, **107**, 131
Stemberg, H.H. **76**
Stevenson, D. 121
Stewart, Mr. 154
Stocks, J.W. **75**
Stokes, W. 67

Tallemache, H.P. **126**
Tamplin, E.A. 115, **117**, 128, 131
Taylor, Alan 119
Taylor, Claude M. **74**
Thomas, F. 97, 253
Thomas, W.M. (Sir Miles) 124, 126, **129**, 132, 254
Thornycroft, Tom 20, **22**, 64, **75**
Tuck, W.G. 242
Turcat, L. 51

Underwood, D.L. 131

VanNamens, R. 93, 94
Verney, R.H. **74**
Villiers, Amherst 131
Vinson, W. Nash **88**, 93

Wadham, J.H. 103, **110**
Waite, Capt. Arthur 147
Walford, Eric 52
Walker, A. Huntley 40
Wallace, Roger 251
Warren-Lambert, Major A. **115**, 122
Warren-Lambert, Mrs. 98, **100**, 121, 131
Wason, C. 78
Watson, S. 119, 120
Watson, Thos. **75**
Watson, W. **74**
Weller, John 147
Westall, S.C. 128, 141
White, H.R. 104
White, L. 148
White, W.H. **35**
Wild, E.W. 126
Wilding, H.R. 125,131
Wilson, Cathcart 78

Winchelsea, Lord 240
Wisdom, Tommy 256
Wood, J.T. 104, **106**
Woollen, T.H. 31, 69
Wright, Warwick J. 31, 40, 71

Zborowski, Count 147, 157

South Harting Hill Climb

APPENDIX X

Index of Motor Cars
Years entered 19'

A.B.C. 22, 23
A.C. 14, 19, 20, 21, 22, 23, 24
Adams 07
Adams-Hewitt 06,
Adamson 14
Albert 22
Alvis 21, 22, 23, 24
Alldays 05, 06, 07
Amilcar 22, 23
Ansaldo 24
Ariel 23
Ariel-Simplex 07
Argyll 06
Armstrong 13
Arrol-Johnstone 07
Ashton 20
Aston-Martin 21, 22, 23, 24
Austro-Daimler 14, 22
Austin 23, 24
A.V. 19, 20, 21, 22
Aviette 14

B.A.C.S. 05
Beardmore 24
Beaufort Princess 06
Beeston Humber 05, 06, 07
Benz 14

Berliet 05, 06, 07, 14
Bifort 14, 19
Bleriot-Whippet 20
Brooke 07
Buckingham 14
Bugatti 14, 20, 21, 22, 23, 24
Buick 07

Cadillac 07
Calcott 14
Calthorpe 14, 21, 22
Carden 13, 14, 21
Charronette 14, 19
Charron-Laycock 20, 21
Chater Lea 13, 14
Chiribiri 19
Chota 13
Clegg-Darracq 14
Clement-Talbot 06, 07
Climax 05, 07
Cooper 23
Coventry Humber 05, 06
Crawford 14
Crouch 13, 14, 24
Crypto 06
Cycar 13

Daimler 05, 06, 07
Darracq 05, 06, 24
Deasy 07
De Dion Bouton 05, 07
De Dietrich 06
Deemster 20, 21, 23
Dennis 04
De P 14
Dixi 05
Douglas 21
Duo 13

Elswick 04
Enfield-Allday 22
Eric-Campbell 19, 21, 22, 23

Florentia 05, 06
Ford 07
Fraschini 06
Frazer Nash 23, 24
F.S. 23

Germain 06, 07
G.N. 13, 14, 19, 20, 21, 22, 23, 24
Gracile 07
G.W.K. 13, 14, 19, 20, 21, 22, 23
Gwynne 23, 24

– 262 –

INDEX OF MOTOR CARS

Hallamshire 05
Hillman 19, 21
Humber 06, 07, 23
Humberette 04, 14
Horstmann 19, 20, 21, 23, 24
Hurtu 20

Iris 06, 07

Jabberwock 14
James & Browne 05, 06
J.L. 20
J.V.C. 22

Lagonda 21, 22, 23
Lancaster 04
Lanchester 14
Lawrence-Jackson 20
Leader 05
Lewis 22
Lindsay 06, 07
Little Greg 21
Lorraine-Dietrich 07

Marlborough 14, 21
Marseal 22
Mass 07, 14
Mathis 14, 20
Maudslay 07
McKenzie 20, 22
Mercedes 04

Metallurgique 14
Minerva 05, 06, 07
M.M.C. 04, 05, 06
Morgan 13, 14, 19, 20, 21, 22, 23, 24
Morris 14
Mors 05

Napier 06, 07
New Carden 23
Nova 14

Oldsmobile 04
Orleans 05
Osterfield 07

Palladium 24
Panhard 04
Peugeot 04, 05, 06, 07, 19
Pipe 06

Reindeer 20
Renault 04, 07
Reo 06
Riley 23, 24
Rochet-Schneider 05, 06
Russell 06

Salmson 23, 24
Scout 07
Simms Welbeck 06

Silver Hawk 20, 21
Singer 07, 13, 14, 19, 23
Speedwell 05, 06
Spyker 05, 06
Standard 19
Stanley 06
Sunbeam 04, 05, 24
Swift 13

Talbot 06, 07, 14, 22, 24
Talbot-Darracq 23, 24
Talbot-Simmins 24
Tamplin 20, 21, 23
Thames 07
Thornycroft 05, 06, 07
Thurlow 14
Turner 13

Vauxhall 14, 24
V.C. 13
Victor 14

Warren-Lambert 14, 20, 21
Welham 13
Westinghouse 06
White (steam) 05, 06, 07
Whitlock Aster 05, 06
Wilton 13
Wolseley 05, 23

Zebra 13

SOUTH HARTING HILL CLIMB 1905-1924

JEREMY BACON COLLECTION

𝐅𝐢𝐧𝐢𝐬